EMBROIDERY
AND NEEDLEWORK

FIRESCREEN DESIGNED BY THE AUTHOR
Embroidery executed by Miss Connie Knowler.

EMBROIDERY AND NEEDLEWORK

BEING A TEXTBOOK ON DESIGN AND TECHNIQUE
WITH NUMEROUS REPRODUCTIONS OF
ORIGINAL DRAWINGS AND
WORKS BY THE
AUTHOR

GLADYS WINDSOR FRY

KING'S PRIZE DESIGNER

FIFTH EDITION

LONDON
SIR ISAAC PITMAN & SONS LTD

First published 1935
Second edition 1936
Third edition 1943
Reprinted 1946
Fourth edition 1950
Reprinted 1953
Fifth edition 1959
Reprinted 1966

SIR ISAAC PITMAN AND SONS LTD
Pitman House, Parker Street, Kingsway, London WC2
The Pitman Press, Bath
Pitman House, Bouverie Street, Carlton, Melbourne
20–25 Beckett's Buildings, President Street, Johannesburg
Associated Companies
PITMAN MEDICAL PUBLISHING COMPANY LTD
46 Charlotte Street, London W1

PITMAN PUBLISHING CORPORATION
20 East 46th Street, New York, N.Y. 10017

SIR ISAAC PITMAN (CANADA) LTD
Pitman House, 381–383 Church Street, Toronto

MADE IN GREAT BRITAIN AT THE PITMAN PRESS, BATH
F6—(G.3084)

TO
MY HUSBAND

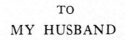

"But while there is pleasure in looking back over accomplishment, the word *happiness* must surely be preserved for that which actually allows us to share in the transformation. No mere knowledge, not even the acquisition of new knowledge, can give this firm delight.

"In it the amateur is joyful, the craftsman content, and the artist free of the weight of age.

"It is the secret of the pleasure women sometimes find in embroidery and men in gardens. Something is made, some combination of thoughts, materials, colours, which was not there before: imperfect as love, it shares with love the only divinity we have; it is our partnership in Creation."

—FREYA STARK, *Perseus In The Wind*, 1948.

"Embrowded was he, as it were a mede
Al ful of fresshe floures, white and reede."

—(Young Squire) Prologue, *Canterbury Tales*.

"Exquisite at her needle."

Epitaph on the tomb of Catherine Sloper, 1620.

"And they did beat the gold into thin plates, and cut it into wires, to work it in the blue, and in the purple, and in the scarlet, and in the fine linen, with cunning work."

—Exodus xxxix, v. 3.

"Fine linen, with broidered work from Egypt, was that which thou spreadest forth to be thy sail."

—Ezekiel xxvii, v. 7.

PREFACE TO THE FIFTH EDITION

My aim in planning this book was to provide a source of reliable information which could be clearly followed by beginners, working either in groups or individually, where no personal help could be counted upon.

It is good to know that this purpose has been both welcomed and well used.

I would like to thank the reviewers of the former editions for their praise and sympathetic understanding of the several aspects of my purpose; and all those teachers, students, and lovers of needlework who have shown appreciation of the sections suited to their need.

In this edition the opportunity has been taken to include additional illustrations in a more modern idiom as well as further examples of traditional work.

Lastly, may I reiterate that none of the "notions" (worked out experimentally by me) are intended as "copies," but as demonstrations for dissection and study; a means in fact of suggesting other and better ideas to the worker according to her personal inspiration and occasion.

All the technical information is here, upon which she may build her own "thing of beauty" within the limits of this most versatile art.

G. W. F.

PREFACE

ONE of the chief ways in early times of showing a sense of decoration was through the means of coloured, or monochromatic, effects on apparel, etc. Prehistoric, and later man, both show embroideries which keep, quite naturally, to all rules of good taste and design.

The means by which these people could evolve such a sense of beauty was leisure, with ample time, simple tools, and workmanship adapted to the material.

We of to-day find ourselves in a position largely the reverse of this; we have far from an abundance of time at our disposal, our aids to knowledge are often confusing, and our sense of beauty is wronged by an apparently unending show of articles made and decorated by machinery which supply all needs for clothes and household use; while "motifs," mechanically embroidered with glasslike artificial silk, are sold to be stuck, incongruously, on our cushions and covers.

Surely no further effort can be made to rob us of the pleasure of self-expression and the joy which comes of a problem personally solved.

Against this threat to true artistry we have the enthusiasm engendered by many excellent classes in needlework, embroidery, and design, which grows as the pleasure of the individually made article, designed to suit its purpose and position, is experienced.

We thus reclaim the delight in creation known to pre-mechanized ages, while having the resources of civilization at our disposal. Also there is an increasing number of good handbooks on needlework. Embroidery and plain needlework, though at one time thought of as separate subjects, have now happily a common interest, largely owing to the teaching of stitchery and other processes through the medium of *decorative* needlework.

Among these books it is hoped that the present work will find a useful place as a clear and practical help in the technicalities of the subject, and prospective candidates, say, for the City and Guilds Examinations will find that all the embroidery dealt with here is dealt with in that syllabus. The chapters open with instructions for the making of various stitches, with a selection of which we must become both familiar and skilled before a work, depending on them, can be truly planned. The illustrations to these are drawn in the most natural position for the worker, and the written instructions for working them face the illustrations so that they may be used for working from at sight.

We then study methods of work built upon the threads of the ground fabric (an important influence), as thus we acquire accuracy, knowledge of the use of our tools, and, at the same time, the making of decoration. Those of us who feel they cannot draw need have no fear, because drawing, as such, is not needed in work which is planned directly in the material. Also a right manipulation of the needle, thread, and fabric will give confidence and a sense of that valuable restraint shared by all crafts alike, namely, the limitations imposed by the material.

The many characteristic effects possible under the heading of "by the thread" methods will be noted with interest.

Next comes an introduction to those processes, necessary for decoration, which sweep over the surface without dependence on the warp and weft in their construction. These nearly all need working drawings on paper before the needlework can begin: here again, for those who declare they have no original ideas, we have alternative suggestions. Good existing patterns can be adapted, specimens from a museum may be re-designed by a new treatment or change of technique, and, last but not necessarily least, interesting patterns may be made by compass and ruler.

Thus it happens that no one, having once planned a piece of work, will tolerate designs so discreditable to the art of needlework as those typified by the weak, wild roses wilting on sapless stems which are still to be bought among those transfers to "iron off."

But, doubtless, the worker of to-day will not have far to seek for strong and useful suggestions from both Nature and Art.

Directions for embroidery with wools and other stout threads follow, including couching, open filling treatments, and the use of Turkey rug wool as an embroidery thread.

The seventeenth century worsted work known as "Jacobean" is touched upon in this section as an outstandingly good example of English secular embroidery. Unfortunately, these lovely hangings have suffered cruel misuse by debased reproductions, lacking in all the endearing qualities of the original works, which have been accepted by virtue of their retention of a name.

Under the heading of "white and self-coloured embroideries," details of the particular techniques which will simplify the making of this exacting work are carefully explained.

"Applied work," its technical procedure and endless decorative possibilities, is dealt with next.

Some guidance in the matter of embroidered lettering is given. Rightly used, lettering can greatly enrich the effect of a work, and, weakly treated, it can as easily ruin it. Careful attention to this subject is therefore well repaid.

A special chapter is devoted to details in the making of "Lingerie," a study made fascinating by the fact that the handmade garment has again come into its own.

Net and pin-stitch appliqué, shadow work, rouleau, and a new method for inserting and sewing on lace, are included, as well as crossway binding, piping, closed and open seams, and treatment for edges and hems and the decorations of various materials. A section is given for the teaching of needlework to juveniles, and is so planned that construction and decoration go side by side. The illustrations, as arranged here, would be useful for blackboard demonstrations to large classes.

Further technical details and instructions are given in the chapter entitled "Odds and Ends."

Suggestions for the specialized uses of embroidery frames and the mounting of work thereon are given.

The section on "Notions" shows various and finished works and traces the ideas back to their conception, not with the intention of the same lines being followed, but as a matter of interest and on the theory that ideas beget ideas.

Colour and design are dealt with throughout the book as occasion requires. In each class of work directing hints are given as to the type of design best suited to it, and also some practical help with regard to the making of them. A few famous historical examples are cited when it is impossible to leave them unmentioned, less for their history than for the standard they set. For permission to reproduce these pieces my thanks are due to the authorities of the Victoria and Albert Museum.

The illustrations have been made, with but few exceptions, especially for the book, and in every case they are selected with a view to their practical helpfulness to new workers; and it is hoped that they will, in the majority of cases, show a clear intent even without the aid of letterpress.

The writer hopes that the book will serve as a practical guide for those who are beyond the reach of important museums, but, above all, that the student who cannot acclaim her work as excellent, may at least say, "A poor thing but *mine own*."

GLADYS WINDSOR FRY

CONTENTS

CONTENTS

ILLUSTRATIONS

CHAPTER I
STITCHES

PLATE 1
AN INDIVIDUAL SAMPLER

CHAPTER I

STITCHES are a means to an end in needlework, not an end in themselves. They are the words of our needle language; without them we cannot speak. Yet there are those who regard the making of a sampler with contempt, as a mere waste of time. Perhaps this is due to their failure to recognize its uses, or it may be due to an unconscious memory of the eye-destroying exercises which little children were given to do, with fine needles upon fine linen—

When I was young
And in my prime
Here you may see
How I spent my time.

Sarah Pelham finished
this sampler in the 6th
year of her age.
8th Nov., 18—

Fortunately, we no longer regard a sampler as evidence of our diligence, but rather as a record for personal use, and in this sense it is hard to overrate its value.

The Use of a Sampler The first stitches, presumably, were made by prehistoric man when he joined leaves, fibrous vegetable material, and, later, hides, with a rudimentary needle and some kind of thong to form a garment. As soon as these stitches fell into definite order, they made decoration, and embroidery had begun. "Need will teach a naked woman to spin," says a Danish proverb, but it is reasonable to suppose the art of sewing preceded that of spinning and weaving. Efficient-looking bone needles have been found among the debris of the Neolithic cavemen's graves, pointing to the existence of needlework in Britain at a very early period. Bronze needles have been recovered from the ancient Egyptian tombs, and some gold ones from Scandinavia. A bronze needle in a silver case was found in the tomb of a woman of the Viking Age in Scotland. Steel needles were first made in England by an Indian, in 1545, whose successor, Christopher Greening, set up a workshop in 1560 at Long Crendon, Buckinghamshire, where it existed for more than three hundred years.

Possessing, as we do, so wealthy a heritage from the past in the matter of stitch variations, few of us would dare to claim acquaintance with them all. Let us choose from among them, and make practical notes upon material, which, planned according to our desire, becomes our sampler—an individual affair. A collection made in this way will be invaluable for future reference, and if, as often happens, we have forgotten how our technique was arrived at, we turn to the back of the sampler and watch our threads; if this fails to tell us what we need to know, we can undo a few stitches, following the passage of the thread.

A needlework notebook should be a companion to the sampler. In it may be noted miscellaneous information of interest to the owner, and time will **Needlework Notebook** prove its justification. A convenient notebook can be made of ordinary notepaper. Buy a few quires of this and some graph paper. Cut and fold a few sheets of the latter to the same size as the notepaper, and stitch about twelve sheets together with thread at the fold.

Make a cover of two pieces of thin cardboard joined at the back by a strip of linen (pasted), and tie the leaves with thread to the cover. When filled, the leaves can be removed and kept, and a fresh set put in. Notes on ornament and colour from Nature, historic or modern examples of embroidery or any allied craft, working diagrams of stitches and stitch arrangements, and notes on technical points, may be made. It will be found that something which seems a commonplace to-day will later become an enlightenment.

The question sometimes arises as to the number of different stitches which should be used in one design. Many suggestions have been made—one, that **Stitch Variation** not more than three are needed; again, that there may be nine to know and use. But it is useless to make any rules, for knowledge of stitches comes, as with colour-sense, by experience. It is, however, well to bear in mind that the use of many colours and many different stitches together will probably lead to a confused issue. Simple means make strong effects.

Stitches are more easily memorized when divided into groups, and to group them according to their construction is practical. See opposite Plate showing **Grouping of Stitches** four main groups and the fundamental stitch in each. Stitches which differ in their structure are comparatively few; it is the many and slight variations in the detail that give such different effects. Compare the twisted chain (Plates 8 and 2) with rope stitch (Plates 13 and 2). The one is of uneven edged-line stitch, sometimes called "Snail trail"; the other, a firm band stitch that pads itself, rope-like, in the working. Yet in making these stitches, the action of the hand and the position of the thread in relation to the needle are identical. All this difference in effect is caused in the case of twisted chain by working obliquely across a single-traced line and spacing out the stitches; and with rope stitch by working between two parallel lines and packing the stitches as close as possible.

A selection of stitches follows, illustrated by drawings, in most of which the working process and its effect are seen. When the drawing is devoted entirely to working processes, as in some of the knotted stitches, the effect may be seen in worked examples.

The first stitches dealt with are those that are simplest in construction, wherein the thread lies on the surface of the material, as in darning, couching, and satin stitch, uninterrupted by any linking, looping, or knotting. These are followed by the linked or chained stitches. Then follows buttonhole or blanket stitch and its many variations. After these come the most generally used knot stitches, and, finally, some composite ones that are made of two different stitches interlaced or superimposed. It is well to form the habit of thinking of a stitch as a member of its constructional group; for instance, is it a flat, a chained, a buttonholed, or a knotted stitch?

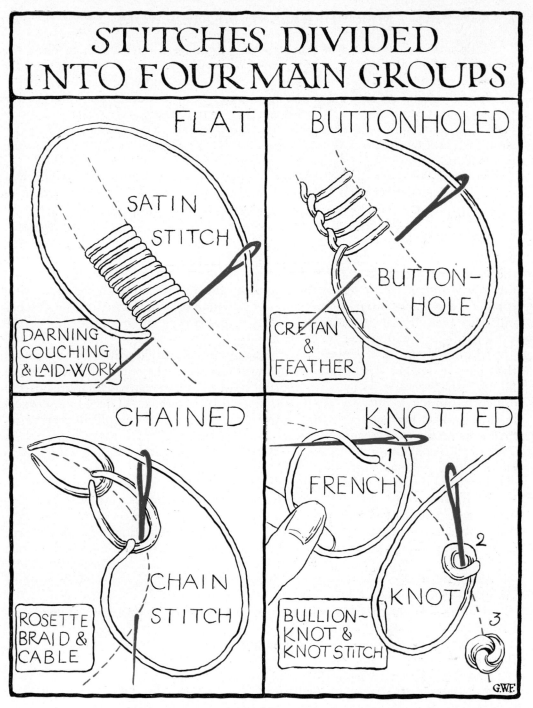

STITCHES DIVIDED INTO FOUR MAIN GROUPS

FLAT

SATIN STITCH

DARNING COUCHING & LAID-WORK

BUTTONHOLED

BUTTON-HOLE

CRETAN & FEATHER

CHAINED

CHAIN STITCH

ROSETTE BRAID & CABLE

KNOTTED

FRENCH

KNOT

BULLION-KNOT & KNOT STITCH

G.W.F.

PLATE 1A

This is the easiest way of remembering them, and does much to clear the confusion of multi-naming. Once these main differences of construction are grasped, stitches give up much of their mystery and settle down to simplicity. In the following diagrams the stitches are shown, as far as possible, in the position most convenient to the worker. It is not necessary to turn the book to realize the action, as is sometimes the case when stitch diagrams are all drawn along horizontal lines. We occasionally work that way, but more often towards us.

In the lower part of the sampler on Plate 2 the working of this stitch is seen. It proceeds from left to right. In the leaves on the left the direction of

Satin Stitch

the stitch is straight across the form (at right angles to the imagined centre vein), while in those on the right it slants obliquely across the leaf—"slanted satin stitch." To work the leaf on the left, begin by running the thread from the base to the tip and pass the needle to the back at the latter point. Bring it out a little to the right on the lower outline, put it in on the upper outline immediately above, and bring it out on the lower line close to the point at which it last emerged. The stitches must lie evenly, side by side, and be as close to each other as the size of the working thread will allow.

Although one of the most used and popular of stitches, it is by no means the easiest to make. Its beauty lies in the evenness of the stitches, which, while filling a shape, must be made to express its outline perfectly. Therein lies the difficulty, and it is only by practice that facility is gained. The Chinese excel in this, and its perfect rendering, both in the simple and complicated arrangements, is seen in their embroideries.

For the remaining illustrations on the plate opposite, the following references will be found of use—

Rosette chain, worked in a ring, is seen between the satin-stitched leaves.

Twisted chain secures the hem at top and sides of the sampler. (For diagrams and details of working see Plate 8.)

Rope stitch is used for the line enclosing the conventional floral pattern. (For working details see Plate 13, and compare with twisted chain—see previous page.)

Buttonholed edge with a group of detached loops finishes the lower edge of sampler. (See Plate 14.)

Braid stitch, shown at top in centre, with needle in position. (Details on Plate 8.)

Tailor's buttonhole, worked in a wheel, is seen in each top corner. (See Plate 14.)

The stitches used within the panel are as follows—

Roumanian stitch, worked in distinct sets of stitches, fills the top flower. (For details of working see Plate 5.)

PLATE 2

SAMPLER SHOWING THE WORKING OF SATIN STITCH AND THE
EFFECT OF CERTAIN OTHER STITCHES

Buttonhole or blanket stitch fills the petals of the lower flower. (See Plate 1A.)

Fishbone stitch, worked in blocks alternating in colour, is used for the leaves. (See Plate 5.)

Stem stitch, in simple lines, is used for the stems. (See Plate 4.) The spots are of buttonhole stitch worked in a wheel.

FLAT STITCHES

Constructionally these are the simplest of stitches. The word "flat" is used to express the fact that the threads lie on the surface as in satin stitch. The threads may overlap or cross each other, but they are still flat, that is to say, not looped, linked, or knotted.

An effective and simple border stitch. In working, the action is similar to that of herring-bone stitch, and it is quickly learned if first practised on a **Chevron Stitch** linen ground in which the threads may be easily counted. The diagram shows a background of threads in red, by which the working of the stitch may be followed.

Bring the needle out at the point marked by an arrow, put it in four threads to the right, and bring it out two threads to the left. The lower horizontal stitch is now made. Next carry the needle straight up over four horizontal threads and put it in at that level, but four threads to the right of where it last came out. Bring it out two threads to the left of this, put it in four threads to the right, and out two threads to the left, and the upper horizontal stitch is made. Now return to the lower line and put the needle in four threads to the right of where it last came out, bring it out two threads to the left of this, and continue as at the beginning. If repeated in horizontal lines, in the manner shown by the diagram, a pleasant filling stitch composed of lozenge shapes is made.

In this stitch three single stitches are worked in succession, radiating from a common centre. The method may be followed from the diagram. It is useful **Fern Stitch** for fine, fern-like sprays, and as a delicate filling for leaves, as it at once expresses the veins. When used on scrolling stems it will be found that the central stitch has to be varied in length to enable it to follow the curved lines.

This is useful for sprays and thorned stems, but is worked in an entirely different manner from the previous stitch. Bring the needle out at the point **Thorn Stitch** marked by an arrow and put it in at the head of the spray, leaving the thread sufficiently loose to lie easily along the curve. Bring the needle out at *A*, and put it in at *B*, just over the traced line, leaving the long thread to the right of it. Bring it out at *C* (the needle in the diagram shows this action), put it in at *D*, bring it out at *E*, and continue as at first.

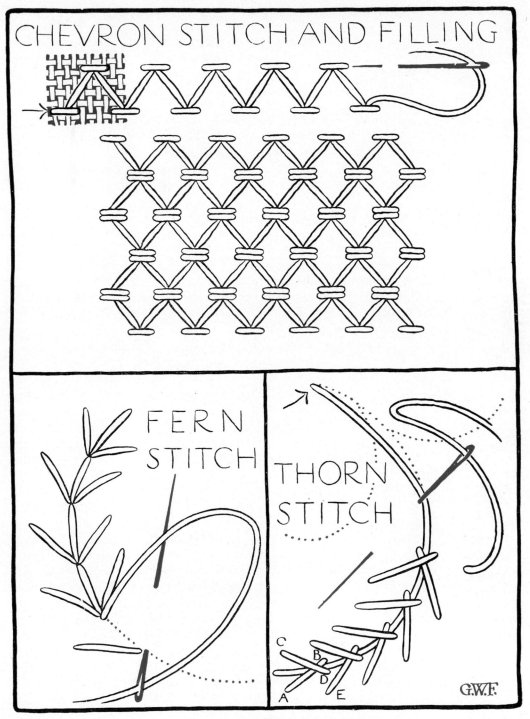

CHEVRON STITCH AND FILLING

FERN STITCH

THORN STITCH

G.W.F.

PLATE 3

The needle enters and is brought out of the material precisely on the line to be worked, giving the effect of a steadily drawn line which, upon close **Back** examination, is found to be composed of small stitches each **Stitch** following closely upon the heels of the other. To work it, bring the needle out upon the traced line at *A* (that is, the length of one stitch from the beginning), put it back at *B*, and bring it out at *C*, which is one step farther on. (See the needle in diagram.) The stitches should be equal in length. Overcast back stitch (see lower diagram) is invaluable for finely drawn lines, and will keep a subtle drawing. It may also be used decoratively with coarser threads, and, overcast with a different colour, will give the effect of a twisted cord.

Also known as "crewel" and "outline" stitch. The amount of material taken up by the needle may vary according to the effect required. In the dia- **Stem** gram a line of medium thickness is in progress; if a broader line **Stitch** is needed, more material must be picked up, while for a fine line the needle may both enter and return exactly on the traced line and pick up material about one-third the length of the stitch. In working, the thread must be kept on the same side of the needle, either to the right or left as is most convenient for the work in hand. As a filling, stem stitch may follow the outline of a form in a succession of rows until it is filled in, which lends itself to a decorative arrangement of shaded colour. The effect of a pattern of diagonal stripes can be contrived by working in straight lines set close together. Begin at the bottom left of the space to be filled and work upwards, making stitches equal in length which both enter and return on the same line. Succeeding lines are begun at the same end, and the stitches in each are placed a step higher than those in the previous line.

Is much used for outlines in fine white work. As shown in the diagram, the padding thread may be either run in the material or left free. In working **Overcast** the overcast stitches, as little as possible of the ground material **Stitch** must be picked up beneath the thread, a precaution which results in a pleasant, fully rounded appearance.

So called because the overcast stitches do not enter the ground material at all, but are worked over a foundation of stem stitches. This method imparts **Detached** a new character to the stitch, and makes it possible for it to pass **Overcast** over other raised forms. In the diagram a tendril is seen which, when finished, will pass over a wide stem. A line of stem stitching is worked loosely at rather long intervals, and as little material as possible is picked by the needle (shown in black on diagram); then a second line is worked (shown in red for the sake of clearness) in the same manner, but a stitch is taken first on one side of the former line and then on the other. It will be seen that the points of attachment of the red line of stem stitch are between, and not beside, those of the black.

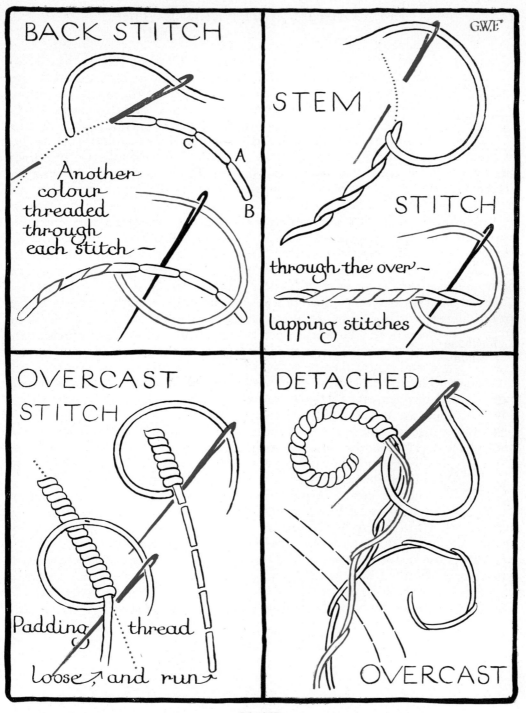

BACK STITCH

C

A

B

Another
colour
threaded
through
each stitch ~

STEM

STITCH

through the over ~

lapping stitches

G.W.E.

OVERCAST
STITCH

Padding thread

Loose and run ~

DETACHED ~

OVERCAST

PLATE 4

This is composed of a long stitch held in position by a short one taken over it at the centre. The effect may be varied by the slope of the stitch, which may

Roumanian Stitch

be straight across as in the diagram, a V-shape as shown by the single one, or any degree between. In any variation the first stitch is set at the slope required and the rest follow suit. When working a pointed petal the small stitch at the top is worked first. The arrow on the left marks the true starting-point for Roumanian stitch; bring the needle out here and put it in on the opposite side, and bring it out a little to the right of the centre line (see needle in diagram), leaving the thread beneath the needle. Pull through, and put the needle in a little to the left of the centre line below the long stitch, bringing it out again on the left side just below the starting-point, and repeat the action. This makes a solid filling, but an open one may be made, by spacing out the stitches. The three flowers at the lower right corner at the centre of *motif* (Plate 116) show the V-shaped variety.

Fishbone stitch is very effective when worked in loosely twisted silk and in groups alternating in colour. It is used for leaf and petal fillings as well as for

Fishbone Stitch

borders. To work a petal, begin with the straight stitch at the bottom and bring the needle out on the right side (see arrow), and repeat the one action shown in the diagram, but on each side alternately. The light plays on the threads arranged thus to peculiar advantage. It will be seen that the stitches overlap at the centre. See the top right flower on Plate 44 and the body of the bird in Plate 113.

Another useful filling stitch for leaves and petals, so called because two lines of back-stitching are formed on the reverse side as the stitch proceeds.

Double Back Stitch

The action in working is the same as in herring-bone stitch, but here the stitches touch each other at the outline. Bring the needle out at *A*, put it in at *B*, and out at *C* (see the needle in diagram). Put it in at *D*, bring it out at *E*, and repeat. On semi-transparent materials this stitch may be worked on the reverse side, making that portion opaque and neatly outlined with back stitch when seen from the front.

This is useful for the solid filling of leaves or petals which are too wide to be conveniently filled with satin stitch. To work it, repeat the action shown in

Flat Stitch

the diagram on each side alternately. A larger space may be filled by working several straight rows adjoining, and in this case the inner edges should be made to interlace. This can be contrived by working a long and a short pair of stitches alternately.

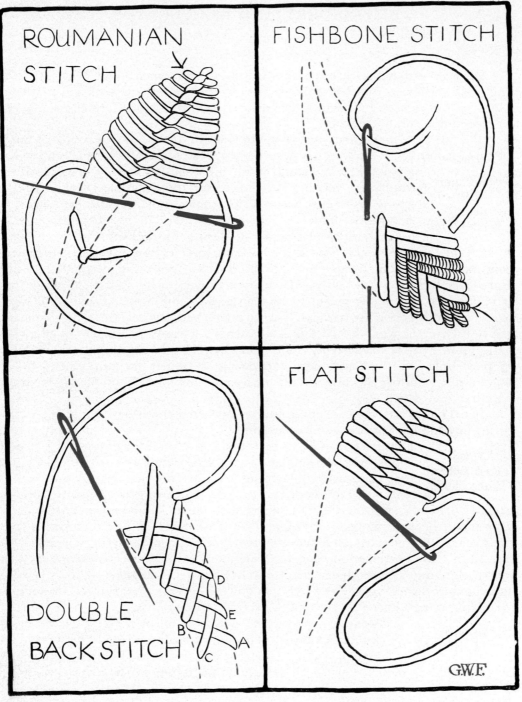

ROUMANIAN STITCH

FISHBONE STITCH

DOUBLE BACK STITCH

FLAT STITCH

G.W.E.

PLATE 5

CHAINED STITCHES

In chain stitch the thread forms a link on the surface and a flat stitch at the back. Eleven varieties follow, having this peculiarity of construction. Chain stitch is neat and strong, and lends itself very readily to the rendering of free and accurate drawing.

The fourteenth-century German white work on Plate 6 is a beautiful example of this quality. It is worked with coarse white linen thread on rough brownish hand-woven linen and mostly in chain stitches. Note the subtle **German 14th-Century White Work** beauty of drawing arrived at by these simple means. In the man's hair, the harness, and the animals' ears, we see how expressive single lines of chain stitch can be. Double chain is used for the wider scrolling stems, the stick upheld by the man to restrain the horses, the horses' manes, and some of the leaves. In the more solid parts the stitch changes to buttonhole. The subject of the panel is "The Pursuit of the Unicorn." It has been used as part of an altar-cloth band, but it is possible that it was meant to be seen against the light. The line of linen left so carefully round the harness, and the man's belt, suggest this, and so placed, the beauty of the work would only be enhanced. Many fine pieces of this type and period exist to-day, having survived the ravages of domestic use and time as pure linen will; indeed, here everything combines for durability—hand-woven linen simply sewn with linen thread—no cutting of background or withdrawing of threads.

The Dutch East Indian embroideries of seventeenth and eighteenth centuries provide another outstanding example of the possibilities of chain stitch. **Dutch East Indian Embroideries** These are worked in very fine silk of many colours and tones of colour, with the smallest of stitches, on a linen ground. In these matters they are in strong contrast to the German fourteenth-century white work, but exquisite drawing is common to them both. Curtains and coverlets are covered with stems sprawling inconsequently over them, bearing flowers, leaves, and buds of every variety of form. From the distance the effect is of a delicately coloured and meandering all-over pattern. On close examination each form is found to be perfectly wrought with line within line of the finest chain stitches until the shape is filled. Quaint animals sometimes sport between the flowers, greatly enlivening the effect. (See No. 1030, 1855, Victoria and Albert Museum.)

Modern Work To-day, when carrying out work all in chain stitch we must bear in mind the load of machine-made embroideries produced in this stitch, and be sure that our treatment holds some distinction of material, colour, or arrangement which will at once proclaim its hand-made quality.

PLATE 6

CHAINED STITCHES. AN EXAMPLE OF XIVᴛʜ-CENTURY WHITE WORK

Part of a linen altar-cloth (German, Westphalian), showing the mythical chase of the unicorn
(symbolizing the Incarnation).

From the Victoria and Albert Museum

In its simple form this is seen on Plate 1. The thread is put to the left side held down with the thumb as each stitch is made, and the needle is both put **Chain Stitch** in and brought out on the traced line, after which it is pulled through in a downward direction with the thread lying beneath it from left to right. In subsequent stitches the needle is always put in the link at the point at which it last came out. The reverse side has the appearance of a line of back-stitching.

Here ordinary chain stitches, instead of being worked in line, are set slant-wise between two lines, the needle pointing first from left to right and then **Zigzag Chain** from right to left. The diagram shows the needle piercing the thread of the last link instead of entering it in the usual way of chain stitches. (Note the position of the other needles on the same page.) This precaution keeps the links in position. Here, especially, accuracy of spacing will make beauty of stitch. The decorative border stitch below is quickly made by the addition of French knots between the stitches.

Also called "Magic" chain, is worked with links of alternating colour. Put two threads in the needle, one of each colour (here grey and white), and **Chequered Chain** bring them out from the back on the traced line. Ignore the grey thread, and putting the white to the left, make a chain stitch, and it will be found that both threads come through together, and that the white has made the stitch. Next take the grey thread and make a stitch, this time throwing the white aside, and continue using each of the threads in turn as though the other were not there. Three lines of stitches worked and arranged as shown in black and red at the foot of the diagram make a pretty chequered border.

This is a speedily worked and decorative band stitch. It can be used for wide and scrolled stems as well as for borders. To work it, bring the needle **Double Chain** out at *A*, put it in at *B* on the opposite side, and out at *C*. (See needle in diagram.) With the thread lying beneath the needle pull through in a downward direction. Throw the thread to the left and make a similar stitch on the opposite side—then to the right, and so on, alternately. It will be seen in the diagram that the second stitch is lower than the first. This is to set the slope, after which the same length of material is picked up on either side for each stitch.

Also called Square Chain. Bring the needle out at *A*, put it in at *B* on the opposite side, and bring it out at *C* with the thread lying from left to **Open Chain** right beneath the needle. Bring it through, but do not pull the stitch tight; then put the needle over the loop now made and take to the opposite side, putting it in at *D* and out at *E*. The worker will soon gauge how loose the thread need be to enable the needle to carry it into position before making the next stitch. The needle in the diagram shows another way of working it; for this a straight stitch is taken on each side in turn.

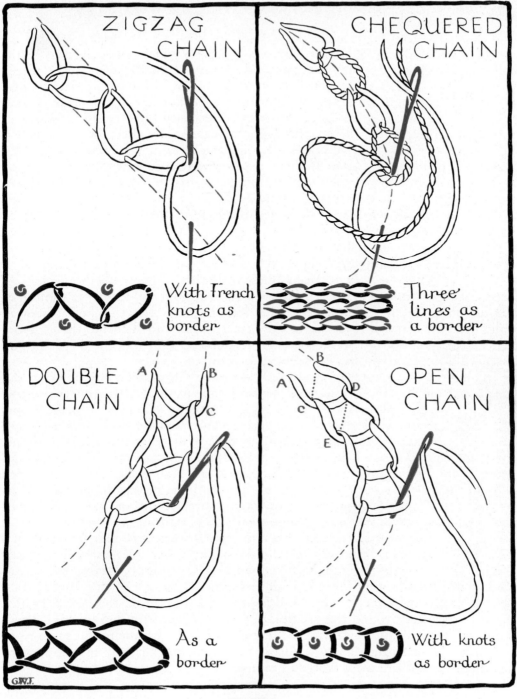

ZIGZAG CHAIN

With French knots as border

CHEQUERED CHAIN

Three lines as a border

DOUBLE CHAIN

As a border

OPEN CHAIN

With knots as border

PLATE 7

Here the links are connected by straight bars, which are arrived at in the following manner. Having brought out the thread at the top of the traced line, hold it down with the left thumb, leaving it slack above. **Cable Chain** Pointing the needle downwards on the left of the slack thread, twist the needle under and over it (until the thread is coiled once round), put the needle in the traced line a little below the point at which it first appeared, and bring it out as seen in the diagram, with the thread lying beneath it from left to right. Pull the needle through in a downward direction and the first straight bar, followed by a link, will appear. This stitch should be worked with a stout, well-twisted thread.

Also called "Snail Trail," is worked from right to left over a single traced line. The effect may be varied by the spacing of the stitches, which can be **Twisted Chain** placed farther apart than those shown in the diagram, resulting in a straggling line stitch that may at times be useful. Worked between two traced lines with the stitches closely packed, it becomes rope stitch (Plate 13). To work it, bring out the thread at the top of the line and, holding it down with the left thumb below this point, take an oblique stitch beneath it and across the traced line, and with the thread lying beneath the point of the needle from left to right, as shown in the diagram, pull the needle towards you in a downward direction.

This firm chain stitch is made by a reverse method. To begin, bring out the thread on the traced line, and working from right to left, put the needle **Broad Chain** in and out once as though a running stitch were being done, but instead of making the second running stitch go back and slip the needle through the already made stitch, put it in beside the point from whence it last came out (the first link will then be made), and bring it out again farther along the line, next slipping the needle under both sides of the link as seen in the diagram. To continue, repeat the process.

This stitch has the appearance of a fancy braid lying on the surface, and shows to the best advantage when worked with a stout, well-twisted thread. **Braid Stitch** It is worked from right to left between two parallel lines. To begin, bring out the thread on the lower line, throw it towards the left and hold it down with the left thumb, leaving the thread slack above it. Pointing the needle downwards on the left of the slack thread, twist it under and over it once. Still holding the thumb on the thread (which is now coiled once round the needle), put the needle in the top line and bring it out on the lower line, and with the thread lying beneath the needle from right to left (as shown in the diagram), finally put the needle through in a downward direction. (See Plate 2 for worked example.)

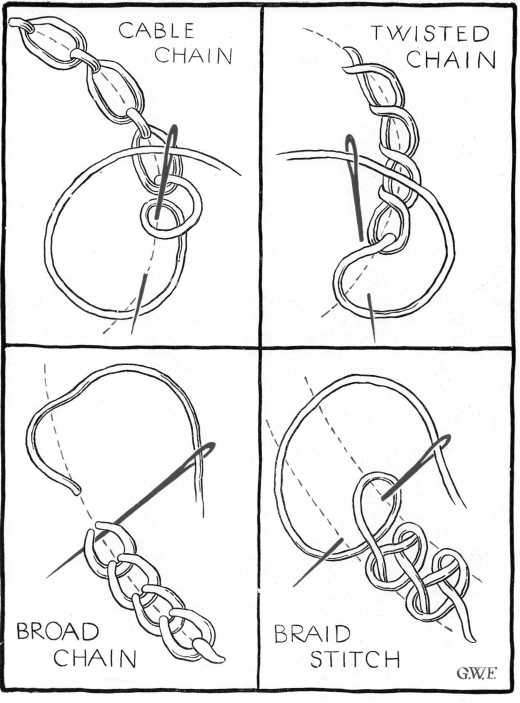

CABLE
CHAIN

TWISTED
CHAIN

BROAD
CHAIN

BRAID
STITCH

G.W.E.

PLATE 8

For the rapid rendering of conventional floral designs this stitch has won a well-deserved popularity. Under the name of "Lazy Daisy Stitch" its beauty

Detached Chain Stitch

has sometimes been sacrificed to rapidity, but when it is rightly used, and in combination with other stitches, many delightful decorations can be made, particularly for dainty things such as children's clothes, and all small articles which can be decorated with a "nosegay" type of pattern. A colour-scheme is essential. In white work the result would be "cheap" and ineffective. A five-pointed flower is shown in the diagram—two detached chain stitches have been worked, and the needle is in the correct position for completing the third and beginning the fourth. The position of the unworked stitches is indicated by dotted lines; actually a dot indicating the centre would be all the marking required. Separate stitches spotted at intervals make a delicate background filling. The diagram shows detached chain stitches combined with fly stitches placed thus. Worked in colours, with the latter in greens, they appear like scattered rosebuds. At the end of the book detached chain stitches are used with others to compose needle-designed borders, that is to say, worked direct on to the material without traced lines. On hand-knitted and woollen fabrics flowers made of detached chain stitches are useful for this reason, for on such textures it is not possible to trace designs, but well-balanced patches of colour may be worked direct.

Also called Y stitch, it is the same as detached chain in construction, but open at the top. The needles show the two actions which go to make the

Fly Stitch

stitch. It is useful combined with various other stitches for the making of needle-designed floral ornament. The effect of successive rows as a diaper pattern is shown in the diagram, also its natural way of making vandykes, which can be put to good account decoratively. Groups of three stitches in alternating colours form the border at the foot of the diagram. On the tea cosy (Plate 23) a line of fly stitch has been worked round the curve to simulate the hemstitching of the straight edge.

Worked in a circle, this stitch makes a complete "rosette" pattern—hence its name. (See Plate 2.) It is worked from right to left in two movements.

Rosette Chain

Trace two parallel lines and bring out the thread on the top line at the right, throw the thread to the left and put the needle in on the top line to the left of where it first appeared, and out on the lower line as shown in the diagram (first movement). With the thread lying beneath the needle from left to right pull through in a downward direction, and a single lop-sided loop is made. Now slip the needle underneath the thread at the top right as shown in the diagram (second movement) and the interlaced link is complete. To continue, follow the diagram of the first movement. This stitch is best worked in a well-twisted thread, whether of silk, linen, or cotton.

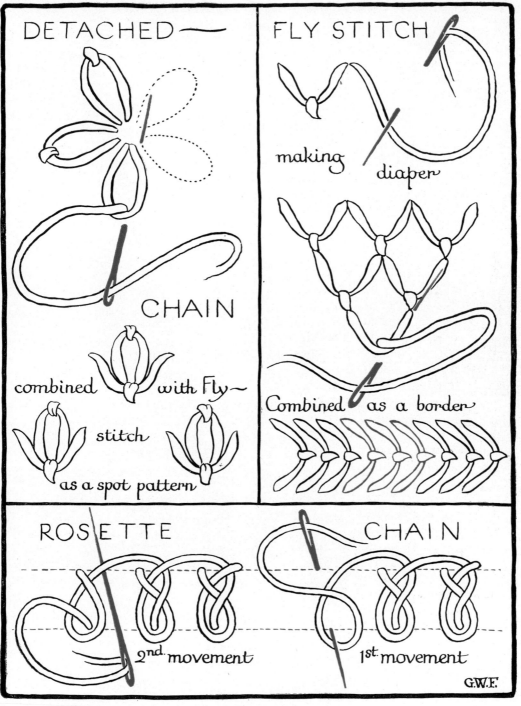

DETACHED—

FLY STITCH

making   diaper

CHAIN

combined   with Fly—
stitch
as a spot pattern

Combined   as a border

ROSETTE   CHAIN

2nd. movement   1st. movement

G.W.F.

PLATE 9

Blanket stitch, commonly known as Buttonhole (though not to be confused with the stitch used for the actual making of buttonholes), is seen on Plate 1.

Buttonhole or Blanket Stitch

It is one of the most generally useful of stitches, fulfilling many purposes. It may be described as being "once removed" from the flat satin stitch. The straight strokes of the latter are developed by the simple process of looping the thread beneath the point of the needle before pulling it through. These loops give the stitch its so-called heading. It is invaluable for the covering of raw edges, which give rise to the scalloped edge, which in its turn creates an opportunity for added decoration beyond the edge in the form of detached loops of buttonholing. It is important as a filling stitch, and in cut work, for bars as well as edges, and is the principal stitch used in needlepoint laces. Opposite it is shown as used for decorative lines.

No. 1. Here the stitches are slanted to form crosses. The needle in the diagram is placed at the angle required for the first stitch; for the second it must be sloped in the opposite direction.

No. 2, an arrangement of three stitches in a group, suggestive of grass decoratively treated. For the first stitch the needle slants from left to right; the second is vertical; the third slants from right to left. (See the needle in diagram.) In the needle-designed borders this stitch is seen combined with a flower of detached chain stitches in centre stem. (See Plate 122.)

No. 3 shows ordinary straight buttonhole stitch worked with a long and a short upright in turn.

No. 4. For this a line of buttonhole stitches placed apart is worked first (red in diagram), followed by a second line (black in diagram) worked just below it, two stitches being placed between each of the former ones. Two colours, or contrasting tones of one colour, are necessary for this.

No. 5. Here the stitches are spaced in pairs, and threads of another colour are afterwards slipped beneath.

No. 6. Three long and three short buttonhole stitches worked in a line, with two threads of another colour darned through them.

No. 7. Interlaced buttonhole stitches, a method which gives a "heading" on both sides of the stitch. In the first row worked, the stitches are placed just enough apart to allow another set of stitches to lie between them. For the second row the work is turned and the stitches dovetailed with the first. The interlaced loops in *motif* No. 5 (Plate 34) are worked in this stitch. For the rendering of "woody" stems, such as apple boughs, this is a useful stitch, the heading on either side suggesting their texture.

No. 8. Here groups of stitches alternating in colour are interlaced. Worked in untwisted floss silk these look like little shells forming a solid border.

Nos. 1 to 6 can be used as edgings. The tray cloths on Plate 28 are finished at the edge by arrangements of buttonhole stitching worked over tiny hems.

BUTTONHOLE VARIATIONS

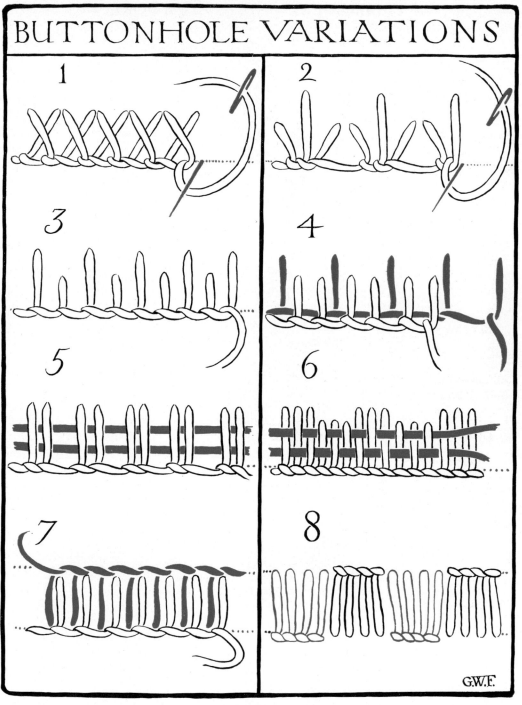

1   2

3   4

5   6

7   8

G.W.F.

PLATE 10

As a filling stitch, buttonhole lends itself to the making of light patterned fillings by spacing the stitches in open and definite order, and to solid fillings by working them closely. Four such arrangements are illus-

Buttonhole as a Filling

trated, in the first it is worked openly in straight lines across the form—each row being worked into the heading of the preceding one. The effect may be elaborated by slipping threads of another colour under the stitches.

Here the stitches are worked closely, and the headings are no longer visible, each being covered by the next row worked into it. This results in a richness

Buttonhole Shading

of texture which is very pleasing. By working alternate rows in a contrasting colour a striped effect is made, and the diagram shows how the method lends itself to shading, or the gradation of colour.

Following the Form

By following the outline of a form with successive rows of buttonholing until it is filled, an outline and a filling are made at the same time. Berries may be decoratively treated by a circle or wheel of buttonhole stitches; the needle enters the centre at the same point for each stitch, and the heading outlines the berry. (See Plate 53.)

Spaced Buttonhole

The fourth illustration differs from the first filling in that the stitches are grouped in pairs and spaced out. Groups of three stitches could be used in the same way, producing another change of pattern. A French knot may be worked in the centre of the spaces if further elaboration is needed. (See centre petals of the *motif* on the top right of Plate 34.)

BUTTONHOLE·AS·A·FILLING·STITCH

PLATE 11

Buttonhole stitch is useful for delicate treatment of backgrounds. The diagram shows the effect of threads afterwards slipped through the buttonhole stitches breaking their severity in a decorative tree-like manner. The perspective of the foreground fields is here suggested by gradation of tone which becomes lighter as the fields recede; but with colour, as well as tone, at the worker's command, such arrangements offer great scope for blending in the former, and giving values in the latter, all worked quite simply in lines following each other. Effects such as these, suggesting trees, fields, and woodlands, come legitimately within the province of needlework in that they are secured by the use of simple stitches frankly arranged in lines. They make no attempt to imitate the landscape of the naturalistic painter, though full use is made of the wealth of tone and colour which dyes can give to the working threads.

PLATE 12

Feather stitch, made use of to such fine effect in the panels and border decorations of the countryman's smock, is buttonhole stitch worked slantwise,

Feather Stitch

first on the right and then on the left, alternately. See the stitch at the centre of the upper diagram opposite.

The effect may be varied by working the stitches closely together or wider apart, by altering the slope of the needle and the length of the side stitches. Two further varieties, double and closed feather stitch, are shown in the diagram, from which the method of working may be followed.

Feather stitch forms part of the needle-designed borders on Plate 122. In the third border it is worked straight with three stitches on each side alternately; in the fifth with a stitch on each side opposite each other, and in the sixth in a waved line with five stitches on each side alternately.

No. 9 on Plate 19 shows feather stitch threaded with another colour about its centre.

Cretan stitch is another form of feather stitch. It is made in the same manner on each side alternately, but instead of reaching the same line at the centre, they

Cretan Stitch

fall short of it and a new effect results. Here it is shown as a petal filling, and the stitches are placed apart in order that the arrangement may be easily followed; for a solid filling they are worked closely. The needle is brought out at the top of the petal and buttonhole stitches are made on the right and left in turn; their length is determined by the shape of the petal.

It will be seen in the diagram that the amount taken up by the needle on either side causes the form of the petal to be repeated in the centre. A variation of this arrangement as a petal filling is seen in the centre flower on Plate 44.

Rope stitch is particularly well adapted to the working of curved and scrolled stems. It has the appearance of slanting satin stitch except that it is

Rope Stitch

more raised on one side, due to the looping of the thread beneath the needle in the manner of buttonhole stitch. It is worked from right to left between two parallel lines, thus: bring out the thread on the lower line and throw it to the left, then put the needle in on the top line a little to the right, and out again on the lower to the left, and close by the point at which it first appeared.

The diagram shows the position of the thread before the needle is pulled through; it is first over the needle (which is natural as it was thrown to the left), and then under the point of it as in buttonhole stitch.

The scrolls in lower left *motif*, Plate 34, and the band enclosing the pocket design on Plate 2 are worked in rope stitch.

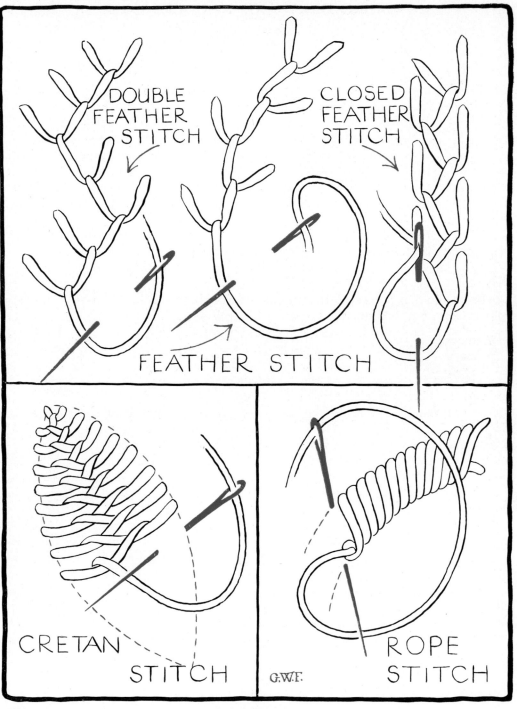

DOUBLE
FEATHER
STITCH

CLOSED
FEATHER
STITCH

FEATHER STITCH

CRETAN
STITCH

G.W.F.

ROPE
STITCH

PLATE 13

Buttonhole Stitches

Tailor's Buttonhole Tailor's buttonhole is worked with an extra twist, which gives it a knot at the edge, and it is easily distinguished from buttonhole stitch, which it resembles, by the firmer and raised heading. It is best worked closely, as the knots need the support of the stitch on either side. To work it, place the needle in the material as if about to make a buttonhole stitch with the thread lying beneath the point from left to right, but before pulling through take hold of the thread near the eye of the needle and place it beneath the needle from right to left as seen in the diagram. Now pull through in a downward direction.

Circles or wheels of this stitch are useful as flower centres and as "spots" in geometrical designs. In working them the needle enters at the same point in the centre for each stitch, and the knotted edge outlines the circle. (See Plate 2.)

Detached Loops From the diagrams at *B* the method of working detached loops for the extra adornment of a scalloped edge may be followed. They are worked, where required, as the scalloping proceeds. Here a group of four are placed in the inlets made by the curved edge; they are worked "in the air," i.e. not through the material, but by means of threads thrown across from side to side where they are attached through the edge of the buttonhole stitch as a foundation.

In diagram No. 1 it will be seen that the buttonholing at the edge of the cloth has been worked just beyond the apex, when the thread is taken back across the angle and passed through the stitch at the edge from back to front, making the foundation of the first loop. Then buttonhole stitches are worked over it until the half-way point is reached, when the thread is again taken back to the edge, making the foundation of the second loop which is buttonholed in turn.

Diagram No. 2 shows this second loop completed, also the second half of the first loop, which is worked next, then the buttonholing of the edge of the cloth is continued and a thread thrown back for the foundation of the third loop.

Diagrams 3 and 4 show how the group is completed. The edge is then continued. (See worked example at foot of Plate 2.) In the diagram the loops are shown worked over a single thread. A foundation of greater strength and stability is made by laying three threads. When the third thread is laid, the needle is in the correct position for beginning the buttonholing over them.

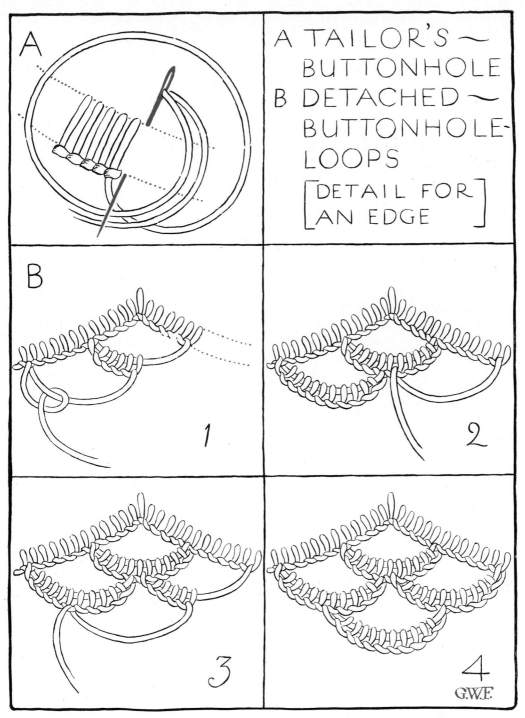

A

A TAILOR'S ~
BUTTONHOLE
B DETACHED ~
BUTTONHOLE-
LOOPS
[DETAIL FOR]
[AN EDGE]

B

1

2

3

4

G.W.E.

PLATE 14

A useful outline stitch, simple and quick to work. Bring the thread out on the traced line at the left, and with the needle pick up a very small piece of the

Knot Stitch

ground material at right angles to the line as seen in the diagram, leaving the thread lying above the needle, its natural position if left to itself. Then take hold of the thread near the eye of the needle and pull it down until it lies under it close to the material. Pull the needle through and bring it up vertically away from the ground. This causes a small knot to tie on the surface. Succeeding knots may be worked so that they touch each other producing a fancy cord-like appearance similar to a line of small beads closely packed, or placed apart when the effect is of beads put at intervals upon a thread. (See the seaweed around the dolphins on Plate 64.) The effect of a double line of knot stitch as an outline is seen in the leaves on Plate 73, and on Plate 34 the lower left *motif* has three lines round the centre petals. When working two or more rows together, as in the last-mentioned examples, the stitches in the first row are placed just far enough apart to admit of the next set being dovetailed between. The seaweed in the border of the cloth on Plate 64 is outlined with knot stitch, with a space between the two rows.

Also called German knot stitch, is worked in three simple movements to a stitch, producing a bold upstanding line of knots. It is advisable to use a well-

Double Knot Stitch

twisted thread, whether of silk, linen, or cotton, to get the best result. The needle enters the ground material once. (See No. 1 in the diagram.) Afterwards it is slipped under the thread. (See Nos. 2 and 3.) This is useful mainly as an outline stitch, and will effectively work border patterns composed of scrolled lines without further addition.

These knots lend themselves to the making of stylized flower forms: roses, rosebuds, daisies, etc. A five-petal flower is seen at No. 5 on Plate 16—three

Bullion Knots

knots for each petal, the inner ones being darker in tone for the best effect. A single French knot makes the centre. So-called roses are made of clusters of knots, five, six, seven or eight, wrapped round the first knot, made after the manner of the two shown. The diagram shows one finished knot and one in the making. Assuming that the knot to be made is to lie between *C–D* (parallel to the knot at *A–B*), bring the needle out at *C*, put it in at *D*, and again out at *C* without pulling it through. While the needle is in this position (as in the diagram) take the thread which is at *C* in the left hand and wind it round the needle as many times as needed to fill the space between *C* and *D*. Place the left thumb on the coil to keep it firm whilst pulling the needle through, putting it in at *D* and gradually pulling the thread through at the back to tighten the knot.

Round-eyed needles having a straight running surface from eye to point are the best to use. Such needles as "crewel" and "chenille," in which the eye

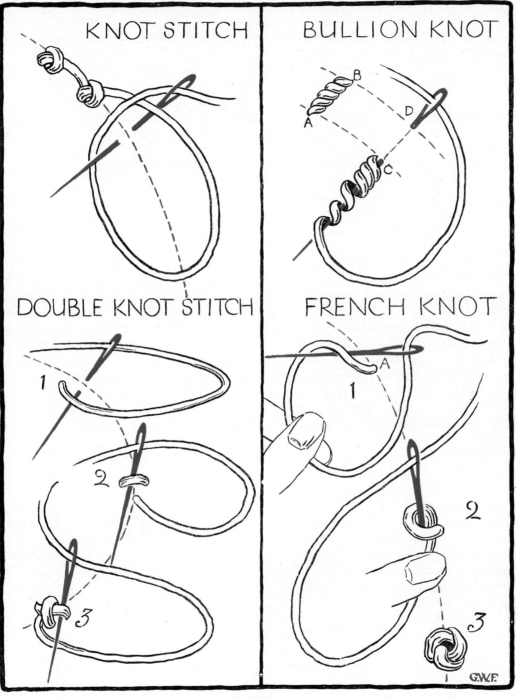

KNOT STITCH

BULLION KNOT

DOUBLE KNOT STITCH

FRENCH KNOT

PLATE 15

is wider than the shaft, spoil the knots, as they cannot be pulled smoothly through the coil.

A French knot should look like a bead lying on its open end. Having secured the thread at some other point, bring the thread out from the back of

French Knots the material at the spot where the knot is to be, *A* on the diagram. While holding the needle in the right hand above the material in the position seen at No. 1, take the thread between the first finger and thumb, twist it round the needle once, bring the needle to an upright position, and put it in close by where it last came out. (See No. 2.) Hold the thread down firmly against the material with the left thumb, whilst pulling the needle through to the back. This is a precaution which must not be omitted, or something other than a French knot will be made. The thread may be twisted once, twice, or three times, but not more, round the needle according to size of knot required.

French knots can aptly suggest the stamens of flowers, and flower centres may be made by a closely packed mass, by an open powdering, or by a circle of knots, to suggest but a few of the many possible ways. Again, the severity of an outline may be modified by a fringe of knots on its outer or inner side. Also backgrounds or ornaments may be patterned by French knots in the manner of a scattering of beads. In Chinese work the decorative value of knotted stitches is seen to perfection. These are not always knotted through the material; sometimes the thread is knotted first and then sewn on, but with great precision of drawing.

In the time of William and Mary and during the reign of Queen Anne the English and Dutch were doing a species of knotted thread work, inspired

Knotted Thread Work originally by Chinese embroideries. The Dutch were large importers from China, and we were in constant communication with the Low Countries at that time. Cream linen thread was knotted by hand, in varying sizes according to the number of strands used. This was sewn on to cream linen as outlines and fillings of boldly formalized designs to which a great variety of detail was added. For large surfaces this method was useful and effective in its own characteristic way, though this was widely different from that which inspired it. The knotting of thread became quite mechanical with practice, as may be judged by Sir Charles Sedley saying of Queen Anne that "when she rode in a coach abroad she was always knotting thread."

Some contemporary uses are seen opposite. No. 1, spot treatments on organdie. No. 2, knot stitch with twisted embroidery silk, light on a dark

Knot-Stitch Specimens semi-transparent material (note the bead-like effect). Nos. 3 and 4 are on very transparent black nylon. The more intense black seen in the *motif* 3, is achieved by applying a piece of the same material at the back, and working through the double thickness. The

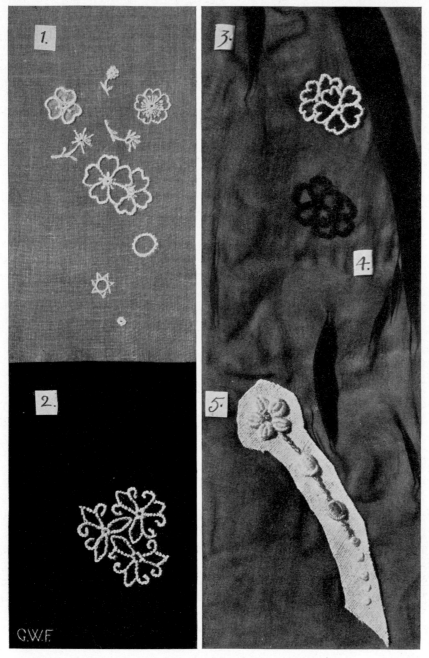

PLATE 16
KNOT STITCHES ON VARIOUS FABRICS

top left organdie spot is treated similarly. (For No. 5, see Bullion Knots, page 32.)

The composite stitches given here are decorative band stitches suitable for conventional and geometric designs of a bold type. In each there is a foundation stitch worked through the ground fabric, upon which another thread is laced in some particular manner. The overcast back and stem stitches on Plate 4 are also composite in construction but "flat," inasmuch as they are neither looped, linked, nor knotted.

A line of back stitching is worked first. With another colour this is threaded in and out as seen on the right of the diagram, making a pretty border stitch.

Threaded Back Stitch The effect on the left is obtained by making a return journey with the lacing thread, passing it in and out of the stitches in the same way. This is a useful method for attaching threads which are unyielding and not adapted to passing in and out of the ground fabric. The foundation, for which chain stitch may be substituted, is done in a workable thread, and the troublesome one threaded through it. (See No. 4 on Plate 19.)

The diagram shows a decorative line stitch composed of herring-bone laced with a thread of another colour. To do this the thread passes perpendicularly

Twisted Lattice Stitch up under one transverse thread (see needle) and down under the next in turn, until the end of the line is reached. Another effect is secured by lacing in the same way upon a foundation of two rows of herring-bone. In this case the stitches are spread more widely than is customary with herring-bone, and the second row of stitches are set between the first, forming a lattice. Two rows of lacing will complete the stitch.

For a filling stitch threads are laid first all in one direction, and a second set is darned in and out of them in the opposite direction to form a network which is laced in the same way as the other stitches. This filling can be worked on a prepared opening without a background, or the ground can be cut away after the filling is done. For either of these ways the network should be worked rather more closely than is otherwise necessary, to give greater strength.

Is worked on a foundation of running, couching, or back stitching. Here the last-named is shown. Another colour is threaded through the stitches in

Pekinese Stitch the manner shown in the diagram, where the thread has been left loose in order that its path may be clearly followed. Actually each stitch, particularly the lower part of it, is pulled fairly tight as the work proceeds. For the finished effect see No. 6 on Plate 19.

COMPOSITE STITCHES

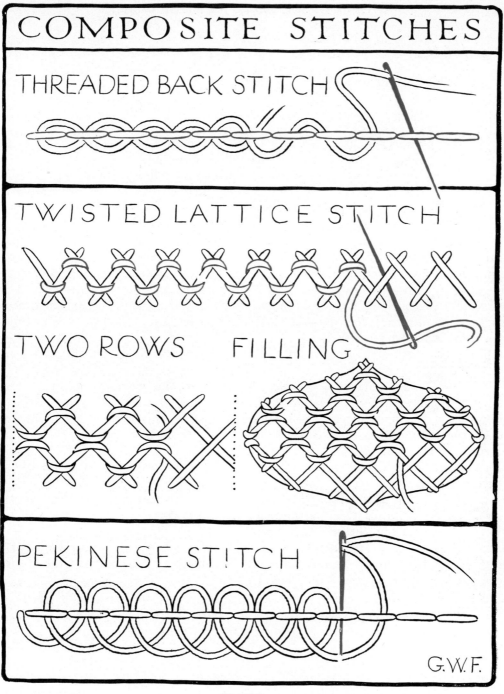

THREADED BACK STITCH

TWISTED LATTICE STITCH

TWO ROWS   FILLING

PEKINESE STITCH

G.W.F.

PLATE 17

Here chevron stitch is worked on a foundation of wedges. These are covered completely by the final stitch which is done with a thread of treble or **Raised Chevron Stitch** even greater thickness, resulting in a line of chevrons in high relief. As a "flat" stitch worked direct on to the material, chevron is seen on Plate 3. For the foundation use a smooth thread which will lie flatly, and bring the needle out at *A* on the right, put it in at *B* and out at *C*, then again in at *A* and out at *D*, and the first wedge is made. The needle enters the material horizontally every time. The position of the thread at the back of the material is indicated in the diagram by a dotted line in red. It is important that the wedges should be accurately placed with the thick thread-work upwards, winding in and out of each wedge in turn, in the manner shown in the diagram. (See worked example No. 7 on Plate 19.)

Interlaced Band Stitch An arrangement of lacing on a foundation of two lines of back stitching.

The diagram at the top shows the relation of the back stitches to each other. They are not opposite but alternate. The lower diagram shows how the final thread is laced and looped; this action is repeated on the opposite side with the thread beneath the needle from left to right of the loop. (See No. 3 on Plate 19 for the effect.)

The group of stitches connecting the links between the two margins of this stitch are three close rows of darning which run the length of the border. With **Guilloche Stitch** another colour these are threaded in and out, as seen on the right of the diagram. The effect is completed by returning the lacing thread, passing it in and out in the opposite direction. The marginal lines are shown in stem stitch, but chain would be equally suitable. A French or a bullion knot may be placed in the centre of the circles. (See worked example No. 8 on Plate 19.)

COMPOSITE STITCHES

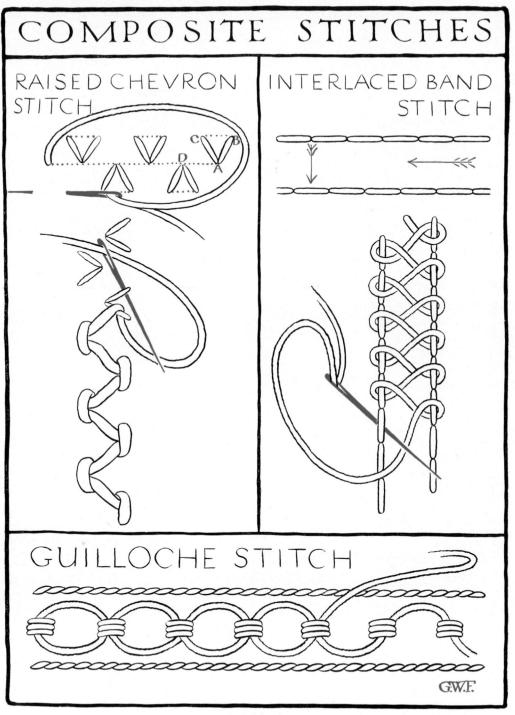

RAISED CHEVRON STITCH

INTERLACED BAND STITCH

GUILLOCHE STITCH

G.W.F.

PLATE 18

DESCRIPTION OF STITCHES ILLUSTRATED ON PLATE 19

1. Herring-bone stitch worked in blue and laced in yellow in the manner illustrated on Plate 17. Buttonhole stitch forms the border on each side.

2. Chequered chain. Worked with two different colours in the one needle. (See Plate 7.)

3. Interlaced band stitch. Yellow silk laced on a foundation of two rows of back stitch in blue. (See Plate 18.)

4. Threaded back stitch. Back stitch in yellow silk with blue threaded in and out of each stitch on the surface. (See Plate 17.)

5. Tied chain stitch. Two rows of chain in blue are worked close together, the links of the second row lying exactly on a level with those of the first. With yellow silk the inner sides of the links are overcast. For this the silk is brought out at the end of the first link of the upper line at the right, and the needle passed beneath the two inner sides of the first pair of links; the same action is repeated in each pair to the end.

6. Pekinese stitch. Blue threaded on a foundation of back stitch in yellow. (See Plate 17.)

7. Chevron stitch. On a foundation of wedges. (For details of working see Plate 18.)

8. Guilloche stitch. Three lines of running in blue at the centre are threaded with yellow silk in two journeys—outwards and the return. A line of stem stitch on each side forms the border. (See Plate 18.)

9. Feather stitch. In blue, threaded at the centre with yellow.

10. Overcast chain stitch. Chain in blue, overcast with yellow silk which passes beneath each stitch in turn without entering the ground material.

11. Herring-bone (two rows). First with yellow, then with blue. In working the latter the needle picks up the spaces between the stitches of the former row, resulting in a crossed appearance.

12. Chain stitch. Blue overcast with yellow on one side only.

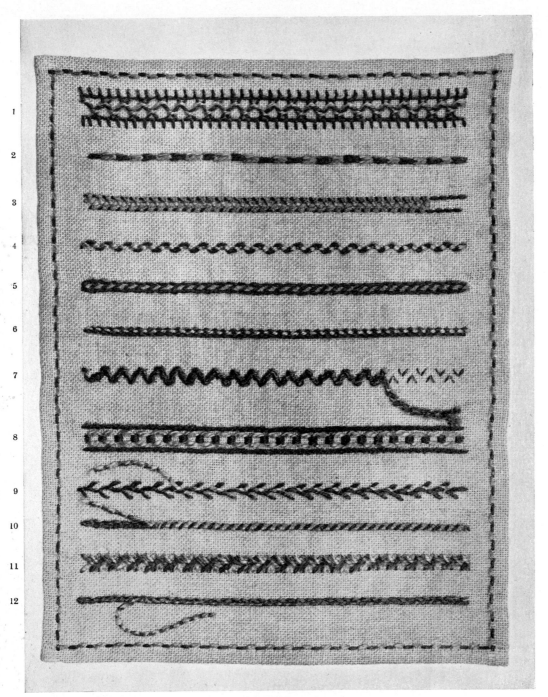

PLATE 19
A COMPOSITE STITCH SAMPLER

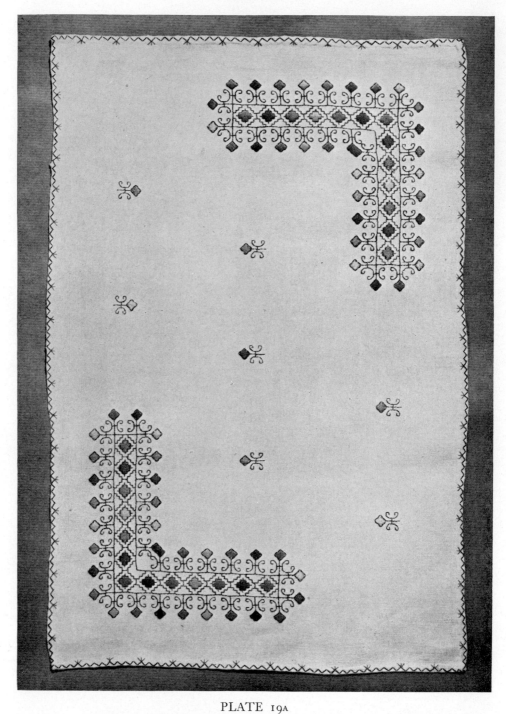

PLATE 19A

EMBROIDERY BY THE THREAD FROM OROPESA, SPAIN

The double running is in black with the solid pieces filled in with
satin stitch in sequences of red, blue, yellow and green.

CHAPTER II

TECHNIQUE INFLUENCED BY THE THREAD OF THE GROUND FABRIC

CHAPTER II

You see, O my modest friend! that your gamut needs not be very wide to begin with. The point is, that within it you learn to play becomingly.

THE above is from a lecture by Sir Arthur Quiller-Couch, delivered at Cambridge, on the practice of writing. Let us suppose it to have been said on the practice of Needlework. Here, to begin with, our gamut need not be wide—proficiency in a few stitches and a whole field of activity opens for us, but the point is that within it we "learn to play becomingly." There are methods of work which, though comparatively simple, are beautiful in their result. Some of the earliest known work is done with coloured threads of wool and flax on linen, and workers who were capable of weaving the linen were ingenious enough to decorate it with patterns in colour.

These patterns were built up by stitches on the warp and weft threads of the material, a method inevitably resulting in that squareness, or angularity, of outline which is so pleasing a factor in textile design, because it is the direct outcome of the tools and material used. Whether such patterns are expressed by an outline as on Plate 28, or solidly as on Plate 31, by filling the background with stitches and leaving the pattern in plain linen as on Plate 26, by darning on the warp threads (the weft having been first withdrawn) as on Plate 23, the result is entirely satisfactory for several reasons, but mainly because the restrictions imposed by the material have been so completely accepted.

This is a consideration which must be carefully observed in all crafts, and in needlework and embroidery not less so. Needle and thread are simple **Limitations of the Material** unpretentious tools with which to make useful and decorative things, and a nice adjustment between needle and thread, thread and stitch, stitch and fabric and design is necessary to ensure a right result. Too small a needle chafes the thread; too large a needle leaves holes showing in the ground material, and, again, if the thread used is not of the right size for the fabric the effect of the stitchery may be lost. In these small matters it is impossible to take too much care, and no time spent on them is wasted, for indeed, most difficulties in workmanship arise from such neglect. Between stitches and ground fabric there is great interdependence, some types of work being possible only on smooth-surfaced, closely woven grounds, as is the case when fine outlines and delicate details are to be expressed, whereas others need loosely woven materials with even threads, and so on. Clearly it is wisest to make the available ground material the starting-point of our design, and this is less of a limitation than at first appears, for in these days every variety of texture can be found. Is this to our advantage? It should be so, for thus we are able to embark upon all types of work. How comes it then that if we take a handful of, say, our contemporary household embroideries and show them beside a similar number of early English, Italian, or other European peasant pieces we find the latter are superior to ours in such matters as appropriateness, proportion, and general harmony? "Think of the many hours they had to spend on it," we say, "hours that we can never give." It was not time alone, but the frankness with which the workers accepted the limitations imposed by the materials which gave the distinction that we are forced to recognize. Their range of backgrounds, though small, were the happy outcome of their own weaving, whilst to dye the threads with which to embroider them must have been a joy in itself. It would seem, therefore, that this limited choice of materials was an aid to artistic results; we would not be without the resources of modern days, though truly we must keep our "eyes skinned," as it were, and be ever wary of going beyond the limitations which our materials impose.

Going Beyond the Limitations   An historical and very obvious example of this fault may be seen in the "Stump Work" which found such favour in Charles I's reign, and continued throughout the Commonwealth into the reign of Charles II. Writing of this so-called "Stump Work" in his book on *English Embroidery*, Mr. Kendrick says—

Its most patent characteristic is perhaps its grotesque ugliness; but another which more effectually differentiates it is the high relief produced by stuffing and padding introduced into many parts of the design. Tent curtains, draperies, etc., are so made that they can be pulled aside, the arms of the figures are modelled in the round, and rockeries are thrown into deep relief. The work is in fact a mockery of sculpture, and departs altogether from the legitimate province of the needle.

It would be difficult to think of a method more unsuitable for the decoration of caskets, work-boxes, and book-covers, yet these were among the things for which it was most frequently used. Technically, this work shows great skill, and is much prized by collectors of curios. To artists and craftsmen, however, it remains an outstanding example of misapplied energy directed by entirely false principles; as do those "needlework pictures" and "portraits" popular in England some hundred years ago, which sought to imitate oil painting. These were worked with fine crewel wools, the high lights rendered in silk stitches, and the whole illusion enhanced by framing and glazing.

Work on the Right Lines   That our work is justified in its aims, and that we enjoy doing it, is the all-important matter, for it is impossible to enjoy doing a thing if all the time we are haunted by the idea that after all it will not have been worth the effort. Selwyn Image said—

The aim of the embroiderer must be not to show 'See how skilful I am!' but simply to make the niceties of his craft tell for the general effectiveness of the design seen at the proper distance.

A dessert doyley or a dressing-table mat may be worked with exquisite details of fine stitchery which will delight us at close quarters, whilst wall-hangings, curtains, and the like must have ornament both bold and steady enough to be effective from a distance. Detail for the mere sake of detail is futile. Now for the considerations that make for this rightness! Here are six points to be considered in planning a piece of work.

1. Appropriateness of conception and design for the purpose for which it is to be used.

Points to be Considered in Planning a Piece of Work

2. Appropriateness of conception and design to the place in which it is to be used.

3. Suitability of material to the above.

4. Balance of colour, or if in monochrome, of tone or texture (i.e. stitch).

5. Stitchery.

6. Rhythm of general effect and finish.

Let us start on the right lines, for in beginning well we end well. What we have of originality will appear in its own time and manner. A piece of work the design of which is controlled by the thread of the ground material makes a good beginning, and has very definite advantages over other methods. It can be worked directly on the material without preliminary drawing, in fact with nothing more than a pencil and a card for marking off distances. It is only through dealing *directly* with the tools and materials of a craft that we learn how they should be handled. Let us start then with linens and threads, and not by drawing on paper. Having successfully accomplished some one kind of work by the thread, we shall have mastered such important matters as a right relation of needle to thread, and thread to fabric, tension of thread and accuracy, and possessing this knowledge, all other methods of needlework will be more easily acquired.

Plate 20 shows some arrangements of straight lines as decoration. Here proportion is an important factor, the more so because of the simplicity of design. Again, if construction in design is clearly grasped, we

Straight Lines as Decoration

are beginning well, and here we have it in its simplest form. These lines may be worked direct on linens or other grounds where the separate threads may be easily seen, and with no other guide than the counted thread for the placing of the stitches. Another way is to mark the position of the lines by withdrawing a thread or threads. The withdrawing of many adjoining threads naturally tends to weaken the fabric, particularly in cases where the final stitch leaves many of the remaining threads exposed, but those stitches in which they are bound together in some manner which covers them entirely give additional strength. Overcast hemstitch, the faggot stitch on Plate 22, and all needle-woven stitches which completely cover the threads, are examples of this. Where such stitches are to be worked in each direction (i.e. along the selvedge and at right angles to it) it is well to choose a material with even threads, that is, with approximately the same number in the warp as in the weft. Where drawn thread line stitches (such as the last three on page 50) intersect each other, little overcast crosses appear, and the ends of the cut threads are secured by buttonholing. (See G on Plate 22.) These decorative incidents resulting from essential stitchery are delightful in themselves.

STRAIGHT · LINES · AS · DECORATION

PLATE 20

PLATE 21

FINISHED WORK, ILLUSTRATING THE USE OF STRAIGHT LINES AS
ORNAMENT

And with the addition of *motifs*.

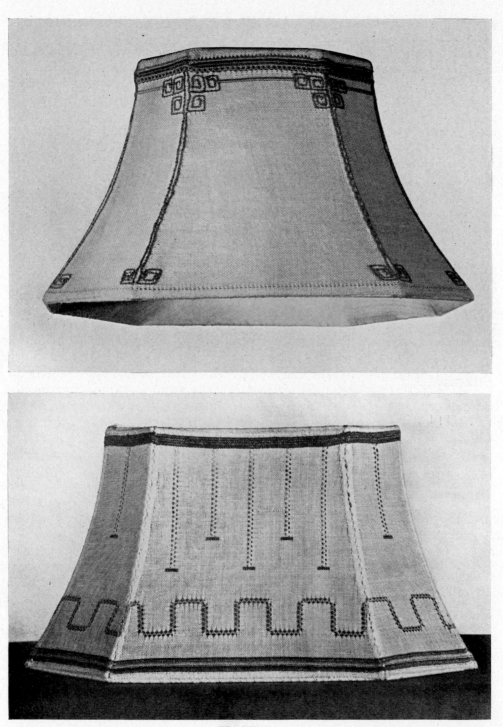

PLATE 21A

LAMPSHADES ON LINEN WITH LINE ORNAMENT

Top: by the author. *Bottom:* by Mrs. Winifred G. Gibbs.

The effect is seen in the side hems of the opposite sampler, and in the right half of the lower hem. It is worked from left to right on the reverse side. The **Hemstitch** top hem is reversed so that by turning the book the working may be followed at the then left side of the lower hem. To begin, secure the end of the thread in the edge of the fold by an oversewing stitch (no knot) and pass the needle behind four upright threads from right to left, pull it through, and then pick up a piece of the edge of the fold. (See needle.) The number of threads picked up varies with the material hemmed and the effect desired.

No. 1. Hemstitch as above on one side of the withdrawn **Bar Stitch** threads, picking up four to a stitch, and again on the opposite side, picking up the same groups of four. No. 2 shows the reverse side on which it is worked, with the needle in position.

No. 3. Pick up an even number of threads, say six, when **Split Hemstitch** hemstitching the first side. On the opposite side take up the same number, but split the clusters, taking three from each, and behold the chevron!

Nos. 4 and 5. Here three threads have been withdrawn, four left, and again three withdrawn; four threads are picked up at the top and at the bottom. **Hemstitch (Alternate)** The action is the same as for herring-bone stitch, but the clusters are not opposite each other. Bring the needle out of the central threads and pick up four threads at the bottom. (See needle.) Next pick up six threads at the top—this sets the clusters alternately, and the stitch is continued by picking up four threads on each side in turn.

No. 6. Hemstitch on each side as for bar stitch (No. 1). The interlacing is done by a thread run through the centre as follows: Secure the thread behind **Interlaced Hemstitch** the buttonhole stitches and bring it out at the centre; divide the clusters of threads in half, and insert the eye of the needle under the second half of the first cluster, and under the first half of the second, and with it hook the farther set of threads under the nearer set; pull through and repeat the action.

No. 7. Withdraw threads as for No. 4. Work on the reverse **Italian Square Hemstitch** side. (See No. 8.) Pick up four threads at the bottom, and at the top pick up those same four threads, then pass the needle behind the central threads vertically (as shown by the needle). Repeat the three actions.

No. 9 is a strong faggot stitch, which can be used to inset lines of colour, in which respect it differs from the previous stitches which depend on the **Faggot Stitch** open-work for their effect rather than upon the thread used. It is worked from right to left in six movements, and is less complicated than would appear. Once the action is grasped, it becomes quite mechanical and can be worked at a good speed. Here three

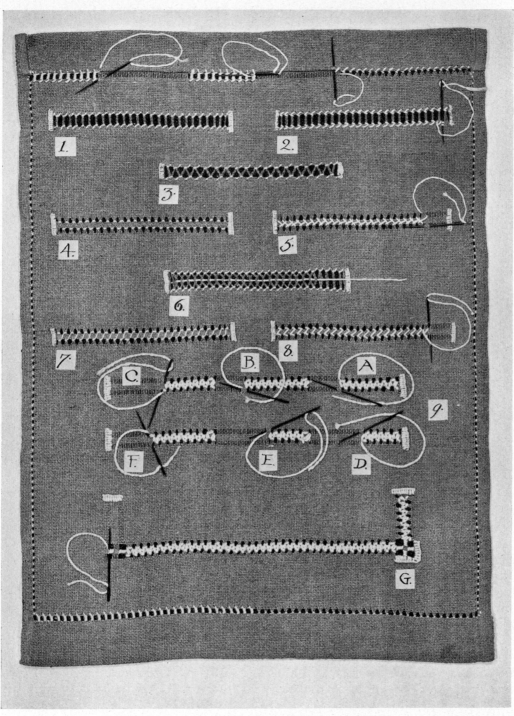

PLATE 22

A SAMPLER OF HEMSTITCHES

threads are withdrawn, four left, and again three withdrawn. The first movement is seen at *A*, where the needle picks up four threads at the bottom. At *B*
the needle is in position for passing the silk round the same threads. At *C* it
passes in at the top and out where the silk is at the bottom. At *D* it picks up
six threads at the top. At *E* it passes the silk round them, and at *F* it passes
in at the bottom and out where the silk is at the top. This is the final movement. To continue, repeat the action at *A*. By picking up six threads at *D*,
the stitch is set alternate; afterwards four are picked up at the bottom and
four at the top in turn. The ends of the cut threads are secured by buttonhole
stitch. At *G* the treatment of a corner is seen. Begin by running a thread
round the angle two threads below the cut edges, and buttonhole from left to
right over it, then pass the needle through the back of these stitches and bring
it out by the central linen threads. Overcast two bars of these and the silk is
in position for beginning the faggot stitch. The same corner treatment can be
used for Nos. 4 and 7.

The working of this stitch is seen in the top hem at the left. The finished
effect is seen in the left half of the lower hem. It is the strongest of the hem-

Overcast Hemstitch stitches. Secure the end of the thread in the hem at the left;
pass the needle behind four upright threads, bringing it out
beneath two horizontal ones (see first needle); now pass the
needle round the four threads a sufficient number of times to cover them entirely
(see second needle), and bring the needle through the fold above the next set
of four threads. This may be used for a wider hemstitch (withdrawing six or
eight threads) without weakening the fabric. (See applied hem on Plate 31, and
pocket on Plate 123.)

Is the name given to the process of darning patterns by needle into the
warp or weft threads of an already woven material, one or other set of threads

Needle-weaving having been first withdrawn. The tray-cloth and cosy opposite
are simple examples of this work, which is decorative in quality
and strong. It is suited to the decoration of table-linen, towel-
ends, chair-backs, and similar articles which suffer hard wear and need frequent
laundering. These examples are worked in two colours, blue and green, on
cream linen. The method of working is explained by a separate sampler,
Plate 24. On the cloth there is a suggestion at one corner for accentuating the
ornament by means of three sets of simple stitches at the angle. A line of
buttonhole stitch is worked first, followed by French knots in green worked
close together. The projecting pieces are in Roumanian stitch. The straight
edges of both cloth and cosy are hemstitched. As this method is not possible
on curved edges, a uniform effect has been preserved by working a line of fly
stitches at the same distance as the hemstitch. First turn back the edge of each
half of the cosy (a single fold is sufficient) and work the fly stitch, which also
serves to catch down the fold. With two threads in the needle work knot stitch
at $\frac{1}{4}$ in. intervals round the edge of each half, and, finally, lace them together

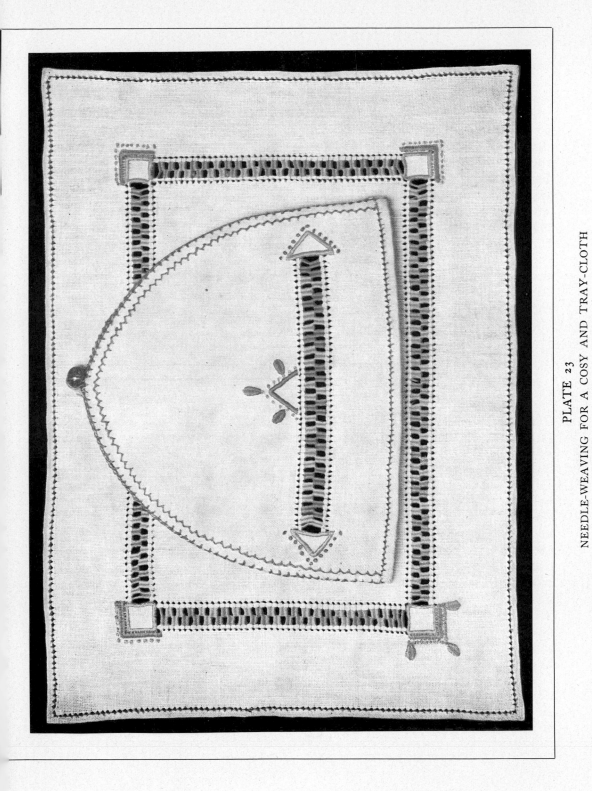

PLATE 23

NEEDLE-WEAVING FOR A COSY AND TRAY-CLOTH

with a double thread through the loops just formed. The bead at the top, which adds finish as a handle, is attached by the lacing thread. To work a border similar to that on the tray cloth on Plate 2 3, first decide at what distance from the hem it is to be placed, and mark this measurement on a strip of paper with a pencil. Using this measure, cut one thread in the middle of each side at the distance decided upon. Pull the cut ends gently until they meet each other at the corners. Cut them at these points and draw out. The outer edge of the border is now defined. Next draw out one thread all round for the inner edge, leaving twenty threads between. These inner threads meet the outer ones, and thus a square is formed at each corner. (See No. 1 opposite, which represents one side.) Next work the four squares; run a thread between the first two threads of the linen, and either buttonhole or satin stitch over this, picking up three threads with the needle, which emerges in the space made by the withdrawn thread (No. 2). More threads may now safely be cut within the boundaries. Next to these draw out one more thread on each side, leave three uncut each side, and withdraw all those between, leaving them arranged thus—

Two withdrawn
Three left
Twelve withdrawn Twenty-two threads.
Three left
Two withdrawn

The stitch at the edge which divides the threads into clusters is worked next (and if done on the reverse side, or back, of the work results in the neater effect seen in No. 4). Secure the end of the thread in the back of the buttonhole stitches, and bring the needle out on the left beneath the three uncut threads. Pick up four threads at the top (see first needle in No. 3), and pass the needle behind the three horizontal threads and between the same two upright ones. (See second needle.) Turn the work and repeat the stitch on the opposite side, and be sure to pick up the clusters accurately. Begin the weaving stitch by overcasting one cluster of four threads to the centre; continue by working over and under two groups of thread (see needle on right No. 4) until the first block is filled. Pass the needle through the centre of one half of this block to get into position for working the second. (See needle in No. 4.) The blocks are worked in groups of three, light and dark alternately. Use two needles, one for each colour. Take a long thread, and on completing a group pass the thread through the stitches at the back of the three horizontal threads in readiness for the next group of that colour.

In the two patterns shown at the top border the ground threads are left exposed in places. This makes for lightness of effect but is less durable. Both are worked over clusters of three threads, divided thus by hemstitch (see Plate 22) worked on each side.

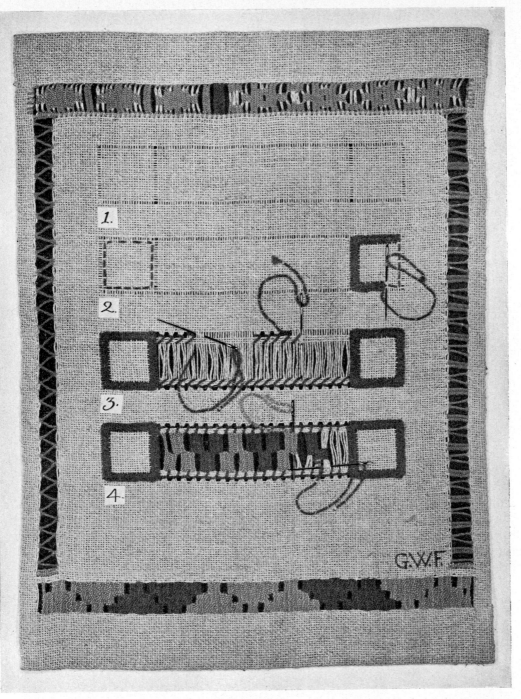

PLATE 24

A SAMPLER OF NEEDLE-WEAVING

The chevron border on the left of Plate 24 is worked by overcasting three threads, taking the final stitch over six threads, thus tying two clusters together at each side. For the border on the right the same method is used, overcasting four threads by straight bars made by weaving over and under two threads.

The border at the bottom is composed of pyramid shapes, each woven over six clusters of four threads. Three light pyramids alternate with two dark ones. The three last-mentioned borders are worked direct without stitching at the sides to divide the threads into groups. On coarse fabrics these thread-grouping stitches are unnecessary, though they may be used where the decorative effect requires them. On fine fabrics they are of practical use, saving time which would otherwise be spent in sorting the threads when weaving.

Another needle-woven border is seen at the foot of Plate 30. Here the threads have been divided into groups of three by means of Italian square hemstitch.

Elaborated Corner Treatments The "stops" used to secure the cut threads at the angles and ends of the needle-woven borders seen on Plate 23 take the form of a square on the tray-cloth and a triangle on the tea-cosy, both simply outlined by satin stitch. On larger work these stops can with advantage be made more important.

Two elaborated corners are illustrated opposite; both are for square cloths on which they connect borders of needle-weaving worked on all four sides. The four larger petals of the flower design (in the lower corner) are enriched by drawn-thread open filling stitches, a different filling being used in each corner of the cloth. The embroidery is in two colours, blue and yellow, on a white linen ground. The flower is edged by buttonhole stitch in blue, the fillings are yellow, and pyramids of each colour alternate in the borders. The upper specimen, with a floral spray within a square stop, is carried out in two tones of wedgwood blue on cream linen, and is finished by an applied hem of blue linen. Instructions for the latter are given on page 172.

Five more woven patterns are shown, two on Plate 1, one on Evenweave linen on Plate 32, and two on Plate 54, carried out with thick threads on suitably coarse material (Celtic cloth).

PLATE 25
ELABORATED CORNER TREATMENTS

Stitches by the counted thread have been popular throughout the ages, and their use has been developed in various ways in both Oriental and European countries. *Points comptées*, the French name for them, is a more descriptive one than ours, namely, canvas stitches, again known in medieval times as *Opus Pulvinarium* (which means "Shrine work" or "cushion" stitches). Still another term, used to embrace all those stitches for which patterns can be worked out on squared paper, is Mosaic stitches, which at once suggests to the mind's eye the special character of work by the counted threads. It has been said that embroidered patterns in crossed and similar stitches preceded tessellated paving and inspired that treatment. The enduring nature of such stitches has always been recognized; hence their use for the ornamentation of chairs, stools, banqueting couches, and other similar articles which must withstand constant friction. Many beautiful pieces of work of this kind, done during the sixteenth and seventeenth centuries, may be seen in our historic houses and museums. These range from small purses in *petit point* to cushions, chairs, panels, and wall hangings, the last-named of a size involving years of labour. In Hardwick Hall there is a panel worked by Mary, Queen of Scots, bearing a monogram of the name MARIA ensigned with a crown. The ground is divided into lozenge shapes, by means of intertwined stems, which enclose in succession a Scots thistle, an English rose, and a French lily. Small ovals, containing illustrations of fables, are inserted into this.

Again, in the latter part of the nineteenth century a set of wall hangings was discovered in a medium-sized house in Hatton Garden, London. The stripping of many wall-papers revealed them stiffened with dirt and barely recognizable in design. A cleansing process was carefully carried out, and they may now be seen on a staircase at the Victoria and Albert Museum, in all their glory. They number six, each measuring 7 ft. 9 in. high by 4 ft. wide, and in all of them the groundwork is completely hidden by stitches. Photographs will show the strength of the design and its suitability in scale to the purpose for which the hangings were made, but to appreciate the bold and skilful technique, in which eight or nine different canvas stitches are used to pattern so large an area and yet give the effect of one rich, flat plane, it is necessary to see the originals. These were made soon after the middle of the seventeenth century. For canvas work and stitches see pages 78 to 82.

Italian Embroideries   In the Italian linen embroideries of the fifteenth and sixteenth centuries we see a perfect rendering of stitches by the counted thread. The designs are often expressed by filling the background with fine stitches which leave the pattern sharply defined in plain linen. These are worked in floss silk, usually red, though blue, green, and pink and blue combined were also used.

Note: the word "Ancestry" appears in the left margin beside the first paragraph.

PLATE 26

"HATTON GARDEN" HANGING

The border illustrated on right is Italian XVIIth Century, red silk on linen; background filled
with stitches.

From the Victoria and Albert Museum

Stitches in silk of one colour only, on linen, are worked with such precision and accuracy, that elaborately decorative subjects are rendered, indeed stories told, by these slender means. In the Victoria and Albert Museum there is a representative collection of Italian embroideries, from which much may be learned. We see beautiful placing, relation of borders, most ingenious finishings, and, in all, the design and materials are perfectly adapted to the purpose for which each work was planned. Thus it will be seen that counted thread work covers a wide field and has a long history to its credit. In the early part of the nineteenth century it fell from grace, bearing the name of "Berlin wool work," when conception of design and colour would go astray to make a hearthrug or footstool the resting-place of a natural lion couched in a bed of natural roses!

The Advantages of Studying Work of Other Countries   A problem may be approached from many different angles, and much may be learned by observing the varied solutions at which the peoples of other countries arrive. It is possible that, had our ancestors of the early nineteenth century been more aware of the development of embroidery in other countries, they might have escaped many of the pitfalls which made the standard of taste at that period deplorable.

In the thirteenth century (roughly between 1270 and 1330) we in England "carried the palm." Ecclesiastical vestments of English work (*opus Anglicanum*) were eagerly sought for by continental countries, and became famous throughout Christendom. Pope Innocent IV, in sending to England for vestments for his choir, gave instructions that they were to be obtained regardless of cost. What praise for perfect craftsmanship! Inventories by our cathedrals and those abroad bear testimony to the existence of quantities of English-made vestments at this period. Of those which survive, the Syon Cope is the best known and most perfect example. It will be of interest to mention here that the coats of arms which form the borders of the cope are worked in cross stitches, which are specially suited to heraldic and all geometric design.

Great English Tradition

The treatment and patterns of the tray-cloths on Plate 28 result from the memory of details seen in old Italian work. Both are embroidered direct by the counted thread and are reversible. The linen used is "Evenweave," made by Messrs. Robinson & Cleaver (Regent Street, London). Here the threads are uniform in size, and the number of them which go to make the warp and weft identical. The separate threads are easily distinguished and counted without difficulty. Pearsall's Mallard Floss is used for the embroidery, in a blunt-tipped wool needle, size 24. The ornament placed right at the edge as shown here is particularly suited to the decoration of luncheon sets, small mats (which will have something stood upon them) or table napkins or towels.

Adaptation of Old Work to Modern Usage

PLATE 27
PORTION OF A LINEN CURTAIN EMBROIDERED IN SILK BY THE
THREAD, SHOWING SATIN, BRICK, DOUBLE RUNNING, AND EYE STITCHES

(For hanging in front of a door opening on the inner court of a house.) Algerian.
XVIIIth–XIXth Century.

From the Victoria and Albert Museum

The cloths shown opposite are edged by narrow hems over which button-hole stitch is worked in different ways. For the red cloth a hem three threads

Orange and Red Cloth

wide (of "Evenweave" linen) is turned, tacked, and secured by hemstitching. For the latter use threads from a spare piece of the linen and pick up three threads to each stitch. In the example illustrated, no thread was withdrawn for the hemstitch. The buttonhole stitch edge is arranged in groups of four stitches, three threads apart, followed by seven stitches worked close together. The first is the width of the hem, the next three each step up one thread, and the final three each step down one. The hemstitching having already charted the threads into groups of three, the placing of the subsequent stitches is simplified. The three *motifs* are in Holbein stitch worked over three threads.

Turn up and tack a hem five threads wide. Over this with blue silk work groups of three adjoining buttonhole stitches, leaving a space of three threads

Blue and Green Cloth

between them. At the corners work the stitches solidly until the angle is turned. Next work a line of double running in green (over three threads) on the cloth and close up to the hem. The *motifs* which spring from the edge are again over three threads.

These tray-cloths depend for their effect on balance of colour. The size of the *motifs* is fixed by the mesh of the linen, and the edge must be arranged in

Balance of Colour

right proportion to them. If the hem is too wide, the colour in the border will look heavy and the *motifs* become poor and mean in consequence. When planning such work it is well to "try out" a piece of the double-run pattern, and then to determine the size of the edge. The colour used must be strong enough to be effective in outline, and if two colours are chosen they must be equal in strength. A light and a dark colour destroy the feeling of a continuous border.

The working of this stitch, known as line, stroke, or Holbein stitch, is shown on the following plate. It is used as an outline stitch on canvas, and on

Line or Holbein Stitch

linen it can be worked so that both sides are alike (as is the case with the example shown opposite). It will be seen that the outline is first followed with a regular running stitch worked over three threads. This works just half the line, which is completed by a return journey of running, this time picking up the stitches made on the outward journey and so filling the gaps between them. This process is also known as "double running." Single stitches branching from the outline are completed on both sides at once, by means of a single satin stitch. The needle in the diagram is in position for making the first of these branches on the return journey, which will complete the unfinished half of the scroll pattern. Patterns worked in this manner appear in some of Holbein's pictures; hence the name.

PLATE 28

REVERSIBLE TRAY-CLOTHS IN LINE OR HOLBEIN STITCH

Note that the lowest border shows how the reverse side of the top one appears.

The fascination of this stitch is that it can be easily worked so that the pattern is identical on the back and front of the material. It is pleasant to work

Two-sided Italian Cross Stitch

and is durable. The animals and the lines forming a border on Plate 31 are worked in this stitch. It should be worked with a blunt-tipped needle on linen with even threads. The thread pulled tightly at each stitch will give an open-work effect. A correct relation between the embroidery, thread, and ground material will ensure the effect. Too thick a thread fills up the holes, but if not thick enough the pulled-up ground threads will show.

The working of the stitch is shown in four movements, beginning at the left. It is helpful to imagine that the ground linen is divided into squares composed of three threads each way, for each complete stitch is made within a square and is composed of a cross-stitch surrounded by four straight stitches.

(1) Bring the thread out in the lower left corner of the square, and make a stitch along the base of it as shown by the needle. The upper corners of the imaginary square are marked by red dots. (2) Put the needle in at the top right corner and out at the lower left. (3) Put the needle in at the top left corner and out at the lower right. (4) Complete the cross by putting the needle in at the top left corner and out at the lower right.

To work so that both sides are identical, make the first three movements only to the end of a line and complete the crossing by a return journey, picking up the side *AB* of each square. The stitches are not complete until the row above is worked (supplying the top sides of the squares). For this reason a pattern must be begun at the bottom and built, line upon line, upwards. When working a pattern the difficulty is to carry the thread from the end of one line of stitches to the point at which the next should be begun. This can be coped with by turning over and working a set of stitches on that side. When this fails, any point may be reached by going over the work done, provided the thread passes over three threads on the slant or three on the straight.

This stitch is worked in two journeys. The first and second diagrams show the actions for the first diagonal line of stitches forming two sides of the squares.

Diagonal Square Stitch

The third diagram shows the needle in position for beginning the second journey, which completes them. It will be seen that the needle passes diagonally behind a square of three threads each time. When used as a drawn-fabric stitch (see Plate 67) the threads must be pulled tightly for each movement. On the reverse side three diagonal lines of straight stitches occur with perforations (caused by the pulled thread) between them.

It is sometimes worked on the back so that this effect may be seen on the right side.

TWO-SIDED ITALIAN CROSS STITCH

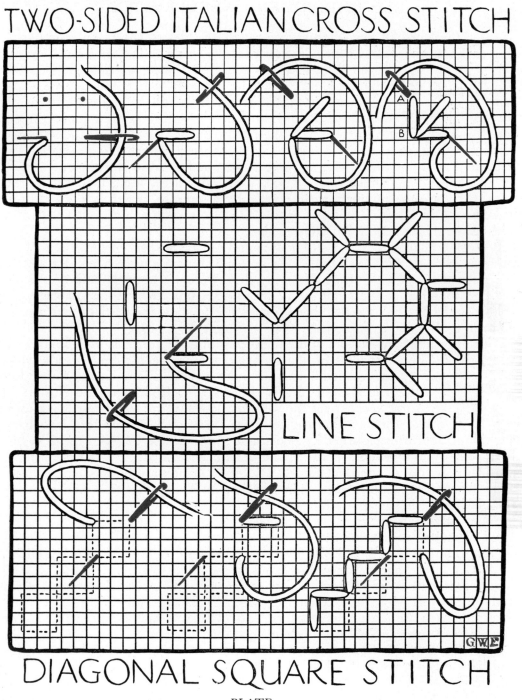

LINE STITCH

DIAGONAL SQUARE STITCH

PLATE 29

For the lace-like hemstitch shown on three sides of the sampler opposite, first make a small rolled hem. The stitches which make the open-work do not

Italian Open-work Hem

secure the hem, so that should be completed first. It is better to withdraw a thread at the place to which the hem is to be rolled, leaving enough linen outside this to roll over twice. It will be found helpful to do the rolling over a loose thread, which is held beneath the fold with the right hand to begin, while the left hand turns the linen over it. Now tack to keep a firm position, and finish by slip-hemming with fine linen thread. Next withdraw the threads for the open-work.

Withdraw one thread, leave three, withdraw three, leave three, withdraw one: these are the numbers withdrawn on the sampler, which is worked upon a coarse "Old Glamis" linen. On fine linens more threads would need to be withdrawn to give an equally open effect.

Work Italian square hemstitch all round on the first set of threads, picking up three threads with the needle. Again work Italian square hemstitch on the inner set of threads, this time arranging that two clusters of the middle threads are tied together as the stitch proceeds. Use a fine linen thread of the same colour as the ground, for the object here is not to show the stitches, but to give an open-work effect.

The border at the bottom of the sampler is in three sections, each six threads wide, flanked by four lines of square hemstitching, each three threads wide.

Border in Three Sections

The completed border occupies a space thirty threads wide. For the centre band the six threads are withdrawn. See clusters of threads ready for the weaving on the right. Overcast one cluster of threads. Weave the next three pairs of clusters into bars, attaching them to each other by one stitch at the centre between the first two bars, and by two stitches between the second and third bars. These stitches are made as the weaving proceeds. The outer bands are embroidered with a series of two threads overcast. The divisions made by the square stitch make the placing of these bars quite easy.

The following *motifs* are from a seventeenth-century Italian sampler—

1. Counted satin stitch.
2. Counted satin stitch with overcast spiral on a foundation of stem stitch.
3. Counted satin stitch with diagonal cross in chain stitch.
4. Here the centre is buttonholed at the end. The central threads are cut and withdrawn, with the exception of two pairs of warp and two pairs of weft threads, which are left uncut and form the foundation of the woven bars. The cut centre is surrounded by a line of diagonal square stitch.
5. The same method is used for the centre here as in No. 4, but the edge and bars are overcast instead of buttonholed.
6. For the bars within the cut centre here a foundation is made by the embroidery thread, which is finished with buttonhole stitch.

PLATE 30

A SAMPLER SHOWING AN OPEN HEM AND ITALIAN *MOTIFS* BY THE
THREAD

Satin stitches worked direct by means of the counted thread in the form of bands, borders, or spot *motifs*, with silk thread on linen grounds, make attrac-

Geometric Satin Stitches

tive decoration. The austere formality of design is softened by the richness of the silk, which retains its full lustre when used in this way. It is by such work that the significance of the name "Satin" stitch is realized. If care is taken with the "fastening in" and "ending off" it is possible to make the work reversible, though not identical on both sides, for the stitches on the reverse side are flatter in appearance.

The satin stitch borders on the opposite plate are adapted from nineteenth-century Persian white work, executed in lustrous while silk in counted thread stitches which entirely cover a loosely woven ground material. Here they take the form of borders, worked with Mallard Floss of delicate colour on cream linen. The top specimen in pale grey-blue is used as a band across the ends of a small runner. The pattern is begun by working the top horizontal line of stitches from left to right over three threads of the ground. This defines the position of the border and the inner pattern follows. This is composed of groups of three horizontal stitches worked over three, and multiples of three, vertical threads up to fifteen. The needle points to the left for each stitch.

To work the diamond, make three stitches over three threads, three over nine threads, three over fifteen, three over nine, and three over three. Next pass the thread in and out of the line to be covered by the lower line of satin stitches, until in position for beginning the little blocks surrounding the diamond. There are five of these, each composed of three stitches worked over six threads. Pass the thread through the back of the finished top line of stitches and work the intervening block composed of three stitches over fifteen threads, three over nine, three over three, three over nine, and three over fifteen. It is convenient to use up ends of threads by working the lower line of satin stitch piecemeal as the inner pattern proceeds. The groups forming the outer orna-ment are begun next, the border line by a stitch over nine threads, followed by stitches decreasing one thread each side until three is reached. Take a second stitch over three and increase one thread each side until nine is reached. De-crease again until three is reached, and pass the thread through the back of the stitches in readiness for the next set. In the lower specimen a border of jade green linen is attached to the cream linen by overcast hemstitch worked with green Mallard Floss. The same silk is used for the counted satin border pat-tern which is placed just above it. The sides of the runner are finished by narrow hemstitched hems which are afterwards laced round and round with green silk to carry the colour through and to keep the same effect on the reverse side.

PLATE 31

GEOMETRIC STITCH BORDERS

The centre border is worked in two-sided Italian cross stitch. (The turned-up corner shows
its reversible nature.) The other borders are in geometric satin stitch.

The lines and animal *motifs* forming the border of the centre cloth shown on Plate 31 are in two-sided Italian cross stitch, the working of which is explained on page 64. The corner is turned up to show that the pattern is identical on both sides. The very narrow hem is tacked up and secured by buttonhole stitches worked over it in groups of about twenty stitches separated by spaces three threads wide.

Two-sided Italian Cross Stitch

The specimen (No. 1) on the opposite plate shows the border of a mat which is part of a luncheon set, composed of geometric satin stitch crosses (see No. 3, Plate 30) spaced between an Italian open hem, and a line of Italian hemstitch. This is a pleasing scheme for linen mats, tray cloths, etc., carried out in écru thread on an off-white ground, or with one good strong colour to suit either table china or room decoration. A full-toned blue, green, venetian red, or old gold would look excellent treated thus, but pastel tints would be ineffective.

Lines and Spots

The interesting corner pattern seen in the centre (No. 2) opposite is built up with triangles of geometric satin stitch and buttonholed eyelets within a line structure worked with Italian square hemstitch and diagonal square stitch. Directions for working the two latter stitches will be found on pages 50 and 64. A buttonhole eyelet, or wheel, is made by putting the needle into the same hole at the centre each time until the wheel is complete. In this case the centre is within a square of ten of the linen threads, so the needle must pick up five threads each time; thus even-sized stitches are made, and the central opening comes by itself when the thread is pulled tightly as each stitch is made. The oblong space left in the satin-stitch triangles adds much to the decorative effect, and is convenient technically, for it occurs just where the stitch would otherwise be too wide for safety. The success of this work depends greatly upon a right adjustment of size of embroidery thread to ground material. As a general guide it is safe to say that the working thread should be equal at least in thickness to that of the ground fabric, and in many cases a trifle thicker will be suitable. Provided this is rightly judged the design will be found to be effective on a fine, medium, or coarse material. On the coarser material, however, it would be well to omit the openwork cross which is worked with an overcast edge and held by an arrangement of overcast bars (the ground material being cut away), because such work is not practicable on fabrics that are likely to fray. (See Nos. 4 and 5, page 66.) Worked with a coarse thread, Anchor Flox, for instance, on Old Glamis linen, for cushions, runners, etc., the arrangement would show to advantage and be sufficiently decorative without the cross. Thread of one colour sufficiently strong in tone to throw up the pattern with distinctness will be the safest scheme to adopt. Changes either of tone or colour (of embroidery thread) spoil the balance.

Geometric Corner Pattern

PLATE 32

LINEN EMBROIDERIES

(1) Border of lines and spots ; (2) Corner pattern, geometric design ; (3) Needlewoven border.

No. 3 shows one end of a table place mat. A similar border of needle-weaving (with a line of Italian square hemstitch on its outer side) occurs at the opposite end of the mat (which measures $25\frac{1}{2}$ in. $\times$ $10\frac{1}{2}$ in.). The whole is finished by an Italian open hem which completes the decoration.

Simple geometric *motifs* such as can be easily arranged within a square or circle, as seen on the opposite plate, look well in combination with straight-line

Motifs for Use with Straight Lines

arrangements, and can be placed within the squares made by the line stitches. (See suggestions on Plates 20, 21, and 21A.) The drawings are shown with the working or construction lines in red. To design similar *motifs*, set the construction lines (this is quickly done if a set-square and a pair of compasses are used) and draw in one section, or repeat, of the proposed pattern. Judge the effect of this by placing a pocket mirror on the centre lines to reflect the repeat. Simple arrangements, needing few lines to express them, are the most satisfactory for needlework. Trace the section and repeat it the necessary number of times to complete the device. In all drawings a fine accuracy is essential, and even so a subtle changing of the lines is bound to occur as the hand-stitching proceeds, and this is a happy effect rightly characteristic of handwork. But the result which comes of careless drawing is always detrimental, and particularly so in designs of a symmetrical character.

The arrangements opposite have been carried out (see Plate 33) on half bleach (écru coloured) linen made by the Old Bleach Linen Company, and embroidered with Clarke's *coton à broder* of exactly the same colour. It is interesting to see how enriched these simple devices may become by stitches used judiciously. Here the effect relies mainly upon change of texture, and cut and drawn work have been enlisted to enliven spaces that might otherwise have appeared insipid.

On Plate 34 these same designs have been embroidered in Pearsall's Mallard Floss, in three colours, gold, blue, and mauve. Quite different stitches are used, and it is interesting to compare the effects.

The lines dividing the coloured *motifs* are worked with Venetian or Italian square hemstitch, and those on Plate 33 with bar hemstitch. The working of both is explained on page 50.

PLATE 32A
WORKING DRAWINGS OF *MOTIFS*

The buttonhole stitch which finishes the two interlaced loops is first padded by two lines of running stitch, picking up as little material as possible with the needle, thus keeping most of the thread on the top surface. The radiating pieces outside the loops are padded by three long stitches, and are finished by satin stitch worked closely across the short way. For the open-work filling stitch, two threads are withdrawn and two left successively across each way (both warp and weft). This is begun by cutting two threads in the middle of the panel to be worked. These are drawn out at the back until stopped by the surrounding stitching. Next, two threads running the opposite way are cut, again at the centre, and are also drawn out at the back. Along the two pathways made thus it is easy to cut alternate pairs of threads with fine-pointed scissors. All the withdrawn threads are cut off "slick" where held by the surrounding stitchery. An open square mesh of threads now appears. From the front of the work these are overcast with embroidery cotton working diagonally, as shown in the example on Plate 63. As a rule, the number of threads withdrawn is a guide to the number of overcast stitches needed between each section.

Motif No. 1

The four centre leaves are outlined with satin stitch worked over two rows of running stitch as padding. (See instructions given for No. 1.) Next the foundation threads for the branched bars are laid; these are thrown across the surface and attached to the material at the outline. The needle is brought out at A (see diagram, Plate 32A) and put in at B, making one long stitch on the surface; then returned to A, so that two threads are laid and lie parallel. The thread is then passed through the back of the satin stitches and finely run along the outline to C, and carried across to E, piercing the laid threads en route at D, and returned to C again via D. It is then run up to F, and the second branched bar is laid in the same manner, and the fine running on the outline completed. The bars are finished by overcasting the laid threads. The linen is then cut down the centre behind the bars, and in order that each half may be folded to the back, cut twice again in the opposite direction. With the linen folded back, the double edge is overcast, working from left to right as in *broderie anglaise*, and the superfluous linen cut away. The dots surrounding the outline are worked in the manner of back stitch, but three stitches are made in the same place for each dot before passing to the next.

Motif No. 2

The four centre leaves are edged with buttonhole stitch worked over two rows of running as padding. On two leaves the "heading" of the stitch is on the inner side, while on the others it is on the outer side, showing that either way is possible when the linen is to be cut away. Cutting against the heading of the stitch is, however, the more general way. The foundation threads for the bars are laid in the manner

Motif No. 3

PLATE 33

MOTIFS (AS SHOWN IN OUTLINE ON PLATE 32A) EMBROIDERED IN
SELF-COLOUR

described for the bars in No. 2, but here they are finished in the weaving stitch, worked over and under the two laid threads. Finally, the linen is cut down the centre and at the edge of the buttonholing. The first incision of the scissors gives the cleanest cut; shaving off by degrees should be avoided. The scrolls are worked in satin stitch, padded by two lines of running stitch.

The bars are worked first. Two threads are laid as a foundation and finished by overcasting. A fine running stitch is worked round the outline of

Motif No. 4

the cut spaces, which are worked by the *broderie anglaise* method, i.e. cut down the centre and across where necessary, so that the linen may be folded back to the outline. The double edge is then overcast, working from left to right. The remaining parts of the outline are worked in satin stitch over a single thread as padding.

Here interlaced buttonhole stitch in gold is used for the two loops (note the "heading" on both sides of the stitch). Begin by running one thread of

Motif No. 5

silk round the edge just within the outer line. For the filling, straight lines of buttonhole stitch in blue are used, each row being worked into the heading of the last. (See Plate 11.) The radiations are detached chain stitches.

A line of knot stitch is worked round the four centre leaves just inside the traced line. A second line is then worked on the outside of this, and each knot

Motif No. 6

is placed between two of the former ones. Two lines of knot stitching interlocked in this way make a raised outline which is both firm and neat. Spaced buttonhole is used for the filling of the leaves, two stitches worked, and the space of two stitches left, and each row worked into the heading of the last. Both filling and outline are in gold silk. The side pieces are in buttonhole stitch worked on the slant (the heading at the centre vein) in groups of mauve and blue alternately. Finally, these are outlined with overcast back stitch in gold.

The centre leaves are outlined by three rows of knot stitching, one of blue between two of mauve. The inner mauve row is worked first, and the two others

Motif No. 7

are interlocked as described for No. 6. The light filling of the leaves is buttonhole stitch in gold, worked openly and on the slant, the two headings meeting at the centre vein. The scrolling pieces, also gold, are worked in rope stitch, which is peculiarly adapted to the purpose, changing as it will easily from a thick to a thin effect at the turn of the scrolls.

Motif No. 8

The outline throughout is worked in chain stitch with gold silk. The diagonal pieces are filled with double back stitch in blue, and satin stitches (also blue) fill the small spaces at the centre. The rounded shapes are filled with darning (of mauve silk), picking up two threads and leaving two.

PLATE 34

MOTIFS (AS SHOWN IN OUTLINE ON PLATE 32A) EMBROIDERED IN
COLOURED SILKS

children's clothes, lingerie, etc.) to large canvas for, say, draught screens. Diagram 1 on the opposite page shows three straight rows of tent stitch as they should appear when finished and completely covering the canvas. For the remaining diagrams a finer thread is used so that its passage in and out of the canvas can be followed. The working of the stitch, which is very simple, is shown at diagram 2. The thread is brought out through the opening marked in red, and passed diagonally over a vertical and a horizontal thread of the canvas. It will be seen that this results in a short stroke on the front and a longer one at the back, which is the correct method. The lines are worked from right to left and left to right, alternately. Diagram 3 shows how the second line is reached, and at 4 the needle is seen in position for making the first stitch of that line. There is nothing against turning the work if held in the hand, and proceeding exactly as shown in diagram 2. Tent stitch can also be worked in diagonal lines, when the principle of a short stitch on the front and a long on the back still holds good. Thus for ascending lines the thread passes diagonally over one vertical and one horizontal (as always for the front of the stitch), the needle being passed horizontally behind two vertical threads for the back. For the descending lines the needle is passed vertically behind two horizontal threads and, whichever way the line of stitches is travelling, the needle always enters into the gaps in the preceding row for each stitch.

The working of cross stitch (or *gros point*) can be followed from the action of the needles in the opposite diagram. To begin, the thread is brought through the opening marked in red. It will be noticed that by this method each cross is completed before the next is begun. By another method, used for grounding, the first half of the stitch is worked along the whole length of a line (see first action) and completed by a return journey identical in action, except that it proceeds from right to left. The crossing must always be in the same direction. The diagram shows the stitch worked over two threads (each way) of single-thread canvas; it can also be worked on one square of Penelope canvas; and over a square of three or more threads, according to convenience, if worked on linens and other fabrics with an even mesh. Cross stitch can be worked in diagonal lines; for an ascending line begin by making the first half of the stitch as shown by first needle in the diagram, and for the second half put the needle in at the top right corner of that square (marked with a red spot), and out of the top left corner (marked with a red stroke). To continue, repeat the first action, putting the needle in at the top left corner of the square (marked by red spot), and out at lower left (marked with red stroke). For a descending line, bring the thread out at the top left corner of the square, and put the needle in at the lower right

Cross Stitch

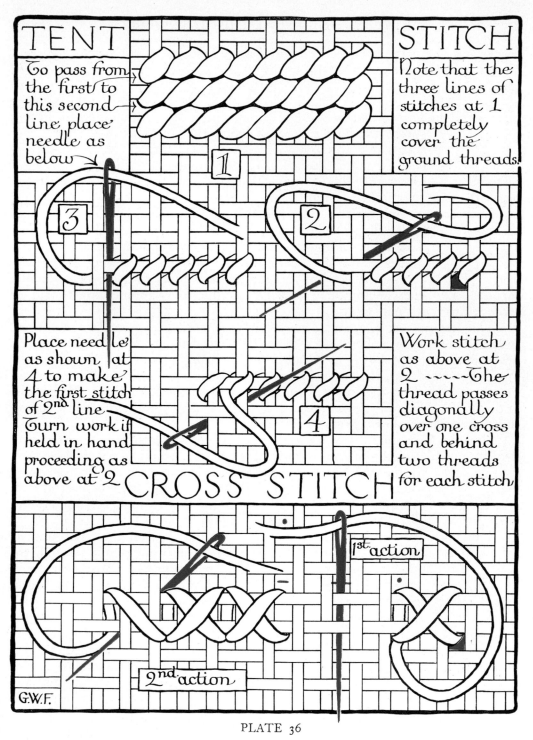

TENT · STITCH

To pass from the first to this second line place needle as below →

Note that the three lines of stitches at 1 completely cover the ground threads.

1

3

2

Place needle as shown at 4 to make the first stitch of 2ⁿᵈ line. Turn work if held in hand proceeding as above at 2

Work stitch as above at 2 ~~~~~The thread passes diagonally over one cross and behind two threads for each stitch

4

CROSS STITCH

1ˢᵗ action

2ⁿᵈ action

G.W.F.

PLATE 36

corner and out at the lower left corner, for the first half of the stitch. To complete it put the needle in at the top right corner and out at the lower right corner.

Gobelin stitch can be worked in several ways. At diagram 4 on the opposite plate it is shown worked in straight rows, end on to each other, as in tent
Gobelin Stitch stitch, the only difference being that in Gobelin the stitch lies across two horizontal and one vertical thread. With this difference in mind, the actions given for tent stitch on the previous plate must be followed. The opening through which the thread is brought to begin the stitch is marked in red.

Encroaching Gobelin is a most useful canvas stitch. It covers the ground threads readily, and the dovetailing of the rows is most helpful for shading.
Encroaching Gobelin The encroaching method may be worked in straight rows if desired, and the height of the stitches increased by passing across one vertical thread and over four, five, or six horizontal threads. The encroaching may be slight, either overlapping one thread or arranged to reach half way.

The diagrams 1, 2, 3, and 4 show how it is worked diagonally—the canvas is less liable to be pulled askew when the stitch is worked thus. Begin a descending line as shown at diagram 1, by bringing out the thread at the opening marked red, pass up over one vertical and two horizontal threads, and put the needle in at that point, bringing out three threads below. (See needle in diagram.) Diagram 2 shows how the needle is placed to begin the ascending row, which is seen in progress at diagram 3.

Upright Gobelin is worked in horizontal rows; each stitch passes over two horizontal threads in the manner of satin stitch, and is never sloped. If
Upright Gobelin by this method the ground is not completely covered, a thread should be laid along the line first, and the stitches worked over it. The process of working over laid lines, known as "tramming," is employed with other canvas stitches in a similar case.

The working of this stitch is shown in the diagram on the right, and its actual appearance in that on the left. The thread is brought out through the
Plait Stitch opening marked red, and the plaited appearance made by taking one stitch forward and one back, in turn—first across two upright threads forward, then across one back. The number of horizontal threads involved may be varied according to the ground used. At the back a single row of upright stitches, two in each place, results. The stitch may be worked on either single or double thread canvas. It is seen worked on linen in sixteenth-century Italian embroideries, filling the background and leaving the pattern plain linen. Italian two-sided cross stitch, given on Plate 29, may be seen used in a like manner—the latter giving an open-work ground effect and the former a solid one.

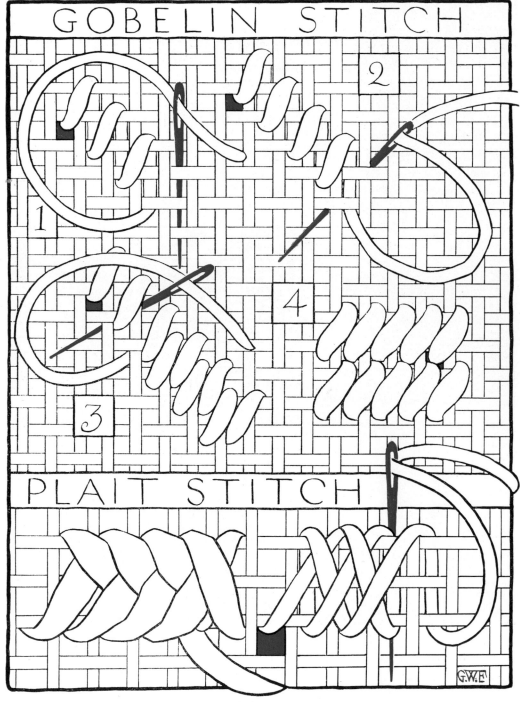

PLATE 37

CORNER OF A CLOTH EMBR[OIDERY]

CHAPTER III

DIRECTLY we depart from the "built up by the thread" types of needlework, we are faced with a new problem—the necessity for making, finding, or adapting a design to suit our purpose. In any case our position will be stronger if we can draw. It is not necessary for all needle-workers to be expert designers, or for all designers to be experts in the technique of the needle; but it is most desirable for each of these to have at least a nodding acquaintance with the work of the other. Embroidery is, after all, "drawing with needle and thread," and it follows, therefore, that the application needed to gain some facility in drawing as such is worthy of the effort. Originality need not be striven for; it is of far greater importance to cultivate true taste. "One fine morning may suffice to burst the bud, but it takes months to develop seed into flower." We can seek inspiration for ideas, at those times when none has sought us, from the works done by other peoples and in other ages, and adapt them to our present use. Experience teaches, and true training should enable us to discriminate and to know which element to use and which to leave out, in order to harmonize rightly with the new surroundings and conditions. (See "Points to be considered in planning a piece of work," page 46.) In sincerely aiming, from the first, at making our work both suitable and beautiful, we shall find ourselves making something of our own.

Some working drawings and arrangements follow, and to these we must accustom ourselves before we can express our ideas or adapt those of others for our practical use.

Working Drawings — A working drawing is a clear outline of the design as it is to appear on the material for working. If it is to be carried out by someone else, instructions as to method, colouring, and stitches must be added. No. 4 on the opposite plate is a working drawing of a border, and Nos. 1, 2, and 3 show the stages of its development as a design. The pattern is constructed upon a waved-line foundation. The lines in red are the scaffolding, as it were, or working lines, upon which a unit of the pattern is made. A unit of the waved line is seen between A and B; this is turned over and traced in the next section, B, C, and again in C, D, and we have the basis on which to build the pattern. In No. 2 the positions of the "masses" or solid parts of the design are indicated, and these are connected with the waved line in the manner of subsidiary stems. In No. 3 the direction of such smaller details as are needed to make an evenly filled band of ornament is indicated, and in No. 4 the completed outline appears. A unit or "repeat" of the whole pattern is contained between the lines E and F, and this can be repeated indefinitely for any length of border. On the next plate the treatment of a corner is shown. A line at an angle of 45 degrees is struck across the border, giving the

86

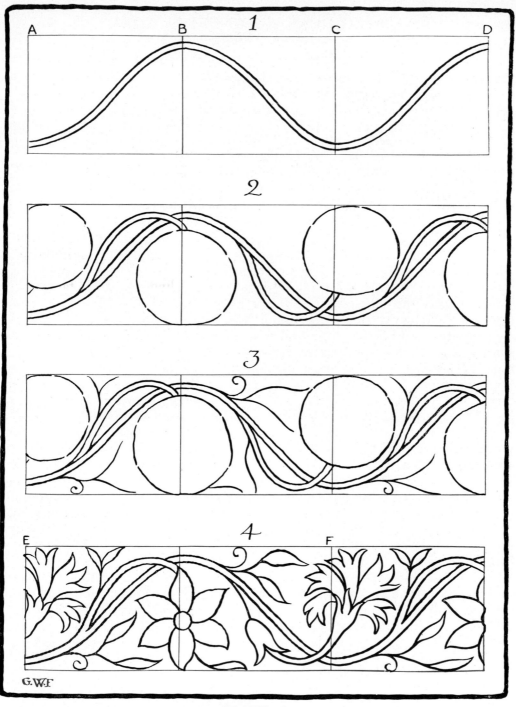

PLATE 38
BORDER DEVELOPED FROM A WAVED LINE

corner. The red dotted line surrounds the part which needed to be redrawn to fill the space pleasantly. The unit is then repeated as before.

The cleanest and most generally useful way of getting a design on to material is by means of a "pricker," "pounce," paint, and brush. First take

How a Drawing is Transferred to Material

a tracing of the working drawing on either tracing or detail paper. Detail paper made of pure linen rag is the most durable of transparent papers, and will serve well for both the original drawing and the pricking, from which a number of impressions may be taken if desired. Place the drawing face downwards on the table, with a piece of felt or any smooth soft material beneath it. Then make a "pricker" by thrusting a needle head first into a piece of soft rubber which serves as a handle, and holding this upright (see opposite), prick carefully along all the lines of the drawing. If the pattern is a fine one, the holes should be set close together; if large and sprawling they may be farther apart.

Now place the material flat on the table and place the pricking on it, rough side up. (The under side is the rough side, that on which the needle entered being quite smooth.) Keep this securely in position by placing an iron or some similar weight at the top. Large drawings will need several weights, for there must be no chance of the paper moving from its correct position. Now take the pounce pad (a strip of cloth rolled round tightly and evenly and tied with thread, or fixed with pins), and dip it in the pounce powder, which may be bought ready prepared (in blue for use on light material, in white for use on dark), and holding the paper down securely at the part nearest you, pass the powder over the whole surface of the pricking. Lift it up, and a clear impression will be found on the material. If too much powder has come through, blow gently to remove it, and with a fine sable brush and any transparent water-colour paint, go over the lines carefully, and then shake the material to rid it thoroughly of the powder. The paint must be mixed to a consistency which will flow with ease on the fabric, giving a clear line. This consistency varies with the texture of the fabric, smooth thin ones needing rather a dry brush, while for thick rough surfaces a loaded brush will be necessary.

Chinese white water-colour is useful for painting the outlines on dark materials, but will not adhere to rough surfaces; for these, white oil paint, thinned with turpentine, should be used. Transparent materials such as *crêpe de Chine*, muslin, etc., may be laid over a clearly outlined design in waterproof ink and painted through. It is possible to fix pounced designs temporarily by ironing the powder through tissue paper. This may be sufficient for work done in a frame; for that held in the hand, lines should be painted for security.

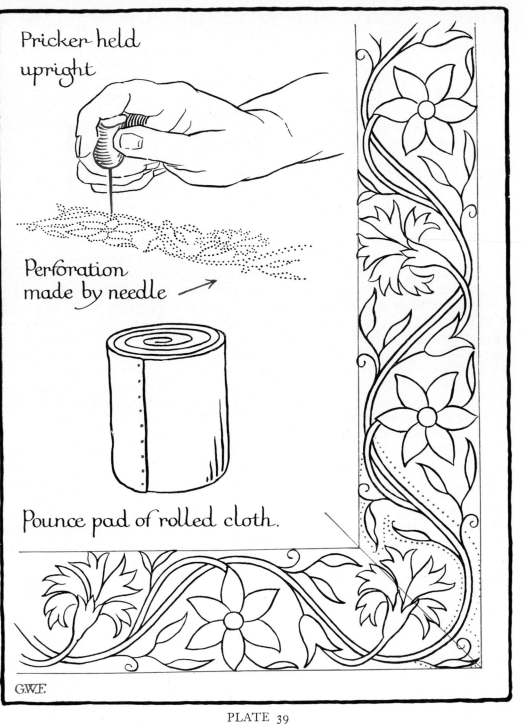

Pricker held upright

Perforation made by needle

Pounce pad of rolled cloth.

G.W.F.

PLATE 39

CONSTRUCTION OF THE CORNER. TRANSFERRING DESIGNS TO MATERIAL

A method of arrangement in design that persists apparently throughout all periods without loss of popularity is the powdered, and the spot and powdered, **Spot and Powdered Patterns** pattern. For the former pattern a small device, complete in itself, is disposed at regular intervals over a surface, while two devices (one much smaller than the other) are placed in alternation in a similar way to make a spot and powdered pattern. One charm of this arrangement lies in the fact that it can be applied to most of the articles we decorate. A dull surface embroidered with a powdered pattern in silk is at once enlivened, even when worked with only one colour—light on dark or dark on light. In either case the gleaming of silk threads dispels its dullness. Again, neutral grounds may be made resplendent with colour by means of a powdered pattern worked in rich colours.

That the idea is no new one for embroiderers is brought home to us by such examples as the Damietta hanging, excavated in lower Egypt in 1898. This work of the fourth century is so comparatively modern in style that it is with amazement that we realize that it was worked some fifteen hundred years ago! The twisted wools with which it is embroidered are still quite bright in places. It is supposed that it was buried soon after it was made. Tree ornaments alternate with a single rose in profile to form its pattern. The treatment of the rose recalls those flowers with which we are familiar in English work of Queen Anne's time. Also it is very interesting to find that stitches which appealed to these workers are those which appeal to us. The above hanging is embroidered in chain stitch, and in other pieces preserved to us from antiquity we find pattern-darning, needle-weaving, and such stitches as back, satin, long and short, and square stitch.

The ancient Egyptians were great embroiderers, and their work had reached a standard of beauty and technique equal to the best we know to-day. Their **Egyptian and Coptic Work** Christian descendants, the Copts, inherited and perpetuated the talent in this and all branches of handwork. When looking at the specimens that so amazingly survive (see collection of Egyptian textiles and embroideries at the Victoria and Albert Museum), what strikes us most, apart from the ingenious workmanship, is the determined way in which natural forms are reduced to ornament. Narrow tapestry-woven borders contain the forms of human figures and animals, including lions, leopards, hares, and ducks, while the vine, a favourite theme, used for panels and borders, is treated with a severity of flatness which is at the same time so rich and satisfying a pattern that it should appeal strongly to designers of twentieth-century interior decorations which call for these particular qualities. It is well for us to remember such examples as these when making our own patterns from natural forms. Nature is inexhaustible as a source of inspiration for design—it is the designer's work to use these inspirations for the making of ornament which is perfectly suited to its purpose.

PLATE 40

EMBROIDERED LINEN HANGING AND COPTIC TAPESTRY

The upper illustration shows a linen hanging, embroidered with coloured wools. There are rows of trees, with rose blossoms in the intervening spaces. Along the top is a border of vines issuing alternately from vases and baskets. This remarkable hanging was excavated by M. Gayet in the winter of 1898–1899, in a burying-ground at Shaikh Shata, Lake Manzala, two miles east of Damietta, Lower Egypt. It was probably embroidered in the IVth or Vth century. The lower illustration is of a tapestry-woven panel in purple wool and linen thread, from a linen tunic. Graeco-Roman period, IVth to Vth century (from Akhmim).

From the Victoria and Albert Museum

For embroidery the floral device is the one which most readily commends itself to our use for powdered patterns. In designing these, if we begin with

The Floral Device

the severity of the Coptic treatments in our mind's eye we shall not make the mistake of confusing groups of flowers drawn direct from Nature, with ornament. For our purpose flowers of one kind may flourish with fruit of another, and spring from the same stem, and other and curious things may be derived, provided the result is good ornament. Nature knows her business; it is for us to know ours. The revivals of decorative art in Europe are traceable to the influence of and contact with Oriental nations. The Mohammedan religious tenet which forbade the actual representation of any object in Nature was of service to design in the above sense.

The Persians, one of the most sensitive and cultured races the world has ever known, devoted their art to the making of useful everyday things, and

Persian Art

were quite untroubled by those distinctions between naturalistic and decorative treatment that we are apt to make. Those of us who were fortunate enough to see the collection of Persian art gathered at Burlington House in 1931 will long remember its magic and beauty. It was as though the description of the seventeenth-century traveller, Sir John Chardin, had been translated into terms of an exquisite art and set down for us in Piccadilly. He says—

Concerning the flowers of Persia. . . . There are all sorts of flowers in Persia that are to be met with in France and in the finest countries of Europe. The flowers of Persia, by the vivacity of their colours, are generally handsomer than those of Europe, and those of India. Hycrania is one of the finest countries for flowers; for there are whole forests of orange trees, single and double jessamines, all the flowers that we have in Europe and several that we have not. The most eastern part of that country, which they call Mazenderan, is nothing but one continued Parterre, from September to the end of April. All the country is at that time covered over with flowers.

It is certainly from Persian traditions that our best elements in floral design are derived.

In England after the Reformation, the demand for the ecclesiastical embroideries, which had hitherto absorbed all the best work, ceased, and was

Sixteenth-Century English Embroidery

followed by an immense output of rich and fanciful embroideries for dress and secular use, and it is to examples of sixteenth-century work that we turn for a peculiar naiveté of expression which characterizes them. The "Great Period" in English embroidery ended with the loss of the Church as its patron, but great impetus was given to design in this new-found freedom of subject. Embroidery was lavished on all articles of dress to a greater extent than ever before. Henry VIII encouraged magnificence at Court and himself wore sumptuous clothes. Queen Elizabeth is said to have possessed over three thousand dresses, most of them profusely embroidered.

PLATE 41

A PERSIAN PRAYER CARPET, XVIIIth OR XIXth CENTURY

Quilted satin embroidered in coloured silks.

From the Victoria and Albert Museum

In the same century books of design were published, and were so successfully received that in a few years French, German, Flemish, Italian, and English publishers brought out books of patterns prepared by their best engravers. Jean Robin opened a garden with conservatories in which he grew plants hitherto little known in Europe, in order that designers might have the opportunity of studying them from Nature. Elizabethan flower studies are especially happy; columbines, pansies, roses, honeysuckle, carnations, strawberries, sweet peas, and tulips combine in gay pattern to cover whole surfaces with needlework. These flowers often grow on spreading scrolling stems, in which a metal thread of gold or silver is introduced, together with the silk. Birds, fish, butterflies, and insects, are sometimes scattered among the flowers and leaves.

Scrolled ornament, long before perfected in China and Persia, came to us in this instance via (in all probability) Spain. The Spanish and black work so popular in England since Catherine of Aragon became Henry VIII's Queen, showed designs arranged in this manner. The Moors, during their occupation of Spain, sent for craftsmen from Persia to make them beautiful things, and were the means of advancing art in Spain above and beyond that of the rest of Europe.

Though Eastern influence is to be found in the design of Elizabethan domestic embroideries, no one upon seeing them would suppose them to be other than English. In the West we have a way of imprinting our individuality upon work, even when inspired by that of Eastern models. Other similar instances are mentioned on page 126 with regard to the worsted hangings, and on page 34 in reference to the knotted thread work. Evidently such assimilation is for the betterment of our native work without the losing of our style and character.

The bodice is chosen for illustration because of the adaptability of its design to other purposes. It may be reconstructed for trays, quilts, etc. Complete **Embroidered Bodice Front** devices of rose, strawberries, honeysuckle, and an unidentified plant fill the lozenge-shapes marked out by sprays of leaves terminating in buds. It is worked on linen in coloured silks, and has a sedate rather than a riotous charm which is exceptional for this playful period.

PLATE 42

ELIZABETHAN EMBROIDERY (LATE XVItH CENTURY)

The upper illustration shows a bodice front embroidered with silk and silver-gilt thread on linen.
Satin, brick, and double back stitches are used. The cushion is also embroidered with silk and
silver-gilt thread, with chain, and long and short stitches. The fringe is modern.

From the Victoria and Albert Museum

To take a flower form as a basis and to work out decorative variations of it is an amusing and instructive exercise in the making of ornament. Opposite

Conventional Rendering of Natural Forms

are shown some conventional variations of a daisy form, that is to say, petals radiating from a common centre and filling a circle—an arrangement supplying the groundwork for seemingly innumerable varieties of pattern, by changing the number and shape of the petals, the proportion of the centre, and sometimes the details within them. To be effective for needlework, the drawings must be kept simple, flat, and clear in line. The circles are divided into six, seven, eight, and twelve sections respectively. The working lines are shown in the central one as a reminder of the method of construction.

The right stitch is one that will work easily the particular shape for which it is chosen, and preserve most clearly the designer's idea of the form. These

Finding the Right Stitch

are the chief considerations, and in fulfilling them perhaps no two workers will happen on identical stitches for working the same form, but each rendering will be "right" if the above conditions are observed. This right choice calls for some experiment, and there is no better means of discovering the possibilities of stitches, for often the very stitch we reject for one purpose supplies the idea for another. There is little advantage in knowing a multitude of stitches unless experience of their application accompanies that knowledge. These examples suggest a method of approach to the use of natural forms as a basis for needle-rendered ornament, and in thus combining design and stitchery, interest is added to both. Any basic flower form, such as honeysuckle, iris, or rose, can be worked out in this way, and leaves, buds, and seed-pods offer further material for the same idea, which by giving full scope to individuality of expression is bound to develop our decorative sense. The design on Plate 46 is the outcome of such study.

Having first learned to conventionalize, rigidly and severely, our treatments may later become more natural, when our knowledge of decoration, and of what stitches can and cannot be made to do will take us safely over the pitfalls awaiting those who attempt to "copy from Nature" without this added sense of design.

These forms can be used in combination with others for designs of the type shown on Plate 46, while in themselves they are sufficiently interesting to form spot patterns, and can be scattered, or more formally arranged, for the decoration of, say, voile sleeves or the borders of a garment.

PLATE 43
WORKING DRAWINGS FOR FLORAL CIRCLES

KEY TO STITCHES USED FOR FLOWERS ON OPPOSITE PLATE

Worked with Twisted Embroidery Silk in Two Tones of Blue on Linen

Top left corner   .   Centre outlined with stem stitch, and filled with laid straight lines couched down by a small stitch across the intersections.
Petals: stem stitch each side, and band of buttonhole stitch at the ends.

Top centre   .   .   Petals filled with satin stitch worked on the slant. Satin stitch spot at the centre with ring of overcast chain stitch.

Top right corner   .   Solid petals in fishbone stitch. Back petals outlined with overcast back stitch. Centre outlined with chain stitch.

Centre left   .   .   Petals: chain stitch worked in lines from centre to tip, first down the centre of petal, then each outline, and finally the gaps between. By this means the pointed tips are preserved without difficulty. Centre outlined chain stitch.

Centre   .   .   .   Solid petals in a variation of Cretan stitch. Back petals outlined in stem stitch. Four petals at centre outlined in knot stitch. Centre filled with flat stitch.

Centre right   .   .   Petals: buttonhole stitch at the tips. The dividing lines are detached chain stitches. Centre: tailor's buttonhole.

Lower left corner   .   Outlined with knot stitch throughout. A satin stitch spot in each petal.

Centre   .   .   .   Petals in double back stitch. Centre ring in satin stitch.

Lower right corner   .   Petals: Roumanian stitch worked in two groups to each petal. Centre rings outlined in stem stitch.
The hemstitch used in the border is the herring-bone variety shown at Nos. 4 and 5 on Plate 22.

PLATE 44
EMBROIDERED FLORAL CIRCLES
See working drawings on Plate 43.

Some leaf, bud, and seed-pod forms rendered in simple stitches are shown on the opposite plate. They are worked with Pearsall's twisted embroidery silk in three tones of one colour on Old Bleach Linen F.T.91. The stitches used are buttonhole, satin, stem, knot, chain, back, overcast-back, seeding, and Roumanian. The trailing leaf at 1 is composed of buttonhole stitch worked in separate sets, so that the heading of the stitch appears on the under-side of each small leaf. The stitch is begun at the tip of the top left leaf and continued to the end of the stem. Then the first leaf on the right is worked, this time beginning where the leaf joins the stem and working to its tip. The forms are easily made by working the leaves on the left from tip to stem, and those on the right from stem to tip. The seed-pod at 3 is also composed of simple buttonhole stitch worked in groups. Again buttonhole is used in the spray at 2 as a filling for the buds worked in straight rows across the form, each row being worked into the heading of the former row. The outline is an overcast back stitch, and the calyx and stems are in satin stitch. The leaf with conventional curling tips at 4 is outlined with knot stitch, and each leaflet has a block of satin stitch within, which repeats the shape of the outer form. The sections of the love-in-a mist seed-pod at 5 are worked in Roumanian stitch, closely for the three light ones, and openly for the darker ones. The stem is outlined with overcast back stitch. The rose leaf at 6 is in satin stitch worked straight across each half-leaf, thus leaving the centre vein clearly defined in the linen. The stems are in back stitch.

Students of seventeenth-century worsted embroideries will recognize the three fat buds at 9, usually worked with a long and short stitch filling within a cup formed of French knots. Here is a new rendering: the cup is worked in buttonhole stitch in two rows, the stitches of the second row entering the heading of the first. The centre spots are wheels, or rather ellipses, of buttonhole stitch connected to the cup by an overcast back stitch. The stems are chain stitch. The tall slender leaf at 10 is worked on each side with slanted buttonhole stitch, with the heading of the stitch towards the centre vein, which is "voided" in the same way as those of the rose leaves at 6. The scrolls are knot stitch worked closely, and the stem is outlined with overcast back stitch. The anemone leaf at 8 is filled with a series of lines of stem stitch worked upwards from the base to the tips. The effect of light and shade is got by using the darker tones on the left and under side, keeping the light threads on the right and upper side. The remaining form at 7 is outlined with chain stitch, with seeding in the centre leaf. The projections and stem are in satin stitch.

PLATE 45
A LEAF AND BUD SAMPLER

The design illustrated opposite is worked with crewel wools on Kirriemuir linen, which has a twilled texture similar to that used for the seventeenth-century wool embroidered hangings.

Light Open Treatment of Floral Designs

Crewels are the finest of embroidery wools. They lend themselves to the expression of detailed drawing, and for this reason are very pleasant to use. Fine wool is to be recommended for first efforts in wool embroidery. The comparative clumsiness of tapestry and "embroidery" wool is apt to be disconcerting at first, but this feeling will be less evident if the worker has prepared the way by beginning with the finer kind. The piece opposite was worked in a frame, and was the student's first attempt at framed embroidery. The colour was not planned beforehand by a sketch on paper, so the central form was worked in first, and the lights and darks of the surrounding flowers carefully balanced round it. Note the importance of the very dark tone used in the bud form at the foot of the design. Had this been worked with the lighter colours the whole spray would have appeared to be falling over to the left, and so lost its pleasant appearance of symmetry. It is interesting as a specimen of semi-solid or light open treatment uniformly observed. In the flower and bud at the bottom, where more weight was needed, this feeling of light treatment is retained by the small spaces of background left within.

The applicability of fishbone stitch to flower and leaf forms may be seen here. It is used for the variegated blue and red petals on the left, for the solid petals of the flower in profile on the right, and for the smaller leaves which surround the centre flower. The two larger leaves show light open treatments. That on the right is outlined by rows of stem stitch in three different greens, two rows of each colour. The vein is filled with satin stitch, which is surrounded by a narrow band of lighter green, and the spotted filling is made with two stitches to each spot. The leaf on the left is edged with long and short stitch, and the inner ornament filled with satin stitch. The stems are in satin stitch worked well on the slant, and the flower petals of orange colour on the left are treated in a similar way. Either stem stitch or couching is used where single outlines occur. The dark blue border of the centre flower is worked with three short and two long satin stitches alternately. It is begun in the centre at the top and worked downwards from left to right, completing one half, and from right to left completing the other. A line of stem stitch in orange is worked on the inner side of the blue, and the long radiating stitches are held down by small transverse ones made rather wider than for the usual couching stitch. Long and short shading is used to fill the centre. Another interesting point is the delicate yet adequate treatment of the calyx of the profile flower on the right, accomplished so simply—merely lines of stem stitch, with little points of mauve placed at their crossing.

PLATE 46
A FLORAL DESIGN EMBROIDERED IN CREWEL WOOLS

Some nineteenth-century Chinese renderings of birds and flowers are shown opposite. They are taken from an embroidered coat worn by a Parsee of India

Birds, Buds, and Flowers Chinese

and are worked in satin stitch throughout, with a voided outline. This voiding requires the greatest skill in working—there is no chance for a misplaced stitch to escape unseen—but no other method gives this particularly crisp result. The sprays are not shown in their relative positions, being merely crowded on to the paper as notes of ornament. A pencil line is drawn round the isolated sprays to show their extent. The first thing we notice in the design is its intense liveliness, or rather "aliveness." Five different birds are shown, and, in each, definite bird action is unmistakably expressed, and this merely by small areas of satin stitch; though it must be added that the direction of the stitches plays a part equal in importance to the precision of outline. This does not appear in the drawing, but in every case the stitches are made to follow the direction most appropriate to the form expressed. In the flowers it is occasionally suggested by the arrangement of the tone. The rose is the only flower of whose identity we are certain, but how vigorous in their delicacy they all are! Though quite flat in treatment, they leave us in no doubt as to the rising of sap in their stems!

This is a further example of embroidery treatments of natural forms, and will be found full of suggestion for designs for dress, lingerie, etc., to be ren-

Other Renderings Suggested

dered in less exacting techniques. Some of the flowers would work charmingly in double back stitch or "shadow" work in the manner of the specimen shown on Plate 86. On coloured organdie muslins they could be worked in coloured filoselles, not solidly but in long and short stitch set closely at the edges and openly within, thus allowing the organdie to show between the lines of stitches. Many other suggestions might be made for white work also, but we give no more than two, for doubtless if the illustration is made use of in this way, each reader will prefer to make her own interpretations. And so history will repeat itself, and some highly individualized embroideries will have arisen from an Eastern source.

Some original embroidered animals by Miss Helen Keen are shown on Plate 54A. They are vigorously and decoratively treated in materials which

Embroidered Animals

are in strong contrast with those used for the opposite plate which is from embroidery in finely split floss on satin, while the animals on Plate 54A are in tapestry wool on linen crash. The latter examples show how drawing and light and shade may be expressed by keeping to a carefully considered outline, and by a judicious change of tone in the wools used, while at the same time adhering to the particularly rigid arrangements of stitchery seen here. Undoubtedly the decorative quality of the lion in this instance is given by the formality of the stitch, while in the case of the zebra the ingenious use made of that animal's striped hide is responsible.

PLATE 47

NOTES OF ORNAMENT ON A COAT (XIXᴛʜ-CENTURY CHINESE)

Showing satin stitch and voided outline.

For quilting, a fine line stitch is worked as an ornamental pattern, through three thicknesses of material, the inner one being of some soft padding substance.

Quilting   This idea of layers of material was probably suggested originally by the need for warmth in a garment, or maybe by the need for a padding to be worn beneath armour, etc. For the latter purpose the stitchery was, one imagines, of a purely utilitarian nature, which, suggesting decorative possibilities, developed by degrees into an art, culminating where dress is concerned in the elaborate waistcoats, jackets, skirts, and other garments fashionable in the seventeenth and eighteenth centuries. For dress we now confine its use to such things as baby bonnets, dressing-gowns and jackets, cushions, and the little adjuncts of the boudoir. As a form of bed-covering, quilting has been in favour in many countries since its inception. Our word "counterpane" is derived from *contrepointe*, a corruption of the French word for "quilting stitch," actually back stitch. The ornament on these covers often took the form of legends or historical events. The well-known fourteenth-century Silician quilt in the Victoria and Albert Museum is a magnificent example of this story-telling type of design, and to leap to another country and a more recent period of history, there are incidents in the lives of the earlier settlers in the United States of America on quilts made by the women, whose descendants living in remote places continue to work in the same tradition.

In our country the tradition has been kept alive in Northern England and South Wales in a most interesting way. The working-class women in county Durham and in Glamorgan and Carmarthenshire have made their own quilts, continuing to do so even when the machine-made manufactured products came so readily to their hand. This is surely a striking illustration of the pleasure to be derived from a love of true craftsmanship.

The specimens illustrated on the opposite plate are typical examples of the work done in these areas. The simple units used in these designs have been handed down the generations, each succeeding worker becoming a designer, when planning out these large surfaces of ornament with no other help than the units and a few chalked or needle-scratched lines on the material. The covers of thin, washable fabric are stretched on large frames, with a padding of wadding or carded sheep's wool laid between them. The running stitch which outlines the pattern, extending over the whole surface of the quilt, keeps the padding in position. The English and Welsh designs have certain similarities, suggesting a common origin now lost to history. The depression in the coal industry, which so seriously affected both these areas, might well have been the death-blow of this lovely craft, but happily by the aid of the Rural Industries Bureau this has been avoided and a widespread activity now exists.

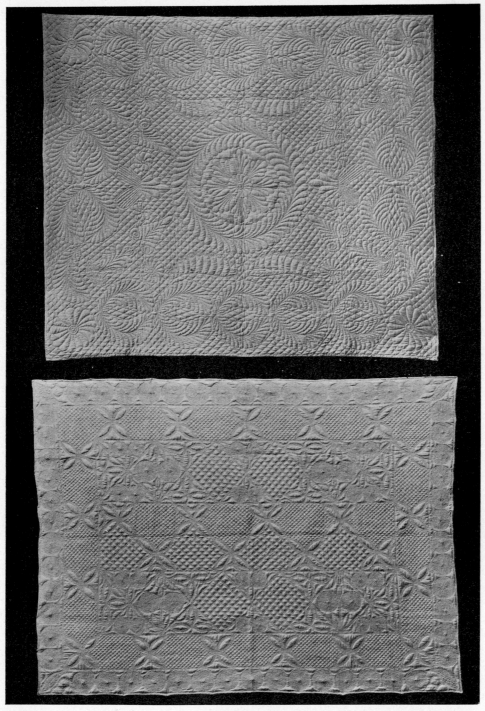

PLATE 48

EXAMPLES OF QUILTING (TRADITIONAL)

The upper illustration shows a Durham quilt with typical feather pattern. The lower illustration
is of a Welsh quilt.

From the Victoria and Albert Museum

By stitching through two thicknesses of material (and an interlining of soft padding) along the outline of an ornamental pattern, the intervening spaces

**Quilting :
Choice of
Design**

become raised, or "puffed" up. Thus, when completely stitched, the effect of a line design has gone and a series of embossed forms appears in its place. It follows, therefore, that when making or selecting a design for this method, we must think in terms of raised spaces rather than of outlines. Many outline designs, pleasing if worked flatly, would be ineffective when quilted. Traditional patterns form the best guide to the kind of treatment needed. Those on Plate 48 will be found helpful. The quilts of the late seventeenth century show the influence of the richly designed fabrics and cottons that our trading ships were then bringing home from China and India. The large exotic leaf shapes and the forms of pines, pomegranates, and other fruit were hailed as boldly flowing quilting subjects.

Thin, strong fabrics of silk, satin, cotton, linen, or artificial furnishing silks can be successfully quilted, whilst domette, cotton-wool (by the yard), fine

**Materials
for Quilting**

flannel, and even old blankets, may, any of them, be used as interlinings. Cotton-wool is suitable for sachets and tea and egg cosies; fine flannel for baby bonnets, coats, and shoes; domette for dressing-gowns and jackets; blanket for hot water jug cosies, and cushions of the heavier type. For backing, fine calico, nainsook, muslin, or any thin, pliable, cotton material may be used. It must be remembered that as the needle has to pass through all three materials for each stitch, thick or stiff materials are to be avoided. Filoselle silk, machine twist, sylko (Clarke's stranded cotton and Star sylko) are all useful threads for stitching.

The three layers of material are kept securely in place by a series of tacking lines worked across their length and breadth, so that they feel as one when the

**Method of
Working, I**

working of the ornamental pattern is in progress. The above-mentioned articles can be worked in the hand quite comfortably without the use of a frame. Running, back stitch, chain, or stem stitch may be used for the quilting, each piece of work being carried out with the one stitch only. For running or stem stitch the design is traced on to the backing material and the quilting done from that side. Running stitch, which is conveniently both sides alike, is the more generally used. With stem stitch, if care be taken to put the needle in and out exactly on the working line (and never obliquely across it) for each stitch, back-stitching will be found on the other side. Chain, worked on the reverse side, has a similar result. Chain and back stitch may be worked from the front, and for these the design must be traced on that side. In the case of delicate fabrics it is preferable to work from the back, so that the risk of marring the upper surface material by the tracing process is avoided.

Thread of the same colour but slightly darker in tone is usual for this method.

PLATE 49

PORTION OF A QUILTED LINEN COVER (ENGLISH, FIRST HALF OF
XVIIIth CENTURY)

Silk quilting in back stitch.

From the Victoria and Albert Museum

By another method, more delicate in effect, the design is stitched through the backing and upper material and the padding inserted afterwards, between **Quilting** the two layers. This is done from the back, with a blunt-tipped **Method II** needle threaded with wool, a soft kind of cotton, or a cord. The backing material must be a rather loosely woven one, to allow the insertion of a needle threaded with several strands of padding thread. Soft tarlatan is an example of the type of texture needed. By the first quilting method described, the effect owes nothing to colour and everything to the play of light and shade, but in this method colour may play a fascinating part. Patterns quilted on semi-transparent silks may be padded with strands of fiercely brilliant coloured wools, which on account of being veiled by the thin silk fabric become delicate pastel colours as they shine through. The idea of coloured padding comes to us from the Persians who, as might be expected, make it an affair of great beauty. A favourite scheme is a white ground stitched with yellow silk, and a padding of blue cord. The yellow stitching has the effect of warming the white to a cream colour, and the blue padding showing through the channels of the ornament with a feeling of coolness gives a subtle and pleasing effect.

The *motif* on the opposite plate is shown in stages 1, 2, 3, and 4 of development, the fourth being the final result. At No. 1 the tarlatan, bearing the traced design, is tacked to Japanese silk on the reverse side, and the running stitch, begun at *A*, has reached its first stopping-place at *B*. The needle is in position for fastening off the thread by overcasting a few of the last stitches (whipped running—see Plate 119). To fasten in the thread, make one running stitch through the two materials and a second in the same place through the tarlatan only.

No. 2 shows the completed running seen from the front.

No. 3 shows the reverse side, again with the work of padding in progress. The needle for this padding is large-eyed, extra long, and blunt-tipped. It is threaded with six whole threads of Arden's "Grove Lustre," used double, so that actually twelve threads pass between the silk and tarlatan at each passage of the needle. This process must be repeated. This has been done in the other padded portions, as may be seen by the cut ends of the threads. Wool or soft cotton make the most suitable padding thread, and as very vivid colours are necessary to make an effect, it is well to choose fast dyes; otherwise accidental contact with moisture may prove disastrous. The thread shown in the plate is a very strong cerise colour, which becomes a soft rose seen through the front silk.

The small triangles are filled with bright emerald green, which, becoming similarly subdued by the Japanese silk covering, looks quite happy with the rose colour.

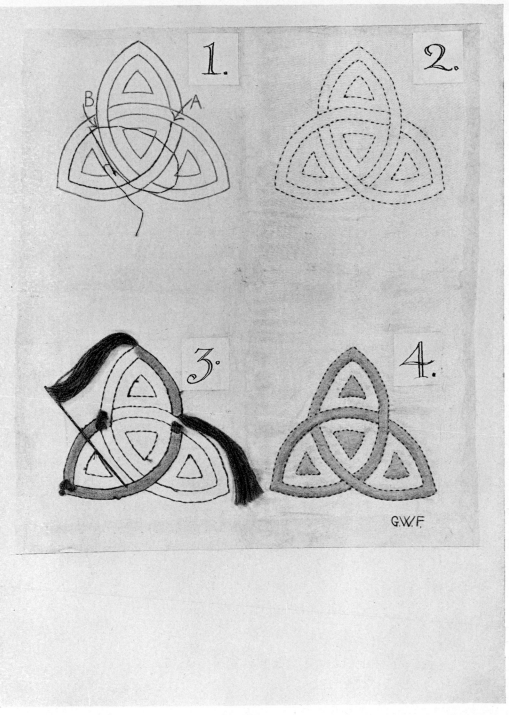

PLATE 50

A SAMPLER OF ITALIAN QUILTING

PLATE 50A
DESIGN FROM A CHINESE STONE PILLOW ADAPTED TO QUILTING

CHAPTER IV

EMBROIDERY WITH WOOLS AND STOUT THREADS

CHAPTER IV

Stout threads call for boldly treated designs; indeed, the thicker the thread the bolder should be the treatment.

Massed conventional floral designs are useful for embroideries in wool. The diagrams opposite suggest the manner of setting about the work. First

Massed Designs indicate the shape the ornament is to fill, be it a square, oblong, triangle, spandrel, or what you will. The first stage on Plate 51 shows a circle with the main "masses" for the flowers all roughly indicated. To this stage add the indication of position of leaves and buds, as shown at second stage. The process should be a rapid one, and no time should be spent on any detail. The final stage shows the complete drawing ready for tracing on to the material. Only such detail as indicated will be helpful to the needlework. In this case it amounts to no more than a few lines breaking up the flower shapes to give them variety, serrated edges to the leaves, and a double line for the veins. The small tendrils in the background spaces serve to complete the mass. The detail in such a design is supplied by the stitches. The three stages are easily made on one drawing, done rapidly and lightly. Any "neatness" or loss of time in "rubbing out" will prove to be a drawback. The final lines may be drawn in clearly and continuously by exerting more pressure on the pencil. Should any confusion of line become hampering, use a coloured pencil, pen and ink, or paint and brush as a remedy.

The design, embroidered in coloured wools, is shown on Plate 52.

The first consideration in all designing is the manner of settling the masses within a design in right relation of parts, making an harmonious whole which

Foundation of Designing will tell at the right distance, whether it be a design on the back of a glove, a wall-hanging, or a banner.

The problem presented by the design illustrated is of so simple a character that it can be carried through in outline. For the larger design it will be found necessary to use tone or silhouette at the outset. By this means the masses may be judged as such—dark against a light ground or light against a dark ground. Study your trials, balancing and adjusting them until the effect is pleasing even in this state of black and white.

See notes on the use of coloured papers on page 172.

The massed circle embroidered in tapestry wools on hand-woven linen on Plate 52 was worked in a frame, and the colour-scheme was a "come by chance" evolved from left-over ends in the work-bag. Five blues, three mauves, three yellows, two shades of flame, and a white are used. The design lends itself equally well to work held in the hand, should other stitches be used. Here the three buds are worked in long and short shading with lines of couching set closely for the cups.

MAKING A MASSED DESIGN

1st stage

2nd stage

Final

G.W.F.

PLATE 51

The stems and tendrils are in stem stitch; the top flower is outlined by wide-set buttonhole stitch in blue, within which a set of single pink buttonhole stitches are worked, followed by a set in yellow, in the same manner. A line of chain stitches in blue surrounds the centre, which is filled by couching a double thread of yellow, in straight lines, with a single thread of a darker shade. It will be seen that the couching stitches are placed between those of the former row like bricks in a wall.

The flower touching the top one is outlined by a double thread of yellow couched by a single one of flame-colour, and the diamond shape within is outlined with a double thread of mauve couched by a single thread of the same. Straight stitches of flame-colour, alternating with shorter ones of mauve, spring from the outline. The centre filling is brick stitch with threads of white slipped beneath the stitches.

The circular flower on the left is outlined with stem stitch in dark blue, within which a double thread of mauve is couched with yellow. The inner rings are in stem stitch, green and yellow. For the centre filling, single stitches in blue are laid across, first in one direction and then in the other, and sewn down by a single oblique stitch at each intersection. A French knot (flame-colour) is worked in each square. Straight stitches in blue, alternating with shorter ones in mauve, radiate from the centre.

The oval flower beneath is outlined with the couched lines, blue, pink, and yellow. These, and also the inner oblong in flame, are double threads couched by a single one of the same colour. The centre is filled by double threads of blue couched by a darker blue. Two needles are used, one for passing the double thread through, and up, at the end of the lines, and the other for the couching thread. The lines branching from the centre are in split stitch.

The remaining flower is outlined by a double thread of purple couched with yellow. The inner ring is a double thread of blue couched with a single one, and the five points springing from it are made with two straight stitches of the same. Each of these points is finished by a French knot in yellow, and a stitch of the same taken from the outline to the centre divides the petals. Long and short stitches in mauve radiate from the centre. The centre is filled by single lines of flame placed openly and couched with dark blue.

A double thread of green couched with blue outlines the leaves, which are filled by straight stitches taken across them from outline to outline, placed about one thickness of wool apart. The long strands are kept in place by the veins, which are laid over them and couched by stitches placed between them. This filling gives an opportunity for shading. A green, a yellow-green, and a green-blue are used, while the vein itself is of a darker green.

PLATE 52

MASSED DESIGN COMPLETED IN WOOLS

See outline on Plate 51.

"Anchor Flox," a loosely twisted and considerably thicker thread than tapestry wool, has the softness of wool, to which is added something of the

Anchor Flox Embroidery sheen of silk. Actually it is mercerized cotton, and apart from its likeness to both silk and wool, it has a quality entirely its own, and lends itself very pleasantly to the decoration of coarse and rough-surfaced fabrics. It does not shrink when washed, and the colours are permanent. For a finer quality of work the thread most resembling Anchor Flox in size is Pearsall's Antyka (pure silk).

The panel opposite is designed to show how well certain familiar stitches adapt themselves to these materials. The ground, a coarse oatmeal-coloured "Old Glamis" linen (No. 261, 05160) in which some harsh straw-like substance is woven, is of a roughness which, while pleasing in appearance, prevents the use of many usual stitches. A size 18 wool (blunt) needle was used for everything but the stem, and for that a sharp-pointed (Chenille) needle was needed to pierce the coarse threads of the fabric in order to preserve a steady outline for the curves.

The colours used are three tones of old rose (1302, 130, and 200) for the flowers, three greens (48, 338, and 69) for the leaves, and green (169) for the stem. The top flower has a solid band of buttonhole stitch worked in the middle tone of rose, outside of which small straight stitches in the dark tone are added, to break the severity of the outline. The inner ellipse is of back stitch in the dark tone, and is connected with the outer by radiating straight stitches of the light tone. In the centre, back stitches are worked crazily with yellow. The flower beneath has two bands of buttonhole stitch, worked openly, the outer of the light tone, the inner of the middle tone. The first of the inner rings of back stitch is dark rose, and the second (and innermost) yellow.

The outer ellipse of the remaining flower is of dark chain stitch, overcast on its outer side with the light tone. The inner ellipse is dark chain stitch, inside of which is a line of back stitch in yellow. The stitches radiating from the centre are made by a ring of fly stitch in the middle tone, and inside each stitch another is worked in the light tone. The berries are wheels of buttonhole stitch; the three tones are used, graduating from dark at the stem to light at the tip. Varieties of chain and feather stitches, Roumanian, and composite stitches built upon chain and back stitch foundations, also work well in these materials.

The method of seaming illustrated on Plate 124 can be effectively done with Anchor Flox on heavy materials. The thread is made in a hundred and twenty colours which are fast to sun and washing.

PLATE 53
A PANEL EMBROIDERED IN ANCHOR FLOX ON COARSE LINEN

PLATE 54
FINISHED RUNNERS EXECUTED IN ANCHOR FLOX
The top specimen is embroidered in cross stitch and the lower ones have needle-woven borders.

PLATE 54A
ANIMALS EMBROIDERED IN WOOL
See page 104.

Couching is the name given to the method of sewing down one or more threads by means of another thread. It is seen in its simplest form on the

Couching

opposite plate, where the needle is shown passing obliquely through the material at the back of the laid thread, making transverse stitches over it. For threads that are non-pliable, too coarse, or too delicate to pass constantly in and out of the material, couching is the most natural method to employ.

Fancy Couching

Couching stitches may be grouped together as shown on the left of the sampler, where, firstly, four transverse stitches set close together are placed at regular intervals; secondly, the stitches are crossed, and thirdly, groups of three stitches are set obliquely, while in the fourth (below) a double thread is laid and sewn with one stitch over both, followed by four stitches over the other single thread, all in succession.

Couching with Embroidery Stitches

The specimen on the right is sewn down with fly stitch. Many other embroidery stitches can be used for the purpose, the most suitable being the open kinds which enter the material at the edges, such as open chain and double back, also the varieties of buttonhole stitch and featherstitch.

By means of couching, boldly decorative embroideries may be carried out with Turkey rug wool. A large "rug wool" needle is used to pass the thick

Turkey Rug Wool Embroidery

ends of wool to the back of the material, which must be woven loosely enough to prevent its being damaged. Tapestry wool is admirably suited for the purpose of sewing down. In the sampler opposite, rug wool is sewn down with a single thread of tapestry wool, except for the heart-shaped leaf where two threads are used, both for the outline and the filling stitch.

The border at the top of the sampler, composed of straight lines of couched wool (three outer and two inner) with scrolls between, suggests a useful method

Couching as a Joining Stitch

of joining heavy fabrics. The join would take place beneath the three outer lines of couching, the fabric being first placed together with the edge of one overlapping that of the other, and tacked through both thicknesses. The laid threads cover the join and the couching stitches secure it. This border would look well against an applied hem of a contrasting colour for the end of a strip, but straight lines of well chosen coloured threads are enough to enhance and, at the same time, join furnishing fabrics which are interesting in themselves.

Use of Couching Threads in Colour Scheme

Many different colours of rug wool are not necessarily needed for embroidering designs. The finer threads used for couching the rug wool and for the filling stitches within the spaces may be many and various, all influencing the colour in such a way that rich effects are possible in schemes in which no more than one, two or three colours of the coarser wool are used.

PLATE 55
A SAMPLER OF COUCHING

It is possible to embroider decorations with rug wool entirely, using a thinner thread for couching purposes only. The heart-shaped leaf and the

Choice of Stitches

border on the previous plate suggest the possibilities of this treatment, which limits the number of filling variations, but variety may be given by fancy couchings (see suggestions on the same plate), and the boldness of such a scheme, rightly placed, may be well justified.

Alternatively, open filling stitches, worked with a finer thread than that composing the outline, can be usefully employed to pattern certain areas of the design where ornament of a somewhat less stark nature is called for.

The hunter illustrated opposite is embroidered with Candlewick Cotton on a linen ground. Star Sylko size 8 was used for the couching, and a thicker one

Embroidery with Candlewick

size 3 (itself couched with size 8) was used for working the arrow, parts of the bow, and the patterns on the man's dress. Here all three threads used are of the same light tone, and matching in colour. Thus the ornament appears in one light tone upon a dark ground. The linen for the latter must be firm in texture and sufficiently openly woven to allow the ends of the candlewick to be passed through to the back. A blunt tipped needle (Tapestry size 18) was used for this purpose, and another smaller one, size 22, for the finer thread used for couching it down. It will be noticed that for the man's topknot the ends of the thread are not passed through to the back, but having been made secure with a couple of transverse stitches, cut off and unravelled to good effect!

Of necessity the drawings for this technique must be both bold and simple. Continuous lines are an advantage with as few points and sharp turns as possible.

Type of Drawing Needed

Patterns which hold their own by means of outline alone, with no dependence upon fine detail for their effect, are the ones to aim for. In fact, it would seem that the very nature of the restrictions imposed by this mode of working becomes a stimulus to the making of good designs.

PLATE 56
EMBROIDERY WITH CANDLEWICK ON LINEN
(Detail from a draught screen.)

The embroidered hangings, curtains, and bed-covers done in England during the last three decades of the seventeenth century, known as Jacobean, **Jacobean Work** of which many survive, are themselves a veritable school of embroidery, comprising innumerable fillings both solid and open, as well as outline and stem treatments. They are embroidered with wools on a twill material of linen and cotton mixture. Some of the wools are of a tightly twisted nature, and all are beautifully dyed. The fact that so many exist to-day in good condition speaks for the quality of the materials, and the fact that they have escaped the ravages of moths is said to be due to their having been kept in constant use, being passed on to servants and dependants when new fashions replaced them.

At one time it was thought that they were made in the reign of James I (soon after the opening of the Far Eastern trade) and so earned their name. The great tree designs, rising from a border of fields or hillocks, and branching large leaves and flowers (sometimes interspersed with tropical birds) over a wide surface, clearly come from the dyed cottons of India and the big tree designs of China. Were further evidence of Oriental influence needed, the presence in the borders of pagodas, eastern figures, and the Persian symbol of the hart (human soul) pursued by the leopard (care) through the tangled forest of life provide it.

The British East India Company received its charter in 1600, but sent no ships to China until 1637, and only four during the next forty years. After that they were frequent, and from 1670 the imitation of Chinese ornament began to be extensive in Europe.

It is interesting to trace to its source the design of these works, but still more so to notice, at the same time, how entirely individual they are. On seeing them we think neither of the East nor of the Indian palampores from which their lines are borrowed, but of the sombre, oak-panelled English rooms which they adorned. Of appropriateness of conception and design to the place in which they are to be used they are an outstanding example. Stretched out flat, some of the designs have a restless and even a clumsy appearance, but hung in folds as intended, and as the chief, perhaps only, decorative incident in a room of the period, they are beautiful. In some, many colours are used; in others a number of different blues and greens, so well managed that at a little distance the effect is rich and mellow, recalling an English countryside on a sunless day.

These are examples from which the modern Embroideress may learn much, but she should be content to emulate and not to copy. She should use her influence so that they may not be embroidered in mutilated sections in anaemic colours for fire- and draught-screens, and cushions, and set side by side with miscellaneous furniture in already overcrowded rooms.

PLATE 57

CURTAIN OF LATE XVIIᴛʜ CENTURY (ENGLISH)

Embroidered in wool on cotton and linen twill material, in long and short, brick, shading, fishbone, satin, chain, and stem stitches, and French knots, with laid and couched work.

From the Victoria and Albert Museum

Various open filling stitches are shown on the opposite sampler. This is a useful way of treating large areas for which solid embroidery would look too

Open Filling Stitches heavy, and in any case, be too laborious to work; but a combination of the two treatments often has a beautiful effect.

The filling stitch may be on the forms themselves, or as a background to them. A strong effect can be gained by outlining a design and filling in the background, as in the petals of the upper flower, one of which is left blank to show the influence of a toned background. The tone of the background, composed of vertical, or maybe, horizontal lines, can be varied by the distance at which the lines are placed from each other. Compare the tone of the top leaf, filled with double threads laid horizontally, with that of the background, filled with single threads set closer together.

Crossed stitches made with a long and a short stitch, and sewn down where they intersect, are scattered over half of the top leaf. Even cross stitches, placed in lines alternately, fill the adjoining petal; and the same, with the addition of French knots in the spaces, that next to it. The petal in the corner is filled with detached fly stitches. For the middle leaf, lines are laid, horizontally, vertically, and diagonally, and then sewn down by single stitches across the intersections. Parallel lines are laid across the petals of the middle flower from centre to edge, and crossed by others at right angles. The effect of placing a French knot in the square spaces is seen in two of the petals. In the lower leaf, groups of two parallel lines are laid at right angles and sewn down at the intersections. The petals of the lower flower are striped by couched double threads laid (from centre to edge) alternately with rows of French knots. The centre is filled with a stitch previously described, but on a smaller scale.

Buttonhole as a filling stitch (open or solid) is illustrated on Plate 11, and geometric satin stitch fillings on Plate 65.

The use of open filling is not of necessity limited to the large in scale, for in the black or Spanish work of the sixteenth century all kinds of finely stitched

Spanish or Black Work open fillings are used. This work is said to have been introduced into England by Catherine of Aragon, through whose own work it became a fashion (in spite of its previous existence),

and it continued to the end of James I's reign.

Leaves and scrolling stems are delicately outlined and diapered with pattern, the whole being worked in black silk on a white linen ground with occasionally a little gold or silver thread introduced.

See contemporary black work sampler, Plate 115.

PLATE 58
A SAMPLER OF OPEN FILLING STITCHES

PLATE 58a

HŌ-HŌ BIRD EMBROIDERED IN VERY FINE WOOLS

Adapted from a Chinese silk tapestry. Ming Dynasty 1368–1644.

CHAPTER V

WHITE AND SELF-COLOURED EMBROIDERY

CHAPTER V

THE idea of working patterns in white thread upon white linen probably originated in coloured work fading through washing, and from that have grown **White-work** all the delicate processes by which the insipid effect of white **Methods** stitching on a white ground may be relieved. These methods include open-work by means of withdrawn threads ("drawn thread"), open-work by means of pulled stitches ("drawn fabric"), pierced holes (*Broderie anglaise*), and cut ornament held together by bars (*Richelieu* and *Renaissance*). The style in which these methods are rendered is frequently revised to suit new fabrics, fashions, and requirements, but their fundamental technical points remain constant, and it is with these that the following pages deal.

Known also as "English," "Eyelet" and "Madeira" work needs to be executed with accuracy to give of its best. If the points emphasized in the **Broderie** working sampler opposite are observed this can be done without **Anglaise** difficulty. The shape to be opened is first outlined with a fine even running stitch, then a single cut is made down the centre from end to end with sharp-pointed scissors. In the case of an eyelet, a second cut is made, again through the centre but transversely. No material is cut out. These cut sections are rolled to the back between the first finger (at the back) and the thumb (at the front) until perforce stopped by the outlining thread. The edge is then finely overcast (from left to right), the needle entering the hole, to be brought through from the back to the front, and the stitches closely packed without overlapping.

Very small holes, which do not admit the insertion of scissor points, may be pierced with a stiletto. Where rows of adjoining eyelets occur it is well to outline alternate halves of the circles, as shown in the sampler, and to complete them by returning in the same manner, so that the crossed threads may strengthen an otherwise delicate place. Raised satin stitch in the form of petals, leaves, spots, and stems, adds interest to eyelet work. Beautiful examples are made in the Island of Madeira, from whence the method is said to have originated. Some form of scalloping in buttonhole stitch, worked over a padding of thread, makes a suitable edging. A running stitch (which by picking up the least possible amount of material keeps most of the thread on the surface) is shown in use on the sampler as padding. Both scallop and leaf are outlined in this way first, and filled in with as many more lines as are wanted for an even under-lay of thread. If the padding stitches define the form accurately, the final satin stitching preserves it. It is easier to start the satin stitch at the fine point of a leaf or petal, and to increase the size of the stitches, than conversely. A satin-stitch spot can be outlined and filled with crossed stitches as padding (see sampler) and is conveniently worked in two halves, by beginning with the longest stitch at the centre and working to the right for the right half, and from the centre to the left to finish.

PLATE 59

A SAMPLER OF *BRODERIE ANGLAISE* TECHNIQUE

In Richelieu and Renaissance embroidery the design is edged with button-hole stitch, and the various parts of the pattern held together by means of needle-worked bars as bridges across those portions that are finally cut away from beneath them. Bars are made by passing the working thread from outline to outline and working back over the foundation thus made, and not through the material.

Richelieu Embroidery

The sampler on the opposite plate shows a small finished border at the top, and beneath (as in the former plate) the method of working. The procedure may be followed from the enlarged four-petalled flower. Begin by running a thread along the inner outline of a petal, and, having reached the first bar, lay its three foundation threads by passing from outline to outline three times. (See needle in top petal.) The needle is then in position for buttonholing back over the threads to the inner line. (See needle in left petal.) Having completed all the bars in this manner, run a thread round the centre ring and work button-hole stitch over it, also round the edges of the four petals (with the heading outwards). The outer line only remains; run a thread round this and button-hole over it with the heading inwards. From the front, with sharp-pointed scissors, cut along the middle of the linen behind the bars. Turn the work over and fold back the cut linen to the worked edge, snicking it here and there to enable this to be done. Finally cut off each piece close to the edge. In the original fifteenth-century work, both edging and bars were of buttonhole, but now overcast, woven, or buttonhole bars are used.

Overcast Bars

Overcasting makes the finest and least obtrusive bar, and may be worked over one, two, or three foundation threads. The working is seen in three stages at the top left of the sampler, and the effect in *motif* 2 on Plate 33, where it is developed to a branched bar.

Woven Bar

For a woven bar an even number of foundation threads must be laid, two or four, and finished by passing the thread over and under the divided threads, as in weaving. (See needle in the left centre illustration.)

Interlaced Bars

See needle in lower left corner. Buttonhole stitch is worked openly over the foundation threads, and again on the other side, this time placing the stitches between those of the former row.

Twisted Bars

Two of these are shown crosswise in a circle. They are worked at the same time as the buttonhole edge. For the bars the thread is thrown across to the opposite side and returned by twisting round itself. The buttonhole edge is then continued and a second bar made. The needle in the specimen is just finishing this.

Single bars may be worked over one, two, or three foundation threads, but if the design contains crossed bars it is well to note the fact before begin-ning, for these must be worked either over one or three threads, and the bars

PLATE 60

A SAMPLER OF RICHELIEU TECHNIQUE

throughout a design must be worked on the same number of threads to keep their size uniform. The working of a crossed bar may be followed from the **Crossed Bars** five squares on the right of Plate 60; in four it is shown in progressive stages, and in the fifth complete. Begin at the top left square and fasten in the thread at the lower left corner; pass it diagonally to the opposite corner, back to the start-point, and again to the opposite corner. Now buttonhole half-way back over these threads, and from that point throw out the foundation threads for a third bar. When pulled through, the needle in the first square will be in position for buttonholing back to the centre. The second square shows this completed, and the needle in position for laying the first foundation thread of the fourth bar. The third square shows this completed, and the needle in position lacing the bars together in the centre of the cross. In the fourth the needle, when pulled through, will be in position for completing the fourth bar.

The same method applies to overcast bars, and either may be worked with three, four, five, or more bars if needed.

Picots are used to enrich bars and buttonholed edging, and are made at the desired intervals as the work proceeds. Four kinds are illustrated on the opposite plate, with the working process on the left and a completed picot on the right. The same can be done going from left to right.

Loop Picot This is a single loop of thread made secure by a buttonhole stitch worked across it. At the required point insert a pin as shown in the diagram, then pass the working thread under the pin, and put the needle into the edge again and make a buttonhole stitch across the loop thus formed.

This is made by the same method as a bullion knot, but is coiled on to the edge of the buttonhole stitch instead of being laid flat on the ground material.

Bullion Picot At the required point pass the needle behind the thread of the last buttonhole stitch and wind it round the needle as many times as the size of picot requires, pull the needle through (meanwhile holding the left thumb on the coiled threads), tighten the knot, and put the needle in again at the same place in the edge and pull through.

Ring Picot Here the thread is looped backwards into the buttonholed edging, and buttonhole stitch worked over the semicircle of thread to the starting-point. If a thicker picot is needed, the thread can be passed to and fro until three threads are laid.

This is begun in the same way as the loop picot. A pin is placed in the material, and the working thread passed under it and into the edge. It is then **Venetian Picot** brought out in the middle of the loop thus made, and passed under the pin again. Then three or four buttonhole stitches are worked upon the loop, bringing the thread into the right position for continuing the edging stitch.

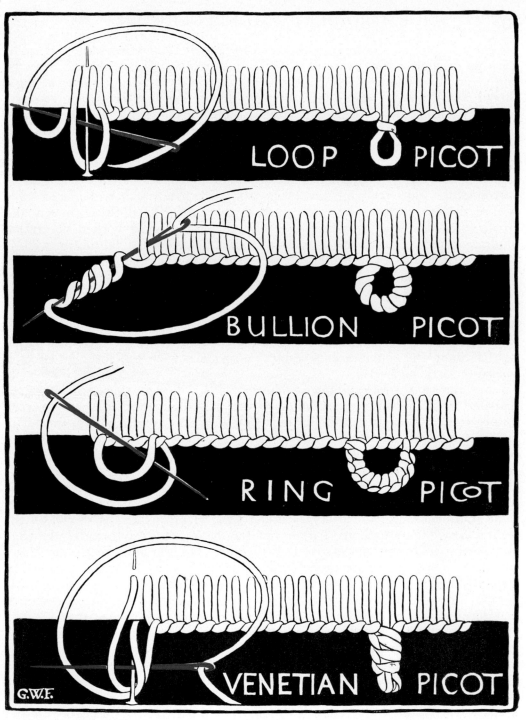

LOOP PICOT

BULLION PICOT

RING PICOT

VENETIAN PICOT

G.W.F.

PLATE 61

Small technical details, such as various kinds of connecting bars, the use or non-use of picots, the treatment of the buttonholed edging (which may be either raised by padding into high relief or kept flat by working over a single thread, and the width varied from thick to thin or kept uniform) all give scope to this work and make possible effects widely differing in character. Again, methods designated "white work," from long association with linens bleached to dead white, are not now necessarily white, but often self-coloured work. Ecru, natural, half-bleach, cream, and indeed the whole gamut of off-white shades are found to be richer in effect and more harmonious with their general surroundings, thus reviving interest in work which might have suffered some eclipse in our growing love for pure, bright colours. Both Richelieu and *Broderie anglaise* have been put to good use for the hand-worked decoration of dresses and lingerie, and successfully used on coloured fabrics as well as white. Arranged with intelligence and restraint, they give a particular kind of quiet enrichment.

There is always a fascination in arranging embroideries which depend solely upon variation of texture plus some form of open-work for their effect, but on some occasions a change of tone in addition is useful. Richelieu work, for instance, may be executed on a dark natural linen with thread of a much lighter tone; the converse arrangement also looks well, but loses its effect if placed on dark surfaces.

For further richness, filling stitches, couched, darned, geometric satin, or diapered in single stitches, are effective, and may be combined with cut-work on occasion. French knots should be avoided, as they are apt to lose their trim appearance when laundered, and the above methods are essentially those for washable things. The specimens on the opposite plate are worked with ecru coloured *coton à broder*, on linen of a slightly darker tone. The first on the left shows a simple treatment with buttonholed bars and outline over a single underlying thread, and eyelets worked as described for *Broderie anglaise*. The same fragment of ornament reversed and more richly treated is shown on the right. Here the buttonholed bars have a foundation of three threads; the edge is more raised (by means of padding threads), and the stitches are set closer together. The spots are worked solidly with raised satin. Threads couched in straight lines fill the upper petal, also the same placed lattice-wise fill the side petals. The solid filling is made by first placing laid threads at equal distances and darning on them, over and under. A piece in the lower corner of this second example is left unfinished, in order that the process may be followed. Cut-work without bars is shown in the third design. (A more complete specimen of this type of design, which must be of perfect fretwork, is shown on Plate 117.) A grouped buttonhole edging—three short and one long—is used here, and the edges of the cut centre-piece are overcast, and have a line of back-stitch seeds worked close up to them. In the last specimen the bars are overcast and

PLATE 62

A SAMPLER OF CUT-WORK DETAILS

have looped picots worked on them. They include crossed and branched bars as well as bars radiating from small buttonhole centres. The latter is a useful and decorative device for connecting more widely spaced pieces of ornament.

Drawn-thread work for border lines, fillings, and backgrounds is another power in the hands of the designer of self-coloured embroideries. By its intro-

Drawn-thread Fillings duction, work of a quite different character from that already mentioned, but quite as definite, becomes possible. It is well to remember that withdrawn threads weaken a fabric. This weakness can be obviated to a great extent by the final workmanship. One kind of drawn-thread work, known as "Teneriffe," has become discredited on account of its impracticability in this respect; also, and perhaps more so, on account of the cheap machine-made imitations of it that at one time flooded the market. These fell completely between two stools, having none of the inherent beauty of hand-made articles, or the dignity of those well-planned and machine-made.

Drawn-thread line stitches and borders are dealt with on pages 50 to 54. On the opposite plate some fillings are shown, and in each a portion is left unfinished, in order that the mesh, on which the pattern is built, may be examined. The boundary line of an area to be filled thus is worked before the filling, and the threads are cut and drawn out when it is completed. This surrounding stitch must be one that will adequately secure the cut ends of the threads. On closely woven textures chain, broad chain, or two rows of knot stitch will do this, while loosely woven open linens will need either satin or buttonhole stitch worked over a padding of chain stitch or lines of running. The number of threads to be withdrawn varies according to the effect required and the kind of linen used, and must be decided by experiment on an odd piece of the material in use. Having settled this point, cut a warp and a weft thread at roughly the centre of the space, and draw them out to the edge in each direction. It will then be easier to cut the remainder of the threads in the openings thus provided. Draw them out on the reverse side to the edge of the surrounding stitchery and cut off.

No. 1 Filling For this stitch the groups of uncut threads must be even in number. In the specimen three have been withdrawn and six left. Groups of three threads (i.e. half of each group) are overcast in straight lines, the needle passing through the back of the surrounding stitches to get from one line of threads to the next.

No. 2 Filling Overcast the first row of threads down its whole length. In the second row, on reaching the middle of the first small bar, carry the working thread across the two adjoining rows, and by twisting round it return to continue the overcasting. Repeat this in the next section; then overcast two bars.

PLATE 63

A SAMPLER OF DRAWN-THREAD FILLINGS

Alternate these two processes until the row is filled. The third row is a repetition of the first, and the fourth of the second. When all the vertical rows are worked thus, the horizontal ones are treated in the same way. This second time the bars composed of the working thread cross those already made, and the pattern is completed.

This square overcast filling is the most generally used. Its direct simplicity of effect is suited to a greater number of occasions than the more elaborate stitches, and can be worked in small and irregularly shaped **No. 3 Filling** spaces with comparative ease. In the specimen (Plate 63) three threads have been withdrawn and three left. The stitch is worked diagonally. Having secured the end of the working thread in the back of the surrounding stitch, work four overcasting stitches over the first horizontal bar, then pass the needle diagonally behind three threads and overcast a vertical bar with the same number of stitches. An isolated line has been worked in order that this process may be followed. The consecutive lines worked in the top left corner show the finished effect. In the lower corner the reverse side of the stitch is shown; its only difference is that the intersections are covered with the working thread which was passed behind them in travelling from bar to bar. If, when using a thread of contrasting tone or colour, the effect of an even tone, rather than a broken one, is desired, the stitch can be done on the reverse side to give the effect.

The bars in this filling are woven; therefore the uncut threads must be even in number. Here five threads have been cut and four left. All the horizontal bars are completed first, working over and under two **No. 4 Filling** threads. The little diamonds are made in alternate squares whilst working the vertical bars. The upper needle is making one of these; on completing the looped diamond continue the weaving until the centre of the next alternate square is reached.

The drawn-thread filling, seen in use as a background in the white-work border on the opposite plate, illustrates the above-mentioned points. (See No. 3 filling.) This border, designed for a square cloth, begins in **Seaweed and Dolphin Cloth** the corner and repeats at the quarter. The seaweed rooted to the shell at the corner scrolls along each side of the cloth until the half-way point is reached, thus filling a quarter of the square. Within the quarter no two fish or groups of seaweed are identical. This restrained variety adds beauty and interest to the pattern, while taking no longer to embroider. This and similarly elaborate designs could be carried out communally, without detriment to their effect—that is, say, if one worker undertook the satin stitch (shell, fish, and spots on seaweed), another the knot-stitch outlines of the seaweed and the chain-stitch filling of the main stems, another the drawn-thread filling, and a fourth worker the seeding and the scales on the fish and shells. By these means a feeling of uniformity

PLATE 64
SEAWEED AND DOLPHIN CLOTH
Showing drawn-thread as a background.

would be preserved which would not be possible if complete sections were carried out by different individuals.

From satin stitches, grouped geometrically, many interesting filling patterns can be evolved. The stitches are worked by the counted thread of the ground

Geometric Satin Stitch Fillings

material, and the effect of definite orderliness given by this method contrasts very pleasantly with the flowing outlines of the forms they fill. The addition of a drawn-thread background to designs treated in the above manner makes a very rich scheme of white or self-coloured embroidery, capable (on fine material) of great delicacy. (See Plate 68.)

Broad chain (see Plate 8) is used for the outline of the design on the opposite plate, which is merely a sampler of the fillings, and not to be regarded as a specimen of the type of work described. The stitches have been worked with a thread of considerably darker tone than the ground, in order that the arrangement may be more clearly seen. It is well to make it a rule to work the fillings as if on transparent material, that is to say, with the threads on the reverse side lying immediately behind those on the front, and when passing the thread from a finished portion to the commencement of a new one to travel through the back of the stitches and not across the ground material. These precautions are not difficult to observe; indeed they are a help to the right management of the stitches, and should the work be placed against the light, as in the case of window curtains, etc., the clarity of the pattern will be found to be perfectly preserved.

The best way to arrive at the working of the stitches is to try them out on linen, using an embroidery thread of about the same thickness (but not finer) as that from which the linen is woven. The vertical stripes of satin stitch in the scrolls and in the leaf on the right will be readily followed. The tooth-edged stripes in the same leaf have six stitches to a tooth, the first and widest across six threads, the remainder decreasing in width to one thread each time. Pairs of stripes, similarly constructed, are worked diagonally across the leaf on the left, and are divided by single lines of diagonal square stitch. (See Plate 29.) The centre petal of the flower is divided into squares by straight lines of square stitch (see No. 7, Plate 22), and completed by a satin-stitch square worked crosswise at the centre of each. In the turned-over top of the right leaf, pairs of vertical satin stitches are worked over four horizontal threads in diagonal lines. This will serve as a key to the working of the stitches in the stem and

Russian Drawn-thread Work

the two outer petals, which are also carried out diagonally, the easiest way to keep the above conditions.

In the Russian embroidery shown on Plate 68 geometric filling stitches are used to pattern the forms, which are further enhanced by means of a drawn-thread background and borders, all worked with white thread on fine white linen.

PLATE 65

A SAMPLER OF GEOMETRIC SATIN FILLING STITCHES

By this method open-work is made without cutting or drawing threads. The stitch, worked in some geometric order and pulled tightly, binds the

Drawn-fabric Stitches

threads of the fabric together, thus creating open spaces. Loosely woven grounds, strong fine thread, and a blunt needle, are the materials required. This work is particularly adapted to things that are seen against the light, as window curtains, or placed over dark surfaces.

Bring the needle out at the point marked *A*, and put it in at *B*, which is a point four threads vertically above and two to the right of it. Pass the needle

Straight-line Stitch

horizontally behind four threads, bringing it out at *C*. Return to point *A*, and, putting the needle in the same hole, again pass it horizontally behind four threads, bringing it out at *D*. (The needle in the diagram illustrates this movement.) Continue thus to the end of the row, pulling the thread tightly after each movement. Succeeding rows can be worked above or below the first row from either end. The diagrams show how the stitches are placed, but not how they appear drawn up by the tightly pulled thread. For this detail see the sampler on Plate 67.

Is a crossed stitch which raises the fabric into high ridges. Bring the needle out at *A* and put it in at a point six threads vertically above it; then

Diagonal Raised Band

pass behind three threads diagonally downwards, bringing it out at *B*. Continue these vertical stitches until the end of the line is reached. Now return down the row, crossing the vertical stitches by horizontal ones, taking the needle down to the left under three threads (see needle in diagram) for the beginning of each new stitch. The needle goes in and out of the holes already made. For the effect see the bird's wings in sampler.

Diagonal Raised Band Combined with Diagonal Square Stitch

For the working of diagonal square stitch see Plate 29. This can be used effectively with raised diagonal band. In the lemon shape on the left of the sampler two rows are worked alternately with one of raised band.

Eye Stitch

For the eye stitch seen on the sampler, bring the needle up at the corner of a square of six threads and work satin stitches from the centre outwards round the four sides of the square until the starting-point is reached. The needle enters the same hole in the centre each time, and is brought out between every thread at the sides.

A buttonholed wheel is made by putting the needle into the same hole at the centre each time until the wheel is complete. A barred wheel is treated in the

Barred Buttonhole Wheel

same way, except that having worked a quarter of the number of stitches necessary to complete the wheel, say, four, a thread is missed out and four more stitches worked, then another thread missed, until sixteen stitches have been made, completing the wheel. In the sampler these form the crest of the bird on the left. In these, two threads have been missed out each time to form the bar.

STRAIGHT~LINE STITCH

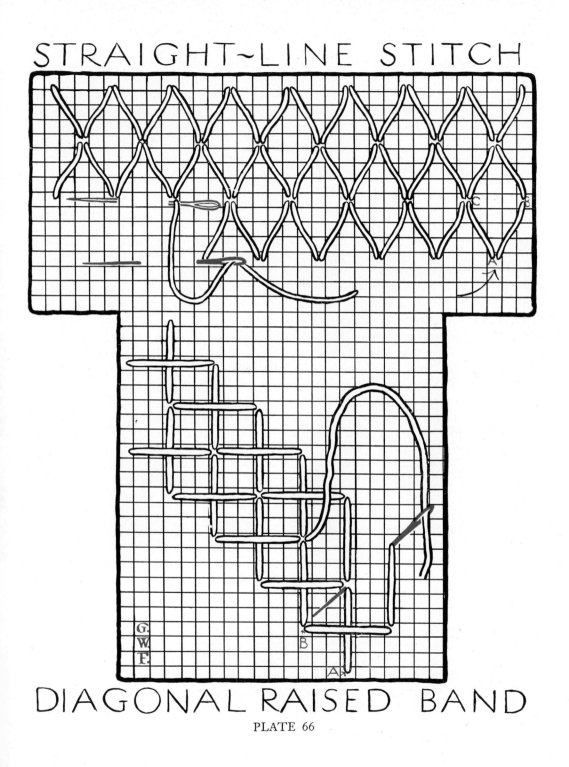

DIAGONAL RAISED BAND

PLATE 66

Drawn-fabric stitches are seen in use as fillings on the opposite plate. This sampler is designed merely to provide spaces to show the fillings. It is, however, full of suggestion for design by this method. Note the use of the eye stitch for the treatment of the bird's crest (on the right), and for the seeds in the split pomegranate. The crest of the bird on the left is expressed by barred buttonhole wheels which also serve for the flowers springing from the ground.

Drawn-fabric Sampler

The ground material is linen scrim; the outlines of the pattern were worked first in overcast chain stitch, with Star Sylko, size 8, and D.M.C. *Lin pour dentelle*, size 40, was used for the fillings. For the fillings the thread must be both fine and strong: fine, for here the object is not to show the thread, but to make the open-work; strong, because in all these stitches the thread is pulled tightly after each movement; hence the name of "pulled" stitches.

Diagonal Raised Band

Is used for the folded wings of the birds. The same stitch is seen in the vase, but there it is spaced out and crossed by a second set of stitches worked in the opposite direction.

Diagonal square stitch (also called diagonal line stitch, see Plate 29), worked over four threads fills the two trefoil leaves and the leaves at the top corners; in one of the latter the stitch is spaced out in stripes. The same stitch is used in the pomegranate and the small curled leaf, but in these it is worked over three threads. In the lemon-shaped fruit on the left, two rows of diagonal square stitch alternate with one of diagonal raised band.

Diagonal Square Stitch

Straight Line Stitch

Fills the mound on which the vase stands, and the two fruits on the right. In the lower of these the peach-like form is helped by changing the direction of the stitch from horizontal in the lower half to vertical in the upper.

Are used for the bodies of the birds. These need no diagram to explain them. In the top bird four threads are bound together by taking a stitch diagonally behind them below four threads and one thread alternately. All the vertical rows are finished in this manner, and crossed by horizontal rows binding together four threads where they come in the vertical rows. One vertical and one horizontal thread is left between each row. The body of bird on right shows a variation of this, two threads instead of one being dropped between the rows of four.

Straight Overcast Stitches

In the birds' tails another overcast stitch is shown, this time worked diagonally. Five overcast stitches are worked horizontally behind four threads and between each of the vertical threads, then five stitches are taken behind four vertical threads and between each of the horizontal ones. A series of rows in steps thus results in overcast squares each enclosing sets of four separate intersecting threads.

Diagonal Overcast

PLATE 67
A SAMPLER OF DRAWN-FABRIC STITCHES

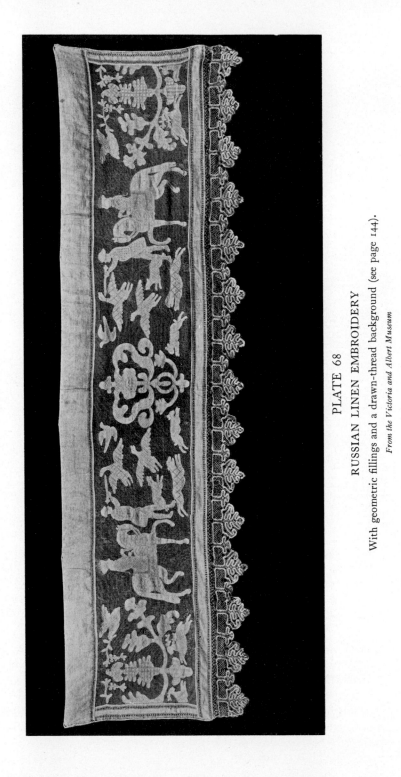

PLATE 68

RUSSIAN LINEN EMBROIDERY

With geometric fillings and a drawn-thread background (see page 144).

From the Victoria and Albert Museum

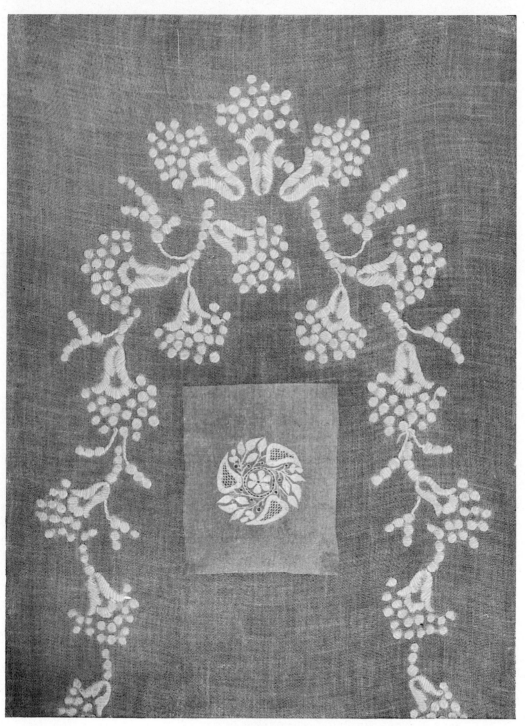

PLATE 69

SATIN STITCH ON VOILE AND A MEDALLION IN "SHADOW" WORK

Muslin lends itself to the execution of delicate embroidery. Fine solid work, combined with open-work (made by drawn-fabric stitches) worked in small areas, gives a filmy, lace-like appearance, quite distinct from lace. On muslin of good quality this work is very durable despite its fragile appearance. A specimen of this kind is seen on the opposite plate. The solid work is in raised satin stitch, including eyelets, spots, and overcast stems; the edge is in buttonhole stitch worked in scallops. The "shadow" eyelets (as seen within the scallop and elsewhere) are arranged by darning in extra rows of padding on one side of the small circle before overcasting. For the final stitching, the needle enters the same hole each time. The drawn fabric or "punched" stitch is worked with very fine cotton in a blunt-tipped wool needle of much larger size than would ordinarily be needed. This helps to accentuate the holes. An explanation of the working of this stitch is given on the following page.

Muslin Embroidery

The wreath embroidered on organdie muslin, illustrated opposite, shows how bold an effect can be secured with satin stitch on these delicate textures. The shapes are uniformly raised, and the satin stitch becomes overcast stitch (see Plate 4) at the stems and fine tips of the flowers. The fine drawing expressed here calls forth all the embroiderer's technical skill. Such work is exquisite for baby paraphernalia and the small, detachable pieces of adult dress; it is always a joy to behold. Designs of this kind are plagiarized by the makers of machine embroideries, who avail themselves of the form but never of the spirit. The inimitableness of hand-work is its great safeguard; the machine that will impart that particular but incalculable feeling has yet to be made.

Ornament of a different and more casual nature, executed in satin stitch, can be used with good effect on voiles for dress decoration. The specimen shown on Plate 69 is part of a large spray, worked with soft white mercerized stranded cotton on flesh-pink voile. It will be seen at a glance how much less exacting this work is technically, compared with the wreath opposite, which is too "precious" in style for other than small quantities. The whole hank of strands is used in the needle, and the forms are filled frankly and rapidly with satin stitch with no under padding. The direction of the stitch gives character to the pattern, and there are no fine points or stems to hamper speedy work. The voile should be stretched in a frame and backed with a special muslin which gives firmness to the work and can be made to disappear from the background by the simple process of pressing with a warm iron.

Another type of muslin embroidery and one that comes between the two former in technical difficulty is seen in the small medallion of Indian work on the same plate. The solid parts of this are worked on the reverse side with double-back stitch. The stems are back stitch worked on the front, and the eyelets are made as described under "eye stitch" on page 146.

PLATE 70
INDIAN MUSLIN EMBROIDERY
The working of the open filling stitch is shown on Plate 71.

The drawn-fabric or "punched" stitch illustrated on the opposite plate is frequently to be seen in Indian work and the English embroideries of the seventeenth and eighteenth centuries. Though similar to the **A Drawn-fabric Stitch for Transparent Materials** diagonal square stitch given on Plate 29 (in that the material is pulled in a series of square shapes) it is worked differently, and, in consequence, is subtly different in result. It is the more suitable of the two for use on muslin and other transparent fabrics, because the working thread is as invisible on the reverse side as it is on the front, so that the transparency of the fabric remains unimpaired by the stitch. The effect of definite open-work in which it results may be seen in the example given on Plate 70. The spots on the illustration indicate the squares of the ground threads upon which the stitch is worked; they also serve to indicate the direction of the warp and weft of the material.

Take a piece of voile or muslin and imagine that the area to be worked is divided into small squares as by the spots in the illustration. Thread a wool needle (size 21) with fine cotton or lace thread and begin a descending line at point *A* marked by an arrow, working thus: Put the needle in at *A* and out at *B*. Repeat this action. Put the needle in at *C* and out at *B*. Put the needle in at *C* and out at *D*. Repeat this action, and continue, putting the needle in at *E* and out at *D*, etc. The thread is drawn tightly after each stitch, which, together with the extra large needle used, results in the spots becoming open holes. This effect is seen in the diagrams showing the positions of the needles. It will be seen that the needle at the top of the page has been put in at *E* and out at *F*, if the lettered key beneath is followed. This action must be repeated; the needle is then put in at *G* and out at *F*. To avoid a confusion of lines in the diagram, this second position of the needle has been shown lower down the diagonal line. This descending line pulls up two sides of each square, and an ascending line must be worked to complete them. For this, follow the diagram at the foot of the page, beginning at *A* marked by the arrow. Put the needle in at *A* and out at *B*. Repeat this action. Put the needle in at *C* and out at *B*. Put the needle in at *C* and out at *D*. Repeat this action, and continue thus as far as required. The lower needle in the diagram has been put in at *E* and out at *F*. This action must be repeated. The needle is then put in at *G* and out at *F*. This action is shown by the needle at the top of the line. The thread is fastened in when beginning, and finally, when finishing, through the back of whatever stitch surrounds the open-work. Sometimes it is necessary to thread the cotton in an ordinary small needle for this purpose.

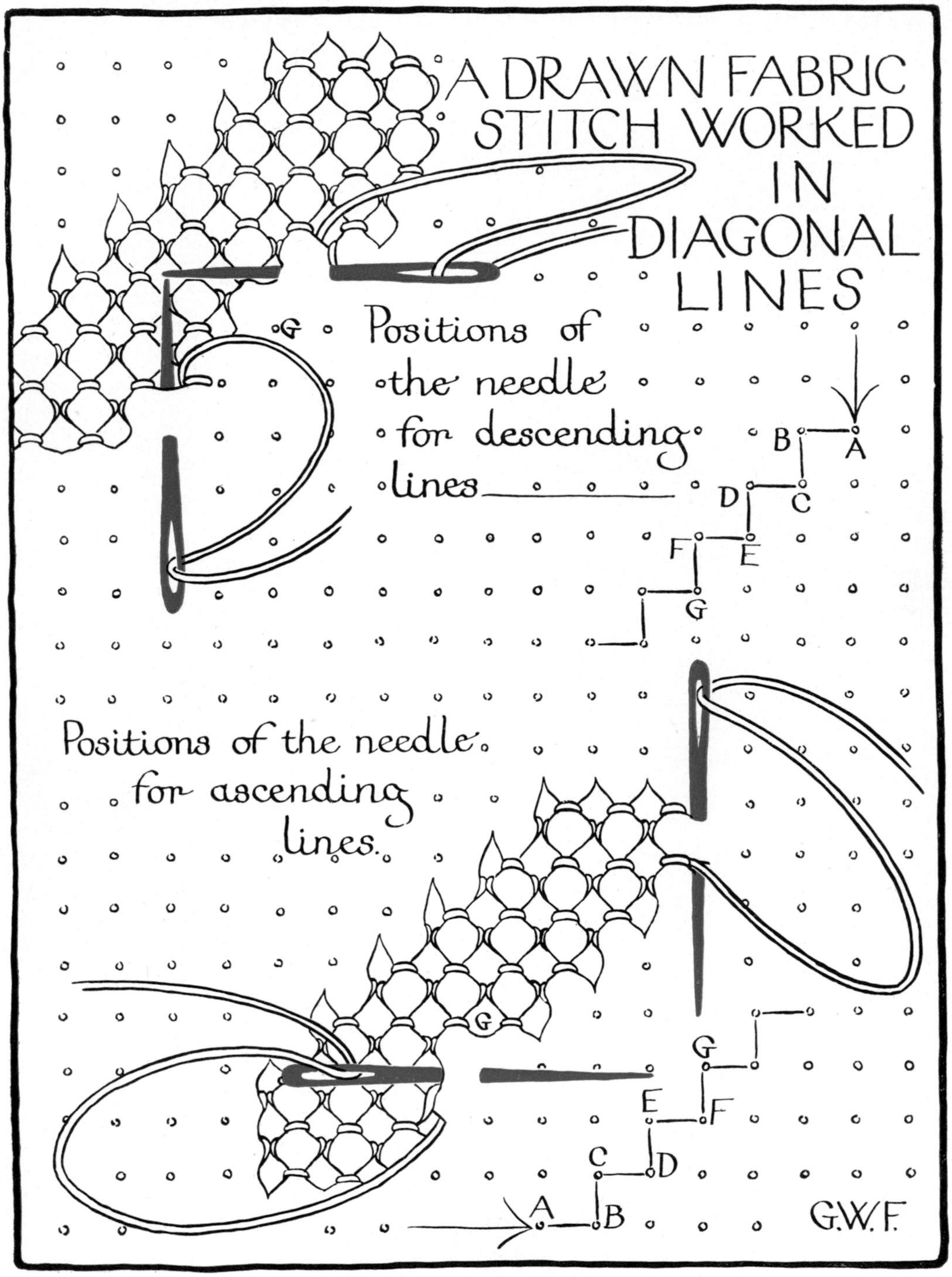

A DRAWN FABRIC
STITCH WORKED
IN
DIAGONAL
LINES

Positions of
the needle
for descending
lines

G

B   A
D   C
F   E
    G

Positions of the needle
for ascending
lines.

G

G
E   F
C   D
A   B

G.W.F.

PLATE 71

Another treatment for transparent fabrics, and one that lends itself to designs of a bolder kind than those previously mentioned, will depend upon the use of

Appliqué Organdie appliqué, or double material, for its broad effect. This is not applied in the usual manner of appliqué work (i.e. on the front, or right side of the material), but as follows. The design is drawn on paper in clear outline, in waterproof ink. The material is laid over this drawing and secured to it and the board by drawing pins. The outline of the design is traced very delicately on to the material with water-colour and a fine brush. The material is taken from the drawing, and laid face downwards on to an ironing sheet, and those parts that are finally to appear in double thickness are evenly smeared with thin starch applied with the tip of the finger. A second piece of material (sufficiently large to cover all the double parts, and lying the same way as the first as to grain) is then laid on the top of the starched piece and pressed down with a warm iron. By this means the applied parts are made to adhere more smoothly and evenly than is possible by means of even careful tacking, and these points are helpful both in the working and to the finished effect.

The embroidery surrounding the double material is completed first, and the unwanted material cut away at the back. The remaining parts of the design are worked on the single thickness. The exotic bird seen on the opposite Plate has been worked on organdie by the method described above. Most of the stitching is Overcast Chain. Buttonhole (or Blanket stitch) will be seen on the short underwing feathers and satin stitch on the top line (bone line) of each wing. Knot stitch outlines the applied tail feathers, and the little fluffy feathers at the back of the bird. A line of spaced back stitches has been worked beside the Overcast Chain in places, to give strength in wear to the applied parts; at the same time adding a richness to the general effect. The eye is a tiny eyelet made by putting the needle into the same hole in the centre and overcasting until the circle is complete.

It must be borne in mind when working on such transparent fabrics as organdie, nylon, Terylene and the like, that threads carried from place to place at the back will be clearly visible from the front. With forethought this can, and indeed must, be avoided. A single thread of filoselle silk, in a No. 6 between needle was used for the embroidery throughout.

PLATE 72
EXOTIC BIRD EMBROIDERED ON ORGANDIE

The lunette for a morning tea-cosy on the opposite plate is another example of the appliqué method described on the preceding page. White bryony, with **Lunette for Cosy** its spreading, decorative stems and tendrils, leaves, and starry flowers, forms the basis of the design, chanticleer symbolizes the awakening day, and the injunction to "fill the cup" conveys its appropriate meaning. The stitches used are satin, knot, chain, overcast back, French knots, and buttonhole. Of these the satin stitch predominates, and its decorative quality when used in narrow bands (in this case stems, veins, and tendrils) throughout a design is exemplified here. The flower petals, lettering, and the outline of the bird, are also of satin stitch. Seeding, worked as explained by the diagram on Plate 74, is used on the breast of the bird. The foremost tail feathers are partially filled with chain stitch. Two rows of knot stitch (dovetailed) outline the leaves; the same stitch is used to secure the circular band, three rows on the outer side and one on the inner. French knots are clustered at the centre of the flowers, and buttonhole stitch is used for the scalloped edge.

It will be seen, from the examples given, that satin stitch can play an important part in white work and muslin embroidery. The medallion on Plate 69 **The Padding of Satin Stitch** is the only piece in which it does not figure. More practice is needed to gain proficiency in the stitch than in any other branch of this work. More than half its difficulties are overcome, however, when the art of padding is understood. If the padding is well arranged, the result in nine cases out of ten will be successful, but if the padding is of indifferent technique it will be impossible to get a correct result by means of the finishing stitches. In all cases of raised work the padding should be carefully modelled to the required form, and when made of laid threads or stitches these should lie in the opposite direction from that to be taken by the finishing stitch. For curved lines the thread is run or darned in (lengthwise) in a succession of rows until the space is filled, but the traced line remains visible on each side of them. The length of the padding stitch is determined by the curves themselves, and the least possible amount of the ground fabric is picked up by the needle in order that the thread may lie as continuously as possible on the surface of it. Further threads may be darned in on top of the first layer, down the centre, and then on either side, in order to raise the satin stitch higher. It must be borne in mind that any discrepancy in the management of the padding will become apparent when the satin stitches are worked across it; these should be set closely, and the thread pulled at each stitch until it lies firmly on the laid threads and reveals the form.

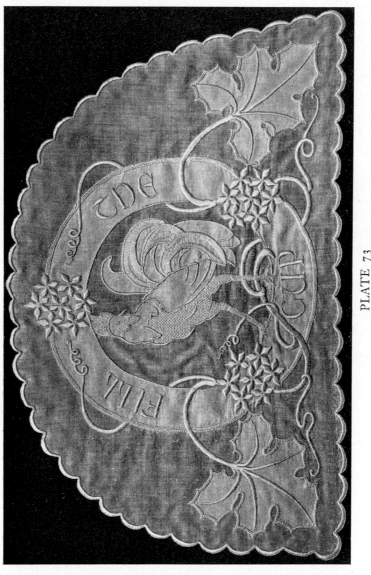

PLATE 73

APPLIQUÉ MUSLIN

Lunette for a tea cosy.

A method of padding by which the threads are made to lie from end to end of the form, wholly upon the surface, is illustrated opposite. Straight forms, of which the uprights in the lettering and the petals of the flowers on the preceding plate are instances, can be accurately and conveniently padded in this way.

The diagram at the top of the opposite plate shows a petal padded with separate threads. The bryony flowers on Plate 73 were worked as described **Padding with** and as follows. Thread a length of embroidery cotton in the **Separate** needle and knot the end. Put the needle in at A, a point to the **Threads** left of the base of the petal, bring it out at B; put it in at C and out at D, a point beyond the tip of the petal. Cut the thread off, leaving enough of it hanging loose to hold between the first finger and thumb. Knot the end of the thread again and lay it in beside the first, and continue thus until the whole petal is filled. The second diagram shows the working of satin stitch over the padding. It will be found convenient to adjust the padding threads as the stitch proceeds; this is easily done by catching up the loose ends together and tightening them as required. When the satin stitch is completed, both knotted and loose ends of the padding threads are cut off against the edge of the petal at the back.

Seeding is back stitch used as a filling; the diagram with the needle on the opposite plate shows how it is worked in straight lines with single stitches. It **Seeding and** will be noticed that the stitches are spaced out and placed alter- **Matting** nately, that is to say, one stitch between two of the row above. Sometimes a single stitch will be found sufficient for each seed, but two stitches worked precisely on the same spot is more usual, while three or more may be needed to produce a similar result when a very fine thread is used. The effect of seeding arranged in straight lines is seen on the breast of the bird on Plate 73. Another effect is obtained by making the lines of stitching follow the outline of the form, as shown in the shell opposite and on Plate 64, where also seeding will be found on the tails and fins of the dolphins. Seeding is often effective used in small spaces, say for the daintiness of little leaves, wherein one half can be filled solidly with satin stitch, and the other outlined and filled with seeding.

The seedings already mentioned have two things in common. They are worked in ordered lines, whether curved or straight, and the stitches are placed **Scattered** alternately. For scattered seeding neither of these rules is **Seeding** observed, the stitches being scattered crazily over the surface with much the same effect as that of seeds scattered by hand upon the ground. This look of apparent carelessness is sometimes useful, but more often as a filling for coloured embroidery than for white work.

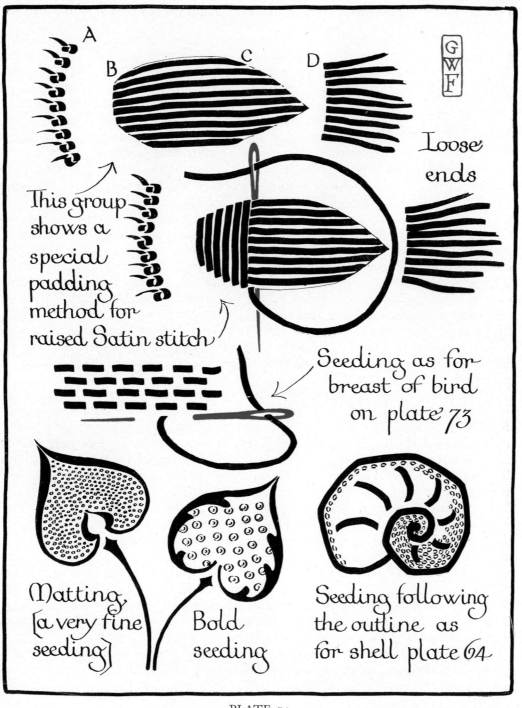

A

B

C

D

Loose ends

This group shows a special padding method for raised Satin stitch

Seeding as for breast of bird on plate 73

Matting (a very fine seeding)

Bold seeding

Seeding following the outline as for shell plate 64

PLATE 74

SPECIAL METHOD OF PADDING.   SEEDING AND MATTING

Punched work can be executed on coarse linen of a loosely woven variety. If it is attempted on too close a texture the punched parts will become puckered **Drawn-fabric** and will not show the flat groundwork, which should be a beauti- **or Punched** ful chequer of alternating squares and holes, this being its chief **Work on** characteristic. A special needle with a thick, straight shaft and **Linen** round eye is used for this purpose. It is threaded with Knox's flax thread of roughly the same thickness as the thread of the linen ground, but no thicker. An ordinary needle is used for fastening the thread on and off, the punching needle being too clumsy for this purpose. The surrounding embroidery stitch is finished before the filling is begun, the latter being worked quite simply by overcasting in straight lines.

The needle is brought out at the top left corner of a square of, say, six threads and put in at the top right corner, out again at the top left and pulled tightly; it is put in again at the top right corner, and out at the lower left corner (passing diagonally behind the square), then into the lower right corner. This process is repeated down the whole of the line. When this has been done over the whole area in one direction, the same process must be repeated in the other direction to complete the squares; this time the needle enters and is brought out in the holes already made. If a similar effect is required on a more firmly woven linen, it can be done by first withdrawing some threads; for instance, draw one and leave four threads each way and punch as above on the prepared mesh.

The *motifs* illustrated opposite are two details taken from an original design on a white linen cloth (kindly lent by Major Hardy-Syms) with English and Scotch emblems. The work is of interest as showing how embroidery with a coarse thread (D.M.C. white embroidery, cotton, size 8, sold in long skeins) may be effectively combined with punched fillings on a loosely woven ground. The embroidery stitches need to be carefully chosen, and those likely to draw the threads of the fabric out of place must be avoided. That treatment is reserved for the punched filling. The rose petals and rose leaves are outlined by simple buttonhole stitch raised by a padding of chain stitch. Interlaced buttonhole is used for the main stem; padded satin stitch for the leaf stems, their veins, and the bracts; the centre of the rose is filled with French knots. The thistle flowers are worked solidly with interlaced buttonhole, and simple buttonhole, padded with chain stitch, is used for the part surrounding the punched work. The leaves are outlined by two rows of chain stitch, overcast together, with a single line of chain stitch for the veins. The two stems, seen between the enfolding leaves, are in raised satin stitch.

A convenient way of designing for work of this kind is to enclose a bold pattern (worked in outline) within a panel shape; this outlined pattern can then have a punched background added.

PLATE 75

MOTIFS SHOWING PUNCHED WORK ON LINEN

CHAPTER VI
APPLIQUÉ

CHAPTER VI

By this method, known by the French term *appliqué*, decoration is made by applying fabric to fabric, the edges being sewn down and made sightly by **Applied Work** some form of stitchery. This method suggests broad surfaces and bold treatment in design, for it is useless to apply small patches of colour which can be easily made by stitches. In the corner design of fruit and leaves opposite, the method of working may be followed. The treatment is of the simplest kind, both in design and stitchery. The ground is brown linen, to which jade green linen is applied for the leaves, and orange for the fruit. The work proceeds thus: first trace the corners on the brown linen, the leaves on the green, and the fruit on the orange, making sure that the grain of the linen, both for the leaves and fruit, will lie in the same direction as that of the ground to which it is to be applied.

Be sure the selvedge of the linens is not lost sight of. Should this be cut off for hemming or shaping, etc., at once pin a label to the remaining material, **Grain of the Material** marking where the selvedge was. Then place the green and orange linens the same way round as the brown, when tracing on them the parts of the design needed. This precaution adds to the beauty of the finished effect, but there is also a practical reason for it. Linen when washed shrinks more in length than width (i.e. between selvedges), so that the whole effect of a bedspread or curtain might be marred by puckering when it is laundered, owing to this neglect.

Cutting Pieces to be Applied In the unfinished specimen on the sampler the traced design is seen with one leaf applied. This is cut with sharp-pointed scissors just outside the traced outline, but it will be noticed that a wider margin of linen is left to lie at the back of the fruit where these overlap it. Cut out all the pieces, noting where these underlying margins should be left, and put them face downwards on paper for starching.

Make some white rice starch in a basin or large cup. Allow it to cool. Then cover the pieces *thinly* and *evenly* with the starch, using the tip of the **Use of Starch** finger; a brush may leave it in ridges. Place the pieces accurately in position on the ground material, and press with a warm (not hot) iron through tissue paper. Lift up the tissue paper and the pieces will be found adhering smoothly to the ground. Starch is admirable for the purpose because it is perfectly clean and will neither spoil the fabric nor impede the laundering of things that are washable. The work can now be mounted in a frame. (See Plate 101.) The edges of the applied pieces must be tacked down with fine cotton (using in this case green and orange) by bringing the needle up in the background and putting it in to the applied piece. The reverse way would tend to fray the edge, whereas this secures it. If the work is to be done in the hand, as at times it must be, the tacking stitch action is the same as for the couching. (See Plate 55.)

PLATE 76

A SAMPLER OF THE TECHNIQUE OF APPLIQUÉ WORK

In the sampler a cord-like thread is couched down with a finer one (Star Sylko, sizes 3 and 8) as an outline. For this, as well as for the tacking, the needle is brought up in the background and put into the applied

Outlining piece. The stouter thread is laid on the edge of the leaf, and the stitches which sew it down are set fairly closely. Note how the leaves are worked vein by vein, which gives them character. (See unfinished single leaf.) The small piece of the outline touching the fruit is worked first, followed by the vein adjoining. The next movement is to pass the cord through to the back at the point it has now reached, and bring it up at the centre vein where the next branched vein starts. Continue this way until the top of the leaf is reached, working the other side similarly (beginning at base of leaf and ending at tip). Finally work the centre vein. It will be seen that by this means the places where the cord is passed to the back are always covered by another flowing over them. For the fruit to look solid and distinguished from the leaves it is outlined by a double thread. All varieties of cord, including gold threads, may be used for outlining, while a softer effect is secured by couching a hank of silk threads (Filoselle for example) which can be made to bell out between the stitches which hold it in place. Buttonholing is the safest way of outlining work done in the hand, and the most durable for things having to stand wear and tear. The fancy varieties (see Plate 10) can be used with good

Extra Stitchery effect. Satin stitch is useful for either hand- or frame-work.

Extra stitchery, apart from that used for outlining, is sometimes added in the form of veins, diapering, etc., but it will be found that the strongest and best designs for this method are those which can be independent of it.

Vital Point in Appliqué Design Any subject is possible as a *motif* for appliqué design, whether it be abstract ornament, fruit and floral subjects, landscape, buildings, interiors, figures, or animals, but it must be expressed in strong and simple terms. This is vital. Success here, as in other arts, comes from the artist adjusting himself to the material.

The panels opposite obey technical and other rules as above indicated. Various coloured silk materials are laid on a linen backing, and outlined with

Landscapes cord, which is supplemented, here and there, by a line of stitchery on its inner or outer side; this, while giving strength to the joining, is used to influence tone and colour. There is little extra stitchery (i.e. apart from the outline) in the top panel, merely the birds in flight and the lines of furrows in the ploughed field. In the lake scene there are flowers on the hill in the foreground, faint light lines on the lake surface, and one shadow (made by stitches) on the left of the snow-capped mountains in the distance. In both these examples the texture of the material plays an important part in the effect. The damask silk (green and golden green) used as a foreground suggests the effect of dappled sunlight on grass.

PLATE 77
APPLIQUÉ LANDSCAPES, COMPOSED OF VARIOUS MATERIALS,
SILKS, VELVETS, ETC.

For the making of banners, appliqué has more in its favour than any other needle method. A banner must convey its message at a glance to be of value

Appliqué Banners
for processional purposes. If it is to be carried out of doors, where it will sway in the wind and be seen from side angles more often than not, how essential it is for the design to be strong and simple!

Added enrichment there may be, provided it is kept subsidiary to the main theme, particularly so for banners of a more permanent nature which are displayed in buildings as decorations. The forms may be subtly effected by the use of a double or triple outline: cord in the centre, a couched line of floss silk on the inner side, of a harmonious or contrasting colour, and another on the outside, either merging the tone gently into the ground or lifting it sharply from it in places. Backgrounds, foregrounds, or the figures themselves can be diapered with patterns of silk stitchery; in fact, anything of this kind which enhances the desired effect is right, while anything which confuses it is wrong.

If materials not strong enough in themselves to stand appliqué work are used, it will be necessary to stretch smooth-surfaced linen or holland in a frame

Framing and Backing
as a backing. This is pasted evenly with starch, and the material, laid on to it, stroked until it is smooth, and then left to dry. If the materials to be applied also need backing, another frame must be prepared in the same way to receive them. When all are dry, the whole design must be traced on the first, and the applied parts on the second. The latter can be loosened from their frame, cut cleanly out, and tacked in place on the framed ground material.

Appliqué can be used for window hangings with a richly decorative result, especially on those windows where houses crowd together, facing blank walls

Window Hangings
or with some equally unpleasant prospect. Here is an opportunity for decorative hangings, dignified in design, and made gay by the use of coloured fabrics through which the light will shine. Across such windows a curtain is usually permanently drawn, so that there is no need of either fullness or draping. It can hang flat, as a wall hanging does, leaving the designer a clear field on which to implant his idea. Materials and colours in this case should be chosen for their ability to transmit light; linens are quite good for this. By judicious use of ambers and golds in the scheme an effect of sunlight can be obtained from windows that are never warmed by it. For such work stiffening is best avoided; pins and tacking can take its place. Put the hanging on a table and fix the applied pieces in position by fine steel pins placed upright in their edges. Then with fine needle and cotton tack across them each way as many times as necessary to prevent puckering.

PLATE 78
SILK APPLIQUÉ BY MRS. JOAN KAMILL

**Coloured
Papers**
Coloured papers are helpful for planning appliqué work. Shapes of these can be cut out, tried, and altered, giving an idea of the breadth of effect to be aimed at, in less time than is spent upon a coloured drawing.

A coloured border may be added to a cloth by means of an applied hem, both as a decoration and as a method of enlargement. For instance, a square cloth made from 36 in. linen will measure less than a yard square when finished, because some of the material must be taken up in finishing the edge, but if a 4½ in. hem be applied to this 36 in. square, the cloth will measure approximately 1¼ yd. This is an effective way of making bedspreads, for which materials must often be joined in some way, few being wide enough in themselves for the purpose. When using linens thus it is worth while being sure that the grain of the linen in the hems lies in the same direction as that of the cloth they surround. To ensure this the two strips for the selvedge sides should be cut along the selvedge way of the material, and the other two across its width.

**Applied
Hems**

On the opposite plate, No. 1 diagram shows a 36 in. square for the centre of a cloth, with a thread withdrawn all round, ¼ in. from the edge. Along the line thus marked the border will be attached by hemstitching. No. 2 shows 1¼ yd. of material, divided into four strips and four corner pieces, for an applied hem 2 in. wide when finished. Measure off 4½ in. and draw a thread, marking where the strip is to be cut. Each strip also has a thread drawn ¼ in. from each edge, marking the amount for turnings. A 4½ in. strip therefore makes a 2 in. finished hem. It will be seen by the diagram that there is linen left over when the necessary amount has been taken for the hem. This can be put to several uses, appliqué ornament for instance, for a tea-cosy, or for hems of tray-cloths and napkins to be used with the cloth. No. 3 shows the cloth with two strips turned in and tacked to the front of it, just level with the space made by the withdrawn thread. These will be turned back and tacked to the other side of the cloth at the same level. Tack the corner pieces in position and finally attach all by hemstitching, taking care that the needle passes through all five thicknesses of linen each time. No. 4 shows a finished corner. On two sides it is hemstitched to the borders; the third is a fold, and on the fourth the ¼ in. is turned in and slip-stitched. By this method the size of a cloth may be increased with linen the same width as itself.

Other specialized methods of appliqué are treated in Chapter VIII on Lingerie.

AN APPLIED HEM

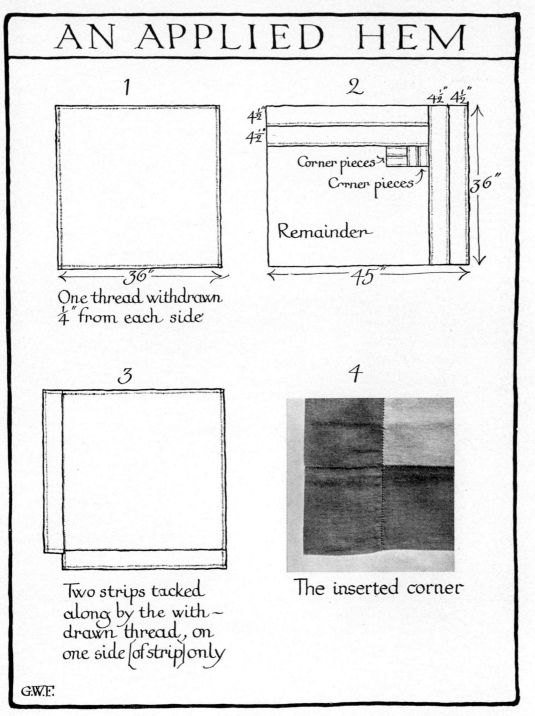

1

36"

One thread withdrawn
¼" from each side

2

4½"
4½"

4½" 4½"

Corner pieces

Corner pieces

Remainder

36"

45"

3

Two strips tacked
along by the with~
drawn thread, on
one side [of strip] only

4

The inserted corner

G.W.F.

PLATE 79

CHAPTER VII
LETTERING

CHAPTER VII

LEGIBILITY, beauty, and character are the essential qualities of lettering, and when arranging it for embroidery we must first suit its type to the subject in hand, and choose a method of working which will best allow these qualities to survive. It is well, therefore, to have a choice of good alphabets from which to select, and no book can be better than Johnston's *Writing and Illuminating and Lettering*. The Roman alphabet, from which all our letters are derived, has been the supreme example for some two thousand years, and craftsmen return again and again for inspiration to the inscription at the foot of the Trajan column, for its perfect proportion. If we, too, keep this example in mind, letter by letter, when adapting it to our various purposes, we shall avoid the mistakes possible without the restraining influence of this ideal.

Letters must be adapted to the materials in which they are to be executed. Take our present instance: if we try to reproduce letters in stitches direct from the Trajan column we find that certain details of formation, so right for chisel, pen or brush, present great difficulties for the needle, as in the case of fine serifs and the inner curve with which the descending upright stroke flows into the base of *B, D, E,* and *L.* It is true that by manipulation these dangers can be avoided, but some of the beauty is necessarily lost.

In large work, as for instance lettering on banners, which may be boldly executed in appliqué outlined with couched cord (see *B* on sampler, Plate 81), we have, by virtue of the size, more chance to emphasize character and preserve form, but for most purposes it is practical to use the round or Lombardic capitals, whose curves, junctures, and terminals present none of the above difficulties for the needle, and may be worked solidly in satin stitch over a padding of threads without loss of either beauty or character.

The alphabet on the opposite page is drawn with special regard to legibility. The letters, though round, are tall and made more slender than usual. This type occasionally (as in MSS.) became so short and thick that D, P, H, and N tended to be indistinguishable, a result to be avoided where legibility is desired.

As most needlework tends to thicken forms, it is well to start with a working drawing, which accentuates the essential character of the letters and should err, if at all, on the side of delicacy. For initials, monograms, and bands of lettering in designs, the letters opposite will be found useful to work from. They are adaptable: the tails (see A, H, and R) may or may not extend below the line; the serif may extend the whole width as in W, H, K, and M, or depth as in E and C, or remain a stroke at the terminal. The letters O and U are not shown separately. For O use Q minus the stroke, and for U the right half of W.

Specimens of worked letters are shown on the next plate. For the initial B the Roman form is chosen to show that it is not impossible to render that type

SUITABLE FORMS FOR EMBROIDERY

G.W.F.

PLATE 80

in needlework, but in a general way it is inadvisable, for the reasons given above. This letter, which is actually a little over 5 in. high, is applied in orange-coloured linen to a cream ground, according to instructions given in the section on appliqué. The edges of the coloured piece are outlined with a couched double thread of a lighter harmonizing colour, which gives the letter its cord-like edge. A line of black is couched close against the outline on the inner side. The thin parts of the letter were the chief difficulty in this instance; many stitches meeting at these places spoilt the appearance of the small amount of coloured linen left between the outlines, and this had to be covered by stitches of an identical colour both at the top and at the centre. Something more approaching a block letter would not have presented this difficulty. The word ANO is worked in double back stitch for the thick parts of the letters, and in stem stitch (which is back stitch reversed) for the thin parts. The transition from the double to the single stitch, or *vice versa*, is not difficult, particularly if it is borne in mind that in either case the needle is making back stitches on the reverse side. This reverse side should show the letters outlined in back stitch, as seen in the reversed N below. By this method letters can be worked on an open-meshed linen with a blunt-tipped needle. For the specimen shown, Mallard Floss and a size 24 wool needle were used, the needle picking up three threads of the ground material for each back stitch.

The beginning of an inscription "To James and ———" shows how the Lombardic forms may be condensed for such a purpose. These are outlined by three threads of Filoselle couched down by a single thread. Couching is best worked in a frame, while for similar lettering, if worked in the hand, overcast back stitch would serve and have much the same effect.

A happy way of treating initial letters, derived probably from illuminated MSS., is to enclose them in panels, and after outlining them to fill in the background with pattern. Couched, darned, and drawn-thread fillings are all suited to this purpose. The letter M shown opposite is outlined by overcast stitch, using a single thread of *coton à broder* over a loose padding of three threads of the same. (See Plate 4.) The panel is outlined in the same way. Alternate sets of four threads are then withdrawn in each direction, and the mesh overcast in diagonal lines as shown on Plate 63. The embroidery thread used exactly matches the half-bleach linen ground in this example, which is strong in effect, owing to the well raised edge and open background. The letters HA, linked and designed into a circle for marking purposes, are worked in satin stitch with two threads of Filoselle over a padding of the same thread. Ciphers and monograms for signing work or marking possessions can be made very attractive in needlework. A cipher is composed of linked or interlaced letters complete in themselves. These may be reversed or repeated if the decorative effect is

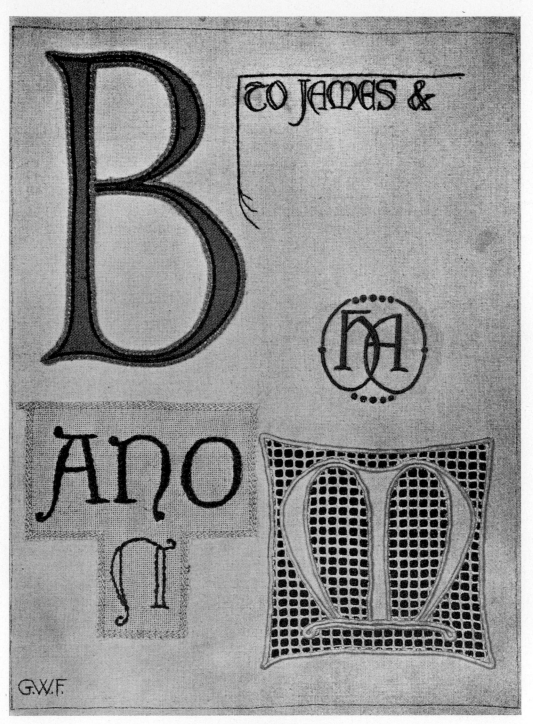

PLATE 81

A SAMPLER OF EMBROIDERED LETTERS

helped by so doing. For instance, the reader will at once notice that a cipher of AA or HH could be made from that of HA as shown here, by removing the unwanted letter, reversing the remaining one, and leaving the rest of the design unaltered. These are particularly legible instances. Sometimes the designs are obscure; a whole word or name can be arranged in this manner as a private mark to be deciphered only by those who are familiar with the device. Again, the rebus, which is an enigmatic representation of a name by pictures, may lend inspiration to designers of needlework. The Abbot Islip's rebus, carved in relief on his chapel in Westminster Abbey, shows an eye, a man falling from a tree, and a slip of foliage, thus depicting his name in two different ways.

For monograms, two or more letters are combined in one form. The G.H. in the centre of the nightdress-case shown on the opposite plate is an instance of this. The design is bordered by two lines from *The Ancient Mariner*:

> O sleep ! it is a gentle thing,
> Beloved from pole to pole !

Horned sea poppies, emblematic of sleep, surround the panel of drawn-thread filling. The condition of this piece, worked on Old Bleach linen, speaks well for the durability of this type of white work, for it has been in constant use for many years, and has had no particular care bestowed upon it. The use of Roumanian stitch for solid filling, where the space is too wide for satin stitch, is seen in the turned-over portions of the flower petals.

Knot stitch, satin stitch, seeding, and French knots complete the number of stitches used in this specimen, in which it will be noticed that the bands of lettering steady and give interest to a design that would be otherwise rather meaningless.

Interesting decoration to be framed and hung on the wall can be made with lettering as its sole ornament. (See Plate 83.) A much-loved quotation from prose or verse enriched by needlework is more intimately individual than one in script or print. The homeliness of the needle's art, and the greater amount of time that must be spent on its execution, make this inevitable. Lettering combined with patterned stitchery may make enchanting wall panels, as exemplified by those exhibited in London in 1934, under the name of "Wessex Stitchery," representing thirty years' work of a lady then in her ninetieth year. In practically all of the hundred and fifty designs shown at this exhibition some finely stitched half-uncial lettering was included, commemorating such things as the seasons, famous words of men and women, outstanding current events, and the worker's own ideas. No two panels were alike, and all were beautiful. That work of this kind, if the standard is sufficiently high, meets with ready appreciation, may be judged from the fact that every piece was sold long before the close of the exhibition, including one acquired for the Victoria and Albert Museum.

In needlework so much fascination lies in the fact that, work as we may, we can never attain to finality of interest.

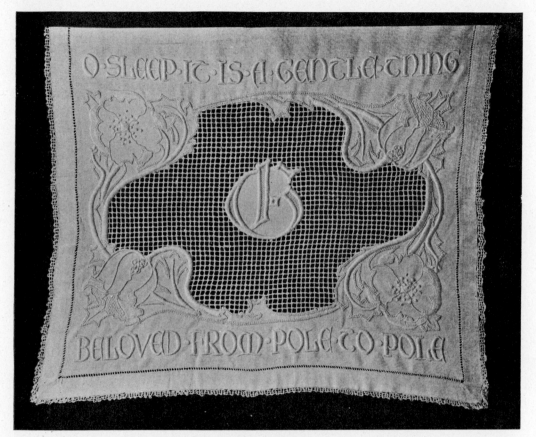

PLATE 82

A DESIGN SHOWING BORDERS OF LETTERING

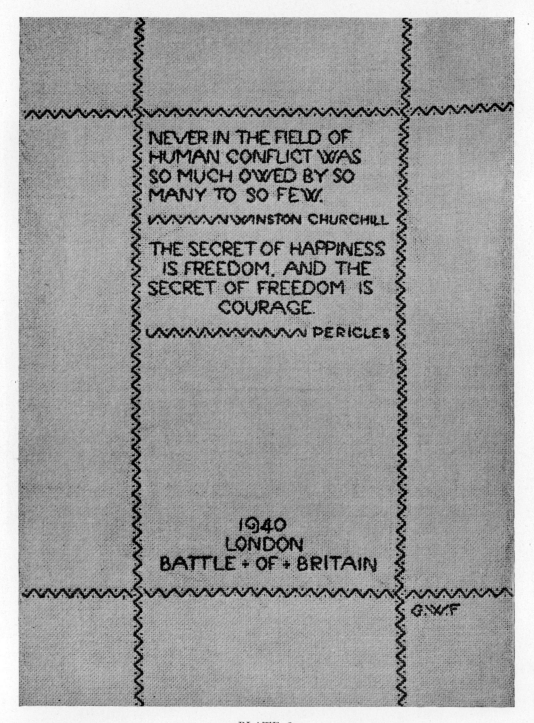

PLATE 83

SAMPLER (BACK-STITCH) WORKED DURING THE BATTLE
OF BRITAIN

CHAPTER VIII
LINGERIE

CHAPTER VIII

THE general cut or shaping of undergarments changes as often as the contour and fashion of outer garments makes a modification necessary. The modern and simple, though much more skilfully conceived, undergarments tend to become more and more elaborate in their finish and decorative treatment, and thus provide a never-ending field for ingenuity and skill in needlecraft. Some methods for the finishing of edges, treatments for seams, and suggested schemes of decoration, are given in the following pages. As in previous instances, the material used should control the treatment; cotton should be treated as cotton, silk as silk, and the special quality of each enhanced by the kind of decoration chosen. This is the whole secret of "good taste" in lingerie design, this oneness or unity of material and its treatment. To realize its absence we have only to recall such instances as spun silk machine-embroidered with artificial silk; or artificial silk stockinette (beautiful in itself) adorned with patches of cotton-encrusted lace.

After the demands of comfort and hygiene are satisfied, the ultimate impression we wish to create is one of elegant simplicity, the finer details delighting us as we become intimate with them. For to-day the designing of lingerie carries with it the blessing of being directly influenced by the contour of the human form, and the resultant beauty of preserving, rather than disguising this, may be seen by comparing the silhouette of the present-day woman with that of her Victorian ancestor, who submitted not only to bulky, but multitudinous, garments.

The treatment of the edge is the first thing to be settled in the making of an undergarment, the type of seam being influenced by this choice. Edges may be bound with strips of the material from which the garment is **Edges** made (Plate 91), hemmed down by embroidery stitches or hem-stitching (Plate 90), or have a separate hem attached by faggot stitch (Plate 94). Again, they may be edged with lace (Plate 86) or finished by buttonhole stitch in any of the variations already given. The use of net on edges is suggested on the following page, pin-stitched lace on Plate 90, appliqué borders on Plates 88 and 89, and finally rouleau on Plates 92, 93, and 94.

Seams may be plainly sewn (see opposite plate), pin-stitched (see Plate 87), piped (Plate 96), or joined ornamentally, either closed (Plate 124) or open (Plates 94 and 95). The method of joining explained opposite, **Seams** known as French seam, is useful for materials that easily fray. Flat seams are preferable for garments next the skin. When joining a bias edge to a straight edge, the former should be kept towards the worker so that it may be eased to the straight edge by the thumb of the left hand. In the case of a felled seam (i.e. hemmed) it is best to tack before hemming, because the turning down of the straight edge to the bias causes puckering.

FRENCH SEAM

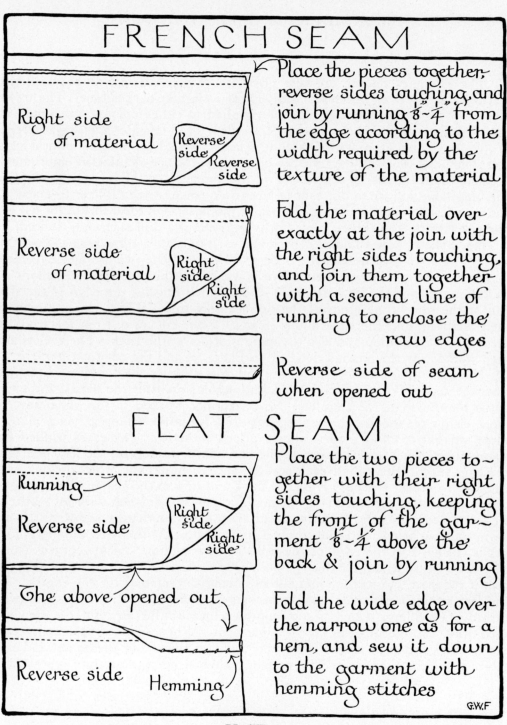

Right side of material

Reverse side

Reverse side

Reverse side of material

Right side

Right side

Place the pieces together, reverse sides touching, and join by running $\frac{1}{8}$–$\frac{1}{4}$ from the edge according to the width required by the texture of the material

Fold the material over exactly at the join with the right sides touching, and join them together with a second line of running to enclose the raw edges

Reverse side of seam when opened out

FLAT SEAM

Running

Reverse side

Right side

Right side

The above opened out

Reverse side

Hemming

Place the two pieces together with their right sides touching, keeping the front of the garment $\frac{1}{8}$–$\frac{1}{4}$ above the back & join by running

Fold the wide edge over the narrow one as for a hem, and sew it down to the garment with hemming stitches

G.W.F

PLATE 84

The examples on the opposite plate are of pale *café au lait* coloured net and *crêpe de Chine* embroidered with silk of a slightly darker tone. The treatment could be suitably applied to other colours and kinds of **Net Edgings** silk lingerie fabric. A single thread of filo floss in a size 6 between sewing needle is used throughout for the embroidery. It is sometimes thought that time can be saved by the use of a thicker embroidery thread. Actually this is not so, for if the thread is unnecessarily thick, the stitching takes longer to do, as it is, in consequence, more difficult to manage, and is at least clumsy in result. Pearsall's filo floss is an ideal thread for use on fine silk fabrics, and can be replaced by Filoselle if a dull surface is desired.

No. 1 shows how a fold of net may be used to soften a line seen against the skin. The net is laid behind the *crêpe de Chine*, and the two are lightly tacked together. A single line of chain stitch is worked within the slender scallops as padding, and covered by buttonhole stitch, which finishes the edge of the silk and at the same time attaches the net securely to it. The tacking thread is then removed, and the superfluous *crêpe de Chine* cut away from the front at the edge of the scallop and also the margin of net at the back. The eyelets are then worked, by the method detailed on Plate 59, and the edge is complete.

No. 2 shows a possible *motif* for use with this edging; the double net becomes a background to flowers worked with buttonhole stitch for the petals, and satin stitch for the stems and eyelets. No. 3 edging, worked in the same way, is more elaborate, though the tracing required is simple enough, being merely three straight rows of plain scallops, placed in series. These are padded by chain stitch, which may be seen in the unfinished portion on the left, one line of chain stitch right round each scallop, and an inner line which begins and ends with running stitches giving the thick and thin to the shape. The upright centre pieces, padded with long tacking stitches, are finished with satin stitch. In the top row the *crêpe de Chine* is cut away from alternate scallops, also from all in the row below, exposing the net underneath. At the back the margin of net is cut close to the edge of the third row of scallops. Sharp curved manicure scissors are useful for this. No. 4 shows a possible *motif* for inside decoration if required, the method and stitches being the same as for the edging. In the last arrangements the net has become a modern substitute for a drawn-thread open filling, which is too lengthy a process for any but the smallest quantities, considering the life of a garment. When inserted in small areas, net is quite strong in wear. It is important that the colour of the net and silk fabric should be alike, or in close harmony, thus avoiding a patched appearance.

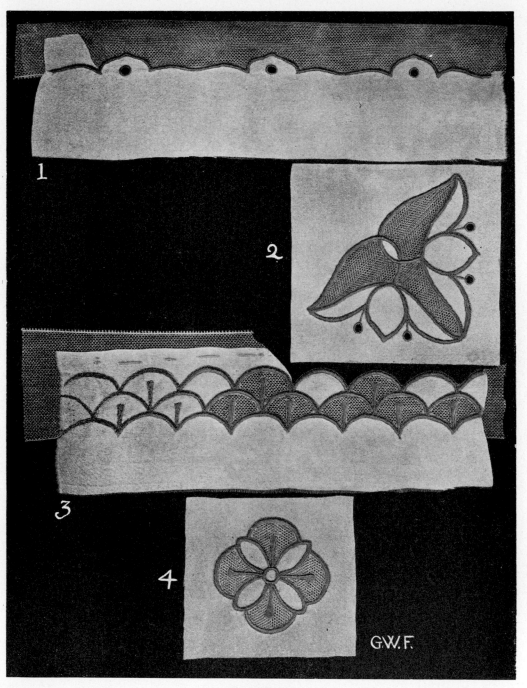

PLATE 85
NET EDGINGS AND *MOTIFS*

Needle-run lace is sometimes used as an edging to *crêpe* silk or washing satin. These materials are rich in themselves apart from such additions, so

Needle-run Lace

care must be taken that the elaborateness is not vulgarized by being overdone. One way of avoiding this is to merge the two materials by letting them flow into one another. In the example shown opposite, the lace, *crêpe de Chine*, and embroidery silk are parchment colour, and alike in tone. The ornament on the silk material is so arranged that the lace is exposed in spaces below and above. Thus the silk partakes of the lace character, and the feeling of unity between the two materials is preserved. In such cases the ornament on the silk should be of a simple character, and the fewer kinds of embroidery stitch used the better. In this instance one is enough. The method of working is similar to that for applied net. The lace is laid in position behind the *crêpe de Chine*; the two are tacked together at the top and round the outside of the ornament. The outlines and veins of the leaves are embroidered with a single thread of filo floss over the whole hank of six threads used as padding. This padding is left loose on the surface of the material, passing through it only in order to begin or finish. (See Overcast Stitch, Plate 4.) Two needles are used, size 6 between sewing needle for the overcast stitch, and size 4 crewel needle for passing the padding threads through. The superfluous *crêpe* is cut away from the lace on the front close against the overcast stitch, and, at the back, the lace from the *crêpe* where it is not needed.

Two kinds of ornament, which have similarities in their working, are seen on the same plate. Here they are worked on silk, but are equally applicable to

Double Back-stitch Motifs

either muslin or linen cambric. The rose spray is worked in double back stitch (see Plate 5) on the reverse side of the material. The stems are worked on the front in back stitch. (See Plate 4.) Again one thread of filo floss is used throughout. On very transparent materials, a delicately veiled effect of colour may be obtained in this way by using brightly coloured silks for stitching at the back. This makes a dainty style of decoration for either underclothes or children's frocks.

For the other ornament, threads are withdrawn to form the squares, which are well suited to the decoration of garments finished with hemstitched hems or by a bind of self-material. The stitch is worked on the back of the squares (see diagram, Plate 87), making on the front an opaque square surrounded by open stitches. In the *motif* illustrated, further threads were finally withdrawn in the centre each way, forming a square mesh finished by overcasting. (See Drawn-thread Fillings, Plate 63.) Some other arrangements of squares for this method are suggested by the diagrams. The effect of the diamond-shaped *motif* can be elongated by means of hemstitched lines dropped from the sides of the squares.

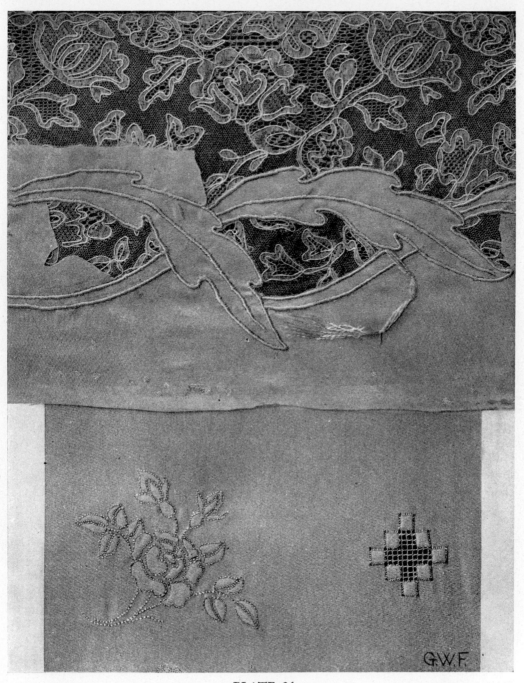

PLATE 86
NEEDLE-RUN LACE AS AN EDGING. "SHADOW" WORK *MOTIFS*
BENEATH

The working may be followed from the diagram on the opposite plate. It proceeds from right to left, as a series of back stitches arranged in minute triangles. Those familiar with the faggot stitch on Plate 22 will

Pin Stitch know the movements required for the stitch, as they are identical. On Plate 22 the stitch is treated as a drawn-thread stitch, and here as a drawn-fabric stitch, where the open effect is secured by using a larger needle than usual, together with a fine working thread. The passage of the thread may be followed in the diagram; it is shown as it would appear when not pulled tightly, and so gives no idea of the effect of the stitch, for which reference must be made to the worked examples on Plates 90 and 88. It will be found that the tightening of the thread enlarges the holes for a zigzag stitch to appear, and that the working thread itself ceases to be noticed.

To begin working, bring the needle out at *A*, put it in at *B* and out at *A*. Repeat the action. Put the needle in at *C* and out at *A*. Put the needle in at *C* and out at *D*. Repeat this action. Put the needle in at *A* and out at *D*. To continue, put the needle in at *A* and out at *E*, and repeat all the former movements in this order successively. As with hemstitching so with pin stitching, the decorative effect may be obtained with nothing more than outlines, but the latter has the advantage of independence of warp and weft, making curved lines possible. Its use for attaching and inserting lace is treated on Plate 90, and for appliqué on Plate 88. It is useful as a joining stitch, and is particularly well adapted to the seams of undergarments made of delicate fabric. The edges of the pieces to be joined are overlapped, and the stitch worked through the two thicknesses. The margins of fabric are afterwards cut away, close against the stitch on each side.

A worked *motif* composed of these squares is shown on Plate 86; stitching on the back gives the solid appearance. A diagram on the opposite plate indi-

Opaque Squares cates the squares for such a *motif*, marked out on the material by the withdrawing of threads in each direction. On fabrics which admit of threads being counted it is well to make the squares measure some multiple of three threads. Many fabrics are too fine for the counting of the threads, and on these the measurement must be made with a card, or better still, spring bow dividers. To work the opaque squares, begin in the lower left corner on the reverse side of the material. Pick up three threads at the bottom and three at the top, alternately, and having reached the point shown by the needle in the diagram of a single enlarged square, pull it through, pick up the remaining three threads at the top, and then put the needle in at the point indicated by the small arrow. It is then in position for working a set of similar stitches between the remaining sides of the square, so completing it.

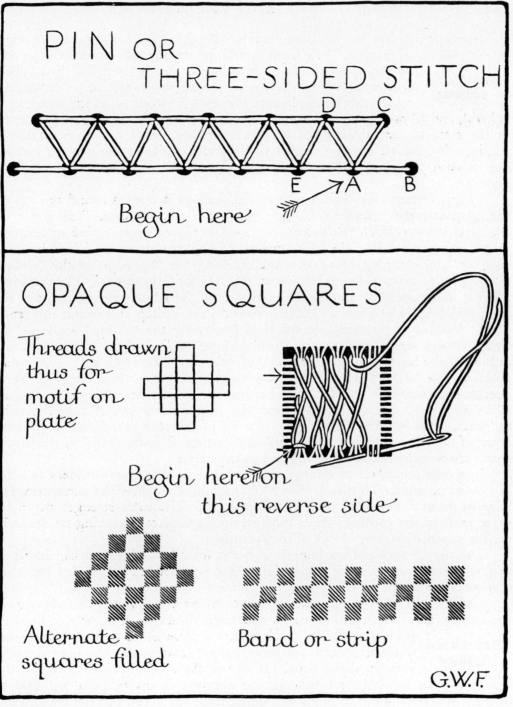

PIN OR THREE-SIDED STITCH

D C

E A B

Begin here

OPAQUE SQUARES

Threads drawn thus for motif on plate

Begin here on this reverse side

Alternate squares filled

Band or strip

G.W.F.

PLATE 87

Appliqué borders and ornament can be effectively used in a variety of ways in the making of lingerie. The front section of a white silk garment is shown

Appliqué for Lingerie

on the opposite plate. A coloured silk is used for the applied ornament; as an alternative arrangement, silk of a contrasting colour can be applied at the back (instead of at the front as it is here), and allowed to shine through. For this to be effective the transparency of the material, and density of the colour applied, must be nicely adjusted. Again, self-coloured schemes similar in style to the illustration may be carried out in satin by using the reverse or dull side of the material for the applied parts.

In this instance the border of inverted scallops is carried round the top of the garment, the ornament falling from it where required. The piece of coloured silk on which the design is traced is placed reverse side uppermost on to the reverse side of the white material. The two pieces are joined by running or back-stitching along the line marking the top edge of the border, about $\frac{1}{8}$ in. of material being left above this line for "turnings." The coloured piece is then turned over on to the right side of the white, pressed flat with an iron, and kept in position by tacking beneath the scallop and round the ornament. With a single thread of filo floss (matching the coloured appliqué) in size 4 crewel needle, pin stitch is worked along the line of the scallop and the outline of the leaves. (For the working of this stitch see Plate 87.) The satin-stitch outline to the berries is worked with a single thread in a size 6 between needle, over a padding of five threads. For the veins overcast back stitch (see Plate 4) is used. Before cutting away the unwanted pieces of coloured silk, the work must be ironed quite flat. If at all puckered it is difficult to cut one layer of silk from another and avoid the cutting of both. Finally, the small stems are worked by the same method as the berries.

It is ever important to arrange that the reverse side of embroidery is kept as neat as possible. This back view is photographed to show the almost reversible nature of the stitches used in this instance. The extra strength given to those parts of the garment where most strain takes place (in taking on and off, etc.) is another point in favour of the treatment.

The use of appliqué for lingerie is not confined to edges; it can be used in many ways for the inside decoration of garments edged by applied hems or cross-way binding.

Small squares or oblong patches turned in (by a withdrawn thread) can be applied by hemstitching. For voiles and linen cambrics, from which threads

Hemstitched Appliqué

are easily withdrawn, it makes a pleasant decoration. On these transparent and semi-transparent fabrics, the turnings should, between them, equal the size of the applied piece, to ensure its being an even tone. Its position on the garment is shown by a withdrawn thread. It is sewn down by hemstitch going from left to right in the usual way.

PLATE 88
PIN STITCH APPLIQUÉ, SHOWING FRONT AND REVERSE SIDE

14—(G.3084)

Hemmed appliqué is similar in appearance to the above, but is less open in effect. It need not follow the thread of the material, and so makes the

Hemmed Appliqué application of diamond shapes possible. The open effect is secured by pulling the threads tightly as for a drawn-fabric stitch. The stitching proceeds from left to right (as for hem-stitching), and simple back stitches are made by inserting the needle from left to right (the reverse of the usual way) parallel to the edge of the patch, with a stitch through the applied material taken from underneath and between each back stitch.

The field for embroidery on the type of Terylene seen opposite is somewhat restricted owing to the material's light weight and slippery texture. The figures

Terylene Treatments illustrated show that the appliqué method can be adapted with ease to these conditions. Place the applied piece at the back of the work and secure it in position by tacking across and down, as many times as are needed to ensure that it will not slip when working. The grain of the two pieces must lie in the same direction. The material is the palest of pinks, worked with a single thread of filoselle, using two tones.

The stitches used were overcast back stitch for the finer outlines, hands, faces, bouquet, frill; chain stitch for the hair, beard and flowers in the bouquet; overcast chain stitch for the remaining outlines.

The narrow nylon lace edging at the bottom of the illustration on the right is attached by pin stitching over the heading of the lace, with a single thread of Terylene "Gossamer thread" in a tapestry needle. The fact that so fine a thread should stand up readily to the pull required by pin stitching bears witness to its strength, as well as to that of the ground material.

The same stitch is used to sew on the wider edging, but here the line of the lace pattern has been followed, and the superfluous lace cut away from the front and Terylene from the back. Chain stitch, using a single thread of filoselle was first worked along the line to be followed, to form a foundation for the pinstitching. A piece of the lace in its original state can be seen on the left.

A convenient edging for armholes, etc., is shown on bottom left. This can be made by folding the material as for a hem about $\frac{1}{8}$ in. wide, and sewing with Terylene thread from right to left in the manner shown for Pinched Rouleau on Plate 93. The working of pin stitch is shown on Plate 87.

PLATE 89
TREATMENTS FOR TERYLENE

Sheer linen, cambric, and kindred materials provide the coolest garments for tropical climates, and stand frequent laundering. Further, they are popular for baby frocks, and lend themselves to delicate needlework treatment. (See Plate 90.) In the lower left side is a hemstitched hem, made without a turning. A single fold is tacked up and threads withdrawn from the double thickness, horizontally and vertically, to form castellations. Hemstitching is worked along each side of the hem and the superfluous material cut away at the back.

Lace sewn on flat by means of pin stitch (see Plate 88), to form an edging, is seen in the top right section. The linen is cut away flush with the edge of the stitching at the back of the lace. This is a neat and strong method **Sewing on and Inserting Lace** of either sewing on or inserting lace. Satin stitch, buttonhole stitch, and whipping are also used for this purpose; but where possible pin stitch will be found to be the more effective method. The lace insertion is attached by the same method, the linen being cut away afterwards from the back. A waved line and a straight line of pin stitching complete the edging. These are marked on the material with a pencil, and in this case, worked over a linen thread (Harris's flax embroidery thread, size E), making the lines equal in weight to the margins of the linen lace. No. 60 cotton in a size 24 wool needle is used for the pin stitching, and a fine sewing needle is needed for fastening the thread in and off, or, better still, these ends can be laid along the top surface and secured by the pin stitching as it proceeds. Both this and the castellated hem are suited for the straight tops of undergarments, or as borders to children's frocks. The strips of lace insertion alternating with lines of pin stitch (or hemstitching if preferred), and the *motif* formed by a fraction of lace inset obliquely and surrounded by a little white embroidery, suggest suitable treatments for the yokes of small frocks.

The top left section shows a hemstitched hem (again without a turning), from which graduated lines of hemstitching spring. The crosses in the open spaces are made by passing the cotton from corner to corner diagonally, and twisting round it to return to the starting-point. The cut ends of the fabric threads are secured by satin stitch spots, for which *coton floche* is used. Alternatively, these may be secured by a few buttonhole stitches with the hemstitching cotton (Plate 22). Well-placed lines of hemstitching and *motifs* of hemstitch form a safe method of decoration for silk, cambric, georgette, voile, or any fabric from which threads can be withdrawn. The fact that these must follow the lines of the warp and weft give them definite character. The severity of this effect can be softened by the use of delicate embroideries of different kinds, the squares on Plate 86 and bullion knot roses among them. The oval *motif* of needlepoint lace is inset by means of pin stitch. Notice how the waved lines and satin stitch spots surrounding it weld it into the fabric.

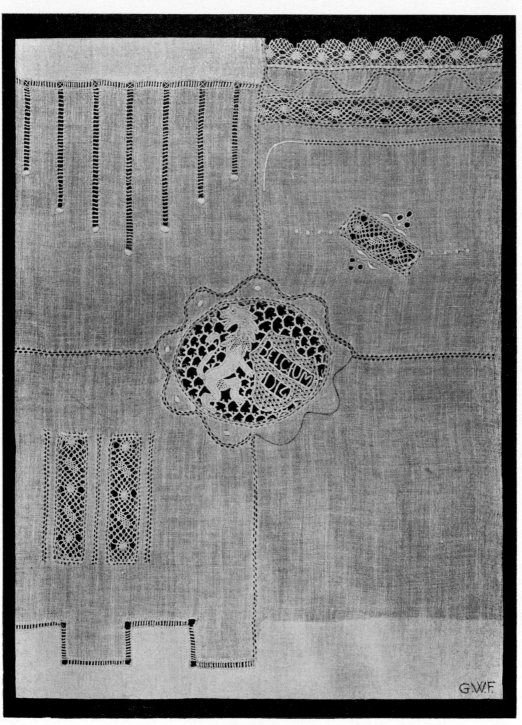

PLATE 90
A SAMPLER OF TREATMENTS FOR LINEN CAMBRIC

The making of a bound edge is illustrated in its several stages on the opposite plate. Instructions for the preparation of crossway strips will be found

Crossway Binding

below. When first running the strip (as seen in diagram No. 1) on a straight-edge (i.e. cut along either the warp or weft) it must be well eased to it; whilst on a crossway edge, also for that of a round or V-shaped neck, it must be stretched as it is being sewn on. These precautions are necessary to prevent the edge from being puckered by the bind. It is in the smooth completeness of a bound edge that its beauty lies. When the first stage is completed, turn the garment round with its reverse side towards you in readiness for the next stage of bringing the strip up and folding it first with its raw edge behind the turnings (diagram 2), and secondly, with its doubled edge over the turnings, to be sewn down to them just above the original running stitches (diagram 3). Either hemming or slip-stitch may be used for the final sewing down, or a swift combination of the two stitches, known as slip-hemming, the aim being to make stitches which are barely visible on the reverse side of the bind, and quite invisible (diagram 4) on the front. Therefore the needle must be kept from slipping right through the triple thickness.

The method shown in diagrams 5 and 6 is preferable for either flimsy or fraying materials, also if a rather heavier edge is required to weight the material down. The crossway strip is folded and pressed in half; it is then placed on the right side of the edge to be bound, with the three raw edges together, and run on as in diagram 5. The garment is then turned round with its reverse side towards you; the double strip is folded over the three turnings (diagram 6) and then sewn down, as in the previous example, just above the original line of running stitches.

Crossway strips folded and made into rouleaux may be curled, twisted, and interlaced without difficulty, and so made to follow the lines of braid-like pat-

Rouleau

terns, by tacking them down to brown paper. The spaces are then filled with faggot stitches, in such a way that the whole is securely held together when the tacking is removed. It is an admirable method for both finishing and decorating lingerie, blouses, dresses, etc. It is delicate in effect, but strong in wear and unimpaired by washing. In addition to these practical considerations, the work, when skilfully executed, gives results that are in excellent taste. There is no possibility of a divorce between decoration and the article decorated, for here the two are one. Supple silk fabrics are best suited to this work, and of these, perhaps, washing satin is the most easily managed.

To define crossway cutting, a few terms must be explained. "Warp" threads are those running the selvedge way of the material. "Weft" threads are those running in a right-angle direction. Material cut along either the warp

CROSSWAY BINDING

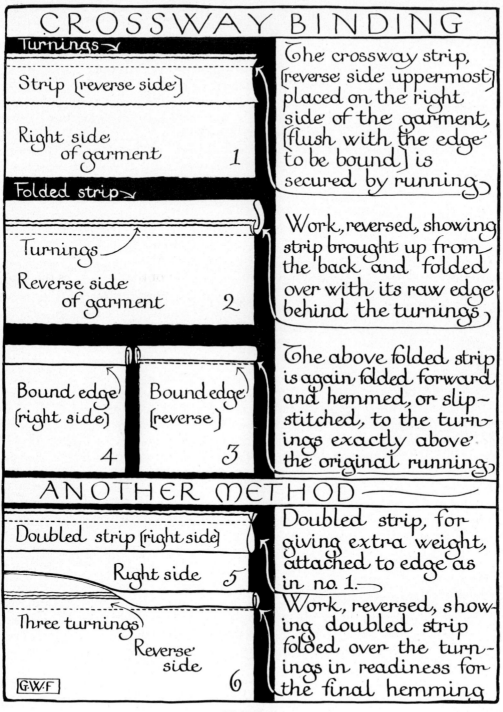

Turnings

Strip [reverse side]

Right side
of garment   1

Folded strip

Turnings

Reverse side
of garment   2

Bound edge   Bound edge
[right side]   [reverse]

        4   3

ANOTHER METHOD

Doubled strip [right side]

Right side   5

Three turnings

Reverse
side   6

G.W.F

The crossway strip,
[reverse side uppermost]
placed on the right
side of the garment,
[flush with the edge
to be bound] is
secured by running

Work, reversed, showing
strip brought up from
the back and folded
over with its raw edge
behind the turnings

The above folded strip
is again folded forward
and hemmed, or slip-
stitched, to the turn-
ings exactly above
the original running

Doubled strip, for
giving extra weight,
attached to edge as
in no. 1.

Work, reversed, show-
ing doubled strip
folded over the turn-
ings in readiness for
the final hemming

PLATE 91

Making Crossway Strips Into Rouleaux

or the weft is said to be cut "on the straight" or "by the thread." Material cut at an angle of 45 degrees to either the warp or the weft is said to be cut "on the direct cross." Material cut neither on the straight nor on the direct cross, but between the two, is said to be cut "on the bias."

Strips used for rouleau decorations are cut on the direct cross. To obtain the angle of 45 degrees, fold the material over until the warp or selvedge threads lie parallel with the weft. Crease the fold, and cut along it. Mark off the width of the strips by means of a card or ruler placed at right angles to this cut edge. Strips from 1 in. to 1$\frac{1}{4}$ in. in width will serve for several sizes of rouleaux. For the smallest, three-quarters of an inch is the minimum size possible. The short ends of the strips must be trimmed straight with the selvedge, so that in joining strip to strip to make a long length, all the seams lie in the same direction; the grain of the material lies the same way throughout.

The method of joining can be followed in the opposite plate. The joined strip is folded, the right side inward, and machine-stitched $\frac{1}{10}$ in. (for the smallest size) below the edge of the fold. With this one exception the process is carried out by hand. The folded strip must be stretched as much as possible while the machine stitching is in progress. This is an important point. Any superfluous raw edge is cut off, but if the material is one that is inclined to fray, a wider margin must be allowed. To reverse the stitched fold, insert a blunt-tipped darning needle in the open end of the fold, and secure it there, by sewing through its eye and over the end of the opening, with a fine needle and cotton. Now push the darning needle forward through the fold, as if using a bodkin, until the ends of the material fastened at its eye follow it into the tube. Continue to push it through, holding by the top of the fold (so that the raw edges are not frayed in the process) until the needle emerges at the other end and the whole of the fold is reversed. Then press the rouleau, stretching it while so doing, and making sure that it is not twisted; it will then be ready for use. Next tack it to brown paper, which has previously been marked for its placing, and iron it once more, this time at the back of the brown paper, so that it is flattened into place.

Edging and Joining Piece Lace

Rouleau and faggot stitch may be usefully and effectively used in making up piece-lace for dress purposes. A single row of straight or pinched rouleau attached by straight faggot stitch gives strength and finish to the edge, while retaining the lace character, and a single row attached on either side to the lace by faggoting becomes a method of joining.

When joining strips of material cut on the cross, first trim the ends of the strips straight with the selvedge, or warp threads as below

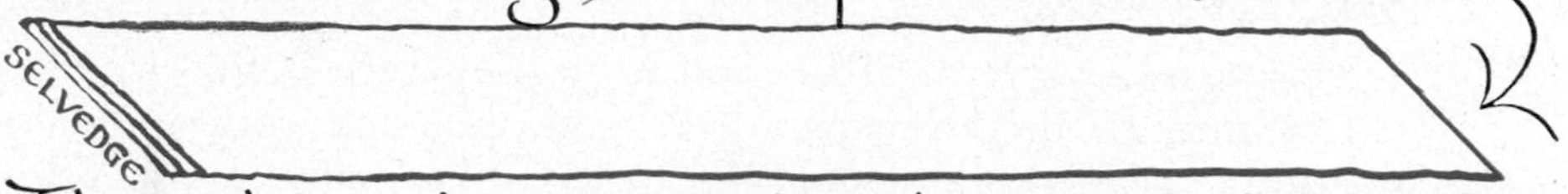

SELVEDGE

Then place the two ends to be joined face to face as below with the points projecting, & run or back stitch along the line marked by the dots, fold back the turnings The reverse side of

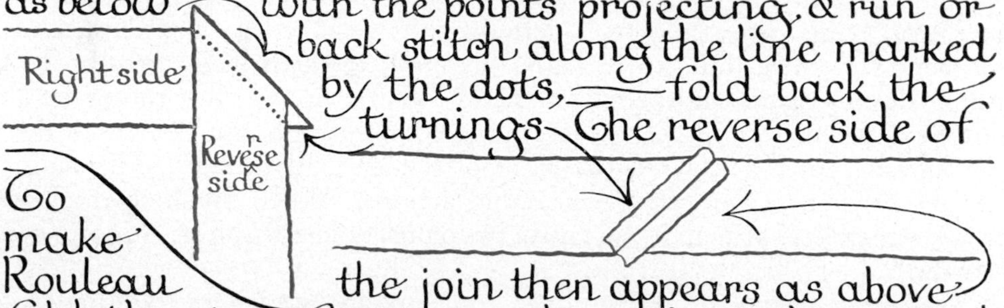

Right side

Revese side

To make Rouleau the join then appears as above fold the strip face inwards and machine stitch 1/16" below the edge of the fold, stretching the folded strip towards you while stitching.

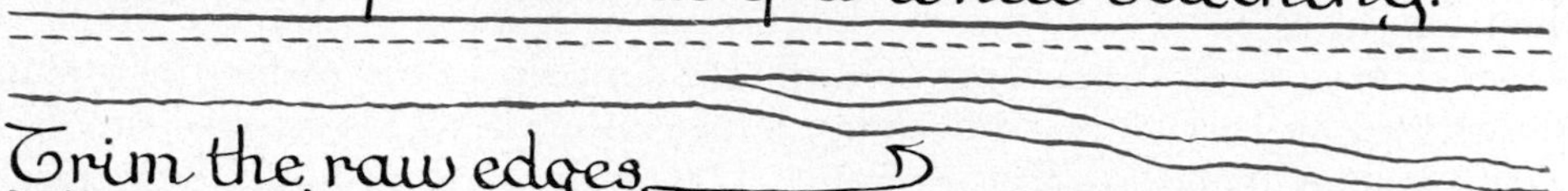

Trim the raw edges.
Fabrics which fray require a wider margin left.
Insert a blunt-tipped 
(enlarged) darning needle in the open end and push it in until its length finishes at the opening. Secure it in this position by sewing through the eye and over the opening with a fine needle threaded with sylko. Then push it through the fold as if using a bodkin until the rouleau emerges as below
Continue 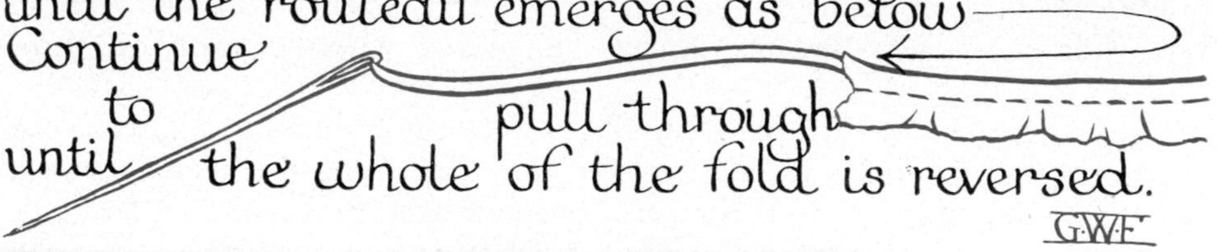
to
until pull through the whole of the fold is reversed.

G·W·F

PLATE 92
THE MAKING OF ROULEAU

By stitching rouleau as shown by the two diagrams on the opposite page, it becomes pinched together at regular intervals and so gives a bead-like appear-

Pinched Rouleau

ance, which is a pleasant variation of the straight kind and combines well with it. The rouleau is prepared in this way before tacking to brown paper. By itself, pinched rouleau makes a good shoulder-strap, being both strong and dainty. To make it, use a double thread of Dewhurst's Sylko, and bring it through to the front in the centre of the rouleau. Put the needle vertically behind the band (not through it) with the thread lying beneath it from left to right as if for a blanket stitch. (See first action.) Then pull it through, up, and towards you tightly. In thus pulling do not strain the thread on the eye of the needle, but rather take hold of it near the material. Next pass the needle through the centre of the fold horizontally, putting it in on the right of the knot just made, and bringing it out $\frac{1}{4}$ in. farther to the left. (See second action.) When finished, the working thread, which should match the fabric in colour, is lost sight of. (See specimens 1 and 2.)

Specimen 3. Straight and pinched rouleaux are used here together to form a simple edging. They are connected by straight faggot stitch. (See the following plate.) When rouleau is used straight, as in this instance (without twisting, curling, or interlacing), it is tacked down with its seam on the inner side; but when curled as in No. 7, it is tacked down with its seam on the outer edge. When satin is used, the reverse or dull side sometimes serves for the ornament, the contrasting surface texture giving added interest. This reverse side is used for the pinched band in the specimen. The straight edge should be kept above while the faggoting is in progress.

Specimen 4. Interlaced ornament is most happily expressed by means of rouleau. The *crêpe* border suggests the possibilities of the style.

Specimens 5 and 6. In No. 5 a twisted rouleau is enclosed by two straight ones. In No. 6 a twisted band is enclosed between waved edges. When tacked to brown paper the twist in No. 5 would be open, and appear similar to that in No. 6. In the latter, the spaces, inner and outer, are filled with twisted faggot stitch (for the working see Plate 94), whereas in the former only the outer spaces are faggoted, so that on being released from the brown paper, the inner spaces fall together as seen in the specimen.

Specimen 7. The rouleau (made of georgette) is connected by straight faggot stitch. For the curled line the rouleau is placed with its seam on the outer side.

The stitch shown in diagram No. 1, on the following plate, is known as faggoting or veining. Its application to rouleau may be seen in specimens 3, 4, and 5. It may be used for joining hems (see diagram 2, Plate 94), also for an open seaming stitch, adapting itself equally to the finest lingerie, the joining of heavy woollen fabrics, and the grades that come between, provided

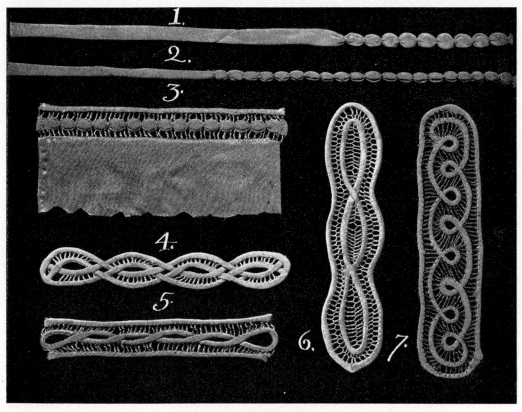

First action

Method of stitching for making — pinched rouleau

Second action

G.W.F.

PLATE 93

PINCHED ROULEAU AND SPECIMENS OF ROULEAU WORK

**Straight
Faggot Stitch**
that the thread used is of the right strength for the material. (A stronger form of open seam, similar in effect, will be found on Plate 95.)

To work straight faggot stitch, bring the needle out at *A* and pick up a piece of the opposite fold at *B*, a point immediately below *A*, and with the thread lying beneath the needle from left to right as seen in the diagram, pull through, up and away from you. This action takes place quickly. The thread is then in the position shown at *C*. To complete the stitch and at the same time to get into position for making another, pass the needle horizontally through the edge of the top fold, putting it in at the point indicated by a black dot at *C*. The needle emerging at *D* shows this second action; on pulling it through, the stitch is completed. When once the straight faggot stitch is mastered, the twisted variation at No. 5 presents no difficulty.

The stitch illustrated at No. 5 is worked vertically downwards, while straight faggot is worked horizontally from right to left. Apart from this difference in

**Twisted
Faggot
Stitch**
position, the action is the same for each. The great difference of effect comes about by making the stitch on each side in turn thus: bring out the needle on the left at *A*, take up a piece on the opposite side a little lower down at *B*, and with the thread lying beneath the needle from left to right pull through, up, and over to the left. Now take up the edge of the left side a little lower down, and with the thread lying beneath the needle, pull up and over to the right. The needle in the diagram is in position for this action. The application of this stitch is seen in specimen 6, Plate 93, where it is seen at its best. It is not suitable for general use as a joining stitch, or for heavier materials. Another way of making the twists in these stitches is to pass the needle round the laid thread as a separate action, but the method described above is the more expeditious, because it combines the two actions. When the double twist arrived at in this way is insufficient for the length of the stitch, additional twists are made by passing the needle round the thread once or twice more. This has been done for the longer stitches in specimen No. 7.

A simple and quickly worked stitch for joining bands of rouleau is shown by the diagram No. 3. Its use should be limited to narrow joins and light-

**Narrow
Joining
Stitch**
weight fabrics. For larger work it would look cheap and ineffective. Diagram 4 suggests the use of this stitch for joining bands which serve as a finish to the neck-line of a dress. For instance, plain alternating bands of the predominating colours in a patterned dress material used as "finishings" might well be joined by this stitch, which is more quickly worked than straight faggot stitch. The action shown by the needle takes place on each side in turn.

FAGGOTING STITCHES

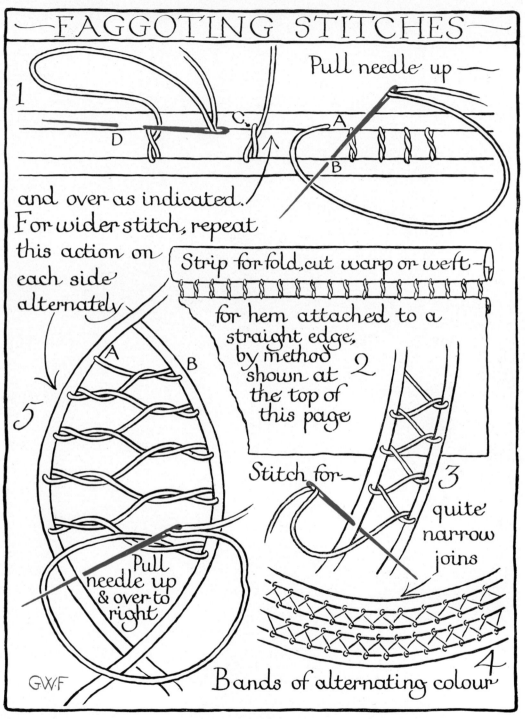

1 Pull needle up

and over as indicated. For wider stitch, repeat this action on each side alternately

Strip for fold, cut warp or weft—

for hem attached to a straight edge, by method shown at the top of this page **2**

Stitch for—

3 quite narrow joins

5

Pull needle up & over to right

G.W.F

Bands of alternating colour **4**

PLATE 94

CHAPTER IX
ODDS AND ENDS

THIS simple open seaming stitch is suitably used on seams for which the veining or faggot stitches given on Plate 94 are felt to be too weak. It has a

Seam of Overcast Bars rightness of effect on the heavy linens sometimes used for coats, skirts, and dresses, for example.

In each of the diagrams opposite, the black part indicates the open space across which two edges of material are to be joined. The material can, when necessary, be tacked to strips of stiff brown paper at the required distance to facilitate working. The making of the overcast bars can be followed by the stages shown in the diagram A. An arrow marks the point of commencement, and the lower needle shows how the thread is slipped through the edge in readiness for the making of another bar.

Buttonhole and Tailor's Buttonhole At B is a seam worked with buttonhole stitches, three on one edge and three on the other, in turn. Any fancy grouping of buttonhole stitches could be used in this way. At C, tailor's buttonhole is shown employed in a similar manner. The hemstitched sides of bags and handkerchief cases, etc., can be joined thus without tacking to brown paper.

Knotted Seam Stitch The working of this stitch may be followed from the diagram. Beginning at the point marked by an arrow, and following the movements shown by the needles, a knotted stitch is made on each side in turn.

To make the insertion stitch, bring the needle out on the right at the point marked by an arrow, put it in the edge opposite, and make five buttonhole

Italian Buttonhole Seam stitches from left to right on the thread thus laid. Take a buttonhole stitch in the right-hand edge lower down as seen in diagram 1, then take another into the left-hand edge a little lower, as seen in diagram 2. Now work three buttonhole stitches from the centre towards the right edge. The needle in diagram 3 is shown in position for making the first of these stitches. This done, the needle picks up the right-hand edge with a buttonhole stitch, and then works three stitches on the double bar from the centre to the left. The needle in diagram 4 is in position for making the first of these stitches. Diagram 5 shows them completed, and the needle making a buttonhole stitch on the left-hand edge. Continue from here as shown in diagram 3. Diagram 6 shows the effect of this insertion, which is particularly suitable for joining hemstitched panels of linen embroidery, and becoming an important part of the decorative scheme. Open and closed seams (Plate 124) can be usefully employed on furnishing fabrics. Cloths may be bordered and curtains lengthened by the insertion of coloured strips decoratively joined. Left-over lengths of various good materials may be pieced together in bold geometric form for the making of cushion-covers, etc. Such gay, mosaic-like arrangements make a relief from the severe effect of much modern furnishing.

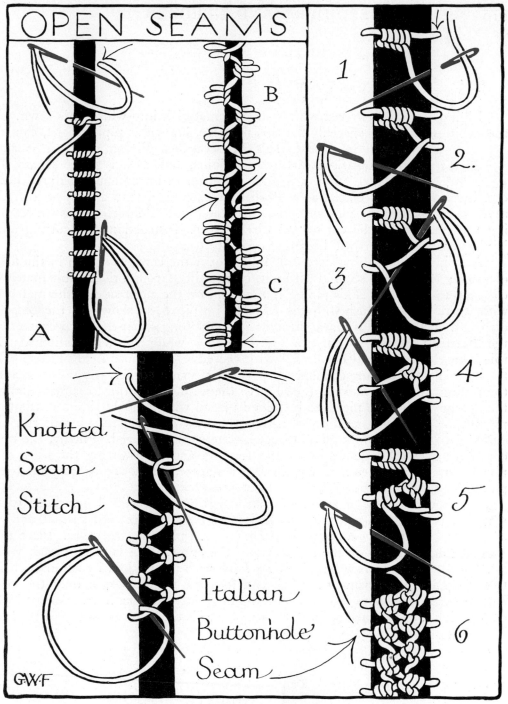

OPEN SEAMS

A

B

C

1

2.

3

4

5

6

Knotted
Seam
Stitch

Italian
Buttonhole
Seam

G.W.F

PLATE 95

Piping is a cord covered with a strip of material, into which it is sewn. A soft white cord made specially for this purpose, known as piping cord, can be bought in sizes to suit all occasions. Piping strengthens and **Piping** gives decision to edges and joins, and, as it is made separately and then applied, is a ready means of introducing coloured border lines. It is often better, as a finish to a bias edge, than a hem or a bind, as the cord holds in the edge and prevents stretching. The strips used for covering the cord should be cut on the direct cross. Instructions for cutting and joining crossway strips will be found on Plate 92.

A strip of the required length is folded over the cord, as shown in the first diagram; this cord is secured within it, by running through the double material close up to the cord. This piping is then laid on the right side of the material with its raw edges flush with the edge to be piped, as shown in the second diagram. If this edge is on the straight (i.e. cut along either the warp or weft of the material) the piping must be eased on to it while it is being stitched; if this is neglected, it will not lie flat with the edge, but cause it to pucker. To follow easily the outline of a curved shape, or turn a corner, the raw edges of the piping must be snicked. (See fourth diagram.) The third diagram shows the second of the two pieces to be joined placed with its right side towards the piping, and its raw edge flush with the other raw edges. This piece is run on close up to the cord through all three thicknesses of material. Finally, the raw edges are overcast together to prevent fraying, and on reversing the work the piped seam is complete. If a plain and a gathered side are to be joined by piping, the gathered side is the last to be attached.

To pipe the edge of an article that is neither to be lined nor faced with material, prepare the piping by folding the strip over the cord so that one of the raw edges projects considerably beyond the other. Place the **Piped Edge** piping on the right side of the edge which is to be piped, with its narrow margin lying flush with it, and join by running close to the cord; then reverse the work and fold the wider margin over the two narrow ones, and sew it down as if making an ordinary hem. For a piped edge which is to be lined or faced the procedure is the same as for a piped seam.

PIPED SEAMS

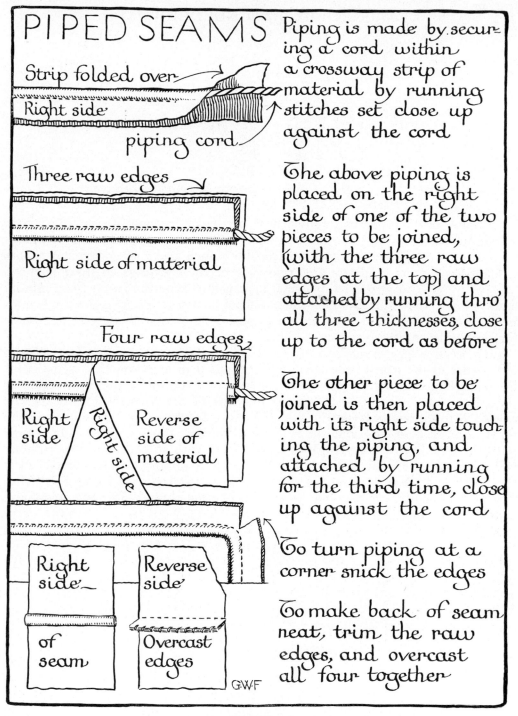

Strip folded over

Right side

piping cord

Three raw edges

Right side of material

Four raw edges

Right side

Right side

Reverse side of material

Right side

Reverse side

of seam

Overcast edges

G.W.F

Piping is made by securing a cord within a crossway strip of material by running stitches set close up against the cord

The above piping is placed on the right side of one of the two pieces to be joined, (with the three raw edges at the top) and attached by running thro' all three thicknesses, close up to the cord as before

The other piece to be joined is then placed with its right side touching the piping, and attached by running for the third time, close up against the cord

To turn piping at a corner snick the edges

To make back of seam neat, trim the raw edges, and overcast all four together

PLATE 96

"Sprat-head" is the name given to a particular method of stitching within a triangle, as shown on the opposite plate. It is a clever device used by tailors to give strength and finish to such parts of a garment as the

Sprat-head   tops of pleats and the ends of the openings to inset pockets.

It is also used by dress, blouse, and lingerie makers (on a minute scale by the last-named) when the mode of construction produces a similar need. The four-pointed *motif* shown opposite suggests the use of sprat-heads for purely decorative purposes.

To work a sprat-head, proceed as follows: Bring the needle out at *A* (the left corner of the base of the triangle), and put it in at *B* (on the right side of the triangle just below the apex). Bring the needle out at *C* (the right corner of the base), and put it in at *D* (on the left side of the triangle, just below the apex). Bring it out at *E* (on the base line close beside *A*), put it in at *F* (on the right side just below *B*), and out at *C*; and continue thus on either side in turn until the base line of the triangle is closely filled with stitches, and the fishbone effect has appeared down the centre, as seen at 4 opposite. The sprat-head is then complete. Nos. 1, 2, and 3 show the work in progressive stages. At No. 5 nine sprat-heads are worked in a pyramid, the threads forming a definite geometric "ground" pattern.

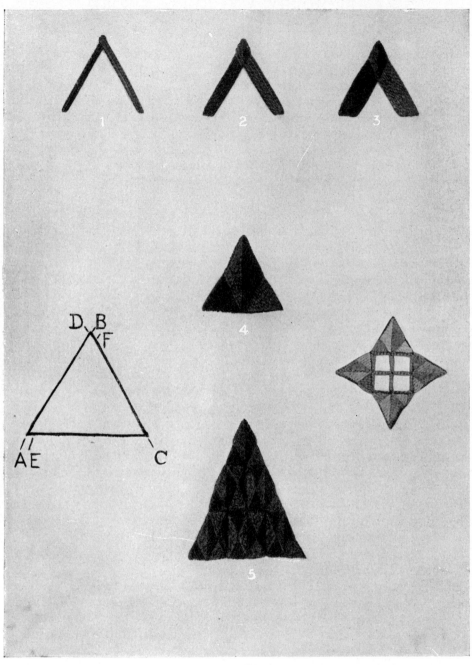

PLATE 97

"SPRAT-HEADS"

One corner of a linen cloth is shown on the opposite plate in the stages necessary for the making of a mitre, which, if carried out on an odd piece of

Hem with Mitred Corner

linen, will be clearly understood. When preparing to hem a linen cloth (or one of any material from which threads may be withdrawn), see that the required size is cut straight by the thread on all four sides. This is most easily done by withdrawing a thread and cutting in the space made by its withdrawal. Now withdraw one thread from each of the four sides at a distance of about $\frac{1}{4}$ in. from the edge. This small margin, known as "turnings," is later folded over to secure the raw edges.

Next mark with pencil on a piece of card or paper a measurement equal to twice the width required for the finished hem; with this, measuring from A (the point in the corner left by the withdrawn threads—see diagram 1), mark along each side points B and C by cutting a single thread at each point and running it out to the edge. Before the mitre can be made, point D, which is the fourth corner of the square $ABCD$, must be found. This is most conveniently done by again measuring off the distance marked on the card, but this time from the centre (approximately) of each side of the cloth, cutting one thread and pulling up the two ends so that they may be found again without difficulty. Ease these threads along until they meet each other at the corners. This is point D. Cut them where they intersect and pull out. This inner line marks the level to which the hem will be sewn. Fold over the corner until point A lies precisely on point D. (See diagram 2.) Crease the edge of the fold so that the diagonal line BC is accurately marked. Lift up the corner, and fold the crease in half, point C lying precisely on point B, as seen in diagram 3.

Beginning at C, backstitch through the doubled material to the edge in the line of the original crease. Now cut off the unwanted piece of material, and diagram 4 shows where the cut is made between the arrows. The portion A is thrown away. Open out the turnings of the backstitch seam, and turn the corner inside out with the fingers; the tip of the corner may be helped by the judicious use of the points of closed scissors. Turn in the $\frac{1}{4}$ in. margins by the withdrawn thread, and place points B and C (now stitched together) to point D.

Diagram 5 shows the hem tacked down in this position. The dotted lines indicate the position of the turnings within the fold of the hem. The hem is sewn down by hemstitch (see Plate 22), one more thread cut at D being withdrawn all round first. Diagram 6 shows the corner of the cloth as seen on its right side when finished by hemstitch, and the tacking threads removed. The two edges of the small open square at the angle are overcast as the hemstitching proceeds.

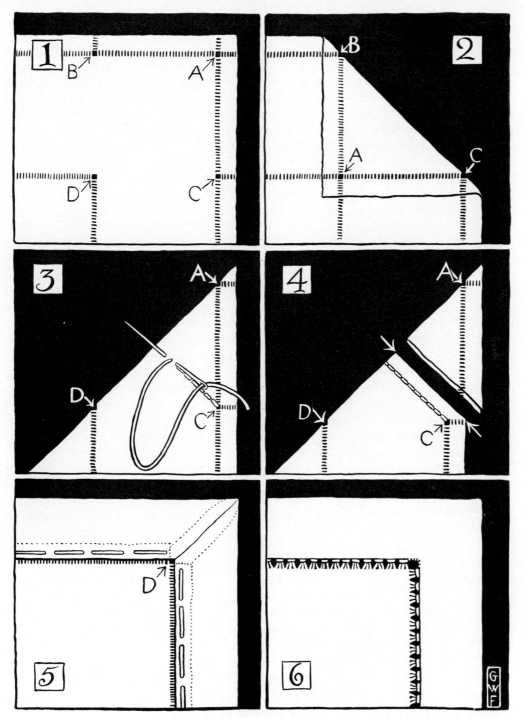

PLATE 98
HOW TO MITRE A CORNER

The country peasant's smock is descended from the Anglo-Saxon tunic which we see in the illuminated MSS. of that period. This is the short garment,

Origin of Smocking

straight and narrow, with an opening just large enough to allow the wearer to put it over his head. It was worn by all grades of society, the differences of rank and fortune being shown by the quality of the material and the richness of the embroidery. Gradually it was cut on more ample lines, for the wearer's comfort, and the ingenious method of embroidery on gathered folds which we call "smocking" was devised to reduce it to a more convenient fit. This smock supplied the needs of British country-men for over a thousand years, from Saxon times to the Industrial Revolution. It vanished then because, with machinery to be handled in farm and field, it became a danger to the wearer.

The few examples which survived are treasured in museums and collections as examples of a beautiful peasant art. It is to these specimens (preferably of the seventeenth and eighteenth centuries) that we go for guidance and inspiration when using smocking on the garments of to-day. Their excellent proportion, and restrained use of stitch and colour, show us how to get the best results. We find that no more than three kinds of stitch are used on one garment for the smocking itself, and that outline stitch is one of these—used to hold the first row of gathers in place, and often to divide into horizontal panels the groups of waved zigzag, V-shaped, or diamond borders made by repeating lines of the more fanciful stitches. The outline stitch gives steadiness and makes for pleasant proportion. It is always safe to smock with a thread of the same colour as that of the material, thus giving the effect of the smocking its full value. If colour is used, the best results are got from primitive colour, red and blue, red and black on white, or simply blue on white or *vice versa*.

The gathers are prepared for smocking by evenly spaced rows of running stitch worked with great regularity. Prepared transfers of dots may be used

Technique of Smocking

by those dubious of trusting to their eyes alone for accuracy. The gathering threads are pulled up on the left side and secured by winding them, two at a time, in a "figure of eight" on a pin placed through the material. The gathers must be quite evenly adjusted before the smocking is begun. When it is completed, the gathering threads are removed. The width of the flat material is reduced by about one-third by the smocking process. The working of embroidery stitches on the gathers can be clearly followed from the diagram opposite (by Mrs. J. D. Rolleston), which

Ornament Found on Old Smocks

is reproduced here by kind permission of the publishers of *The Embroideress*.

The "curiously wrought" ornament found on the collars, cuffs, and shoulder panels of old smocks is worthy of study. Heart, feather, fern, and rosette *motifs* are designed into arabesque-like pattern by lines of simple buttonhole and feather stitching.

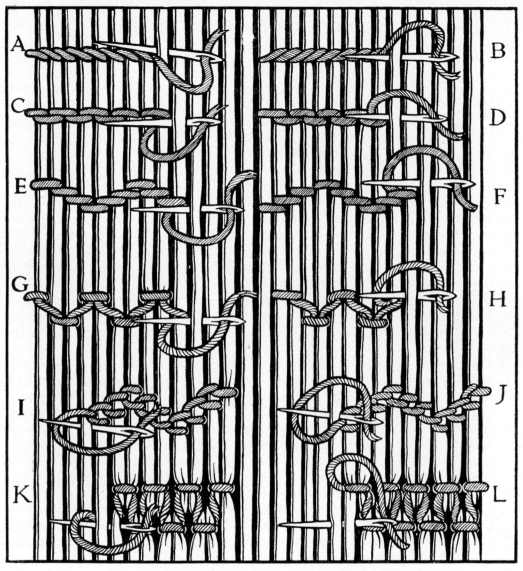

PLATE 99

SMOCKING

A and *B*. OUTLINE STITCH, worked left to right with the thread respectively *below* and *above* the needle.

C, D. CABLE STITCH, worked left to right, one stitch to each pleat. The needle should always be kept in the same straight line with the thread alternately above and below it, as shown in the diagram.

E, F. WAVE STITCH, worked left to right. Beginning at *E*, the top stitch and the two following *down* should be worked with the thread *above* the needle, as outline stitch at *B*. The bottom stitch and two following *up* should be worked with the thread *below* the needle, which is shown in position working the bottom stitch at *E*.

G, H. DIAMOND STITCH, worked left to right. Beginning at *G*, the top stitch is worked with the thread above the needle ; the thread then passes diagonally on to the next pleat, and the bottom stitch is worked about ⅛ in. lower down than the top stitch, with the thread *below* the needle as at *G*.

I, J. FEATHER STITCH, worked right to left in the same way as ordinary feather stitch.

K, L. VANDYKE STITCH, worked right to left. The needle takes up *two* pleats at a time, as shown at *L*. These are held together rather firmly by a back stitch over them, as the needle is shown doing at *K* ; it then passes up about ⅛ in. and repeats the same movements on the top row.

Every care must be taken to keep embroidery threads in perfect condition. Skeins of silk should be wound on to folded cards. This can be done on one's **Care of** own hands without assistance, as follows: Remove the paper **Embroidery** label; untie the knot at the centre of the skein, and unfold or **Threads** shake it out to its full extent. Hang one end on the left thumb with the knot (by which the two ends of thread are tied) resting uppermost at the thumb's base. Place the back of the outstretched right hand in the lower end of the skein, and while holding the threads taut, push the right hand away from you and up over the left hand (without crossing the threads) as many times as are needed to wind the whole skein on to the left hand, finally hitching the end of the skein on to the fingers. The right hand is now free. Pick up the scissors and cut through a single thread of the silk close to the knot (on the thumb). Pick up the folded card and secure one end of the silk within it, and proceed to wind the silk round and round the card until it is entirely removed from the left hand. Both hands are in action, moving freely while the winding takes place. Write the name, colour, and shade number from the paper label, on the end of the card. This precaution will save much time and trouble when the silk needs to be matched; the original labels are invariably lost.

Use needles of good quality, and an emery cushion to keep them bright. Do not use long needlefuls of thread; the work is hampered and the thread roughened before the end. Use a smooth thimble. Old silver ones, worn smooth by time and use, are best of all. New ones can be treated with emery paper. Use small scissors with very sharp points.

Always sit in a good light. When stitches must be unpicked, do not think of saving the thread; it is better to cut it through and pull out the short ends. Unpicked threads are spoiled for further use, and the dragging-through process often damages the ground material.

Do not embroider silk fabrics with coloured mercerized cottons. Cheapness, in whatever material and tools one uses, will spoil both the utility and the artistry of the thing made. In the days of guilds of embroiderers a member was "prohibited from using gold of less value than eight sous" (then a high price). Also he was bound "to use the best silk and never to mix thread with silk because that made work false and bad." Embroidery is essentially an enrichment of material; the least artistic of people immediately resent a mean treatment of a beautiful thing.

When using gold and metal threads extra care must be taken to keep the hands smooth, cool, and dry. Fine pumice stone can be used to take roughnesses from the skin. Frequent washing with a good soap (such as Monsol) and tepid water will keep them clean and cool, and talcum powder lightly dusted will keep them dry.

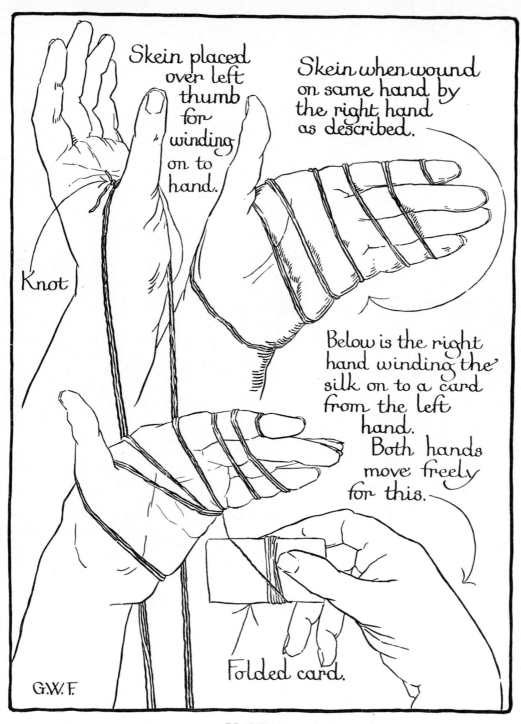

Skein placed over left thumb for winding on to hand.

Skein when wound on same hand by the right hand as described.

Knot

Below is the right hand winding the silk on to a card from the left hand.
Both hands move freely for this.

Folded card.

G.W.F.

PLATE 100

HOW TO WIND A SKEIN OF SILK

CHAPTER X
FRAME WORK

CHAPTER X

CERTAIN types of work cannot be carried out satisfactorily in the hand, but must be first stretched in a frame. These include couched work, gold work, laid work, the solid fillings shown on Plate 102, and most but not every kind of appliqué work. The advantage to be gained by mounting the work on a frame well repays the slight trouble spent on it. When mounted thus the design is spread out smoothly before one, and comparative effects of colour and stitch are realized with more ease. Also both hands are left free for the business of embroidering. One hand is kept beneath the frame and the other on top, and the needle is passed through the material from hand to hand. Two thimbles are worn, one on the middle finger of each hand. Once the unusualness of using both hands for the stitching has worn off, it will be discovered with pleasure that much more rapid work can be done than is possible when one hand is perforce occupied in holding the material.

Use of Embroidery Frame

A simple embroidery frame has two round pieces of wood with a mortise at each end. These are the rollers forming the top and bottom of the frame. A strip of webbing is nailed along the length of the wood between the mortises. For the sides of the frame either two flat pieces of wood with holes pierced at regular intervals to receive pegs, or two long wooden screws with two nuts on each for screwing the rollers at the required distance, are used. Both are shown in the illustration opposite, from which the method of mounting may be followed. The selvedge of all materials except velvet should be placed parallel with the sides of the frame. If the work is too long for one framing it can be rolled round one or both rollers if necessary. In this case a piece of soft material (flannelette), of the exact size of the parts to be rolled up, should be laid on and rolled with them quite smoothly.

Mounting Work in a Frame

In framed work the ends of threads are fastened in and off on the surface of the work at some part of the design that will be finally covered by stitches. To fasten in, the thread is passed through from the front to the back until the merest tail is left on the top surface. This is held down by the first finger of one hand whilst the other hand brings the needle through from the back and sews the end down with a couple of small stitches. And to finish it off, the needle is passed down and up through the material twice, making what in hand work would be two running stitches, and the thread is cut off close to the surface. Unfinished lengths of thread should never be left hanging at the back, but brought through to the front in some unworked portion of the design, from whence they can be recalled when needed. Finished portions of silk work should be kept covered while others are in progress.

To Fasten Threads In and Off

TO MOUNT A FRAME

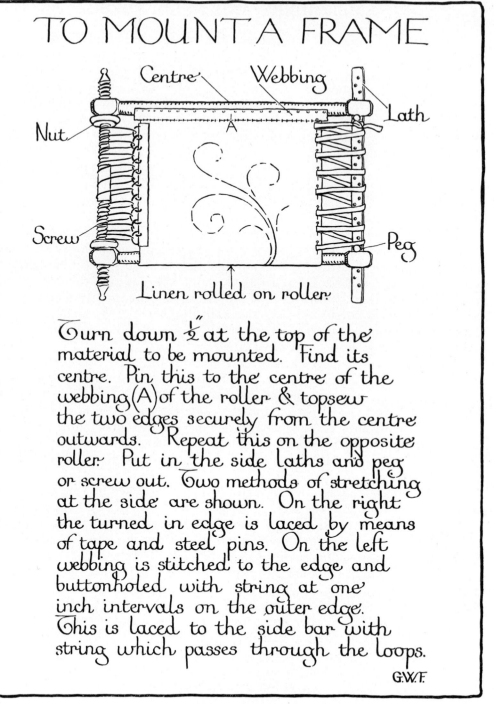

Nut • Screw • Centre • Webbing • A • Lath • Peg • Linen rolled on roller.

Turn down ½" at the top of the material to be mounted. Find its centre. Pin this to the centre of the webbing (A) of the roller & topsew the two edges securely from the centre outwards. Repeat this on the opposite roller. Put in the side laths and peg or screw out. Two methods of stretching at the side are shown. On the right the turned in edge is laced by means of tape and steel pins. On the left webbing is stitched to the edge and buttonholed with string at one inch intervals on the outer edge. This is laced to the side bar with string which passes through the loops.

G.W.F.

PLATE 101

The effect of long and short shading is shown in the middle flower on the sampler opposite. One petal is left unfinished to show how the first set of

Long and Short Shading

stitches are worked. The needle is brought out in the centre of the petal and put in on the outline, and the long and short stitches worked thus until the half is filled. The needle is then brought back to the centre and the other half completed. Whenever there is to be a suggestion of radiation in the direction of the stitches, they should be worked from the centre outwards in two halves. Remember always to put the needle *in* on the outline, for it is easier to put accurately into a line a needle one can see, than it is to bring one through from the back by feeling only. In this work the beauty of the outline depends on the accurate placing of the ends of stitches.

However many sets of stitches are used, the lower ends are always left uneven and lying the right direction for the reception of the next. (See the unfinished petal.) For the second and all subsequent sets of stitches the needle is brought from the back (splitting through the ends of the former set of stitches) and worked downwards. The idea of this method is that the various colours or tones of colour used should intermingle as imperceptibly as possible, as they do in birds' feathers; hence the old name of "plumage stitch" for this style of work. (See lotus flower in Plate 103.)

The top flower is worked in brick stitch shading. By this method stitches are placed with a rigid regularity, and there is no suggestion of radiation. A

Brick Stitch Shading

set of long and short stitches is worked first, as seen in the unfinished petals, and the remaining sets are filled in with satin stitches of equal length. This method may be seen in use on the seventeenth-century worsted hangings. On the specimen opposite, worked in Mallard Floss, two stitches, instead of single ones, have been worked for each brick stitch.

By this method, seen on the right half of the lower flower, the tones are kept quite separate and distinct. The first set of stitches is worked, as in the

Encroaching Block Shading

other examples, by putting the needle in on the outline at the top, and the remaining sets follow the same direction, each encroaching a little on the former one, the needle being put into the silk stitches to form the outline of each new tone. Note that this arrangement makes the stitch-marks apparent, and that, by working the reverse way, as in long and short, they are not seen. (See Plate 103.)

Voided Outline

The above stitch may also be worked without encroaching, that is to say, with the sets just touching each other, or they may be completely separated and show little channels of the ground material between them, as seen in the left half of the lower flower. This is known as "voiding," a method carried to perfection by the Chinese. (See Plate 47.)

PLATE 102

A SAMPLER OF SHADING STITCHES

The embroidery on the opposite plate is worked on the unaltered outline of a design taken from a Chinese porcelain bowl. In the original the free Lotus pattern is carved in the paste under a celadon glaze of olive **Chinese Bowl** tone, and is an example of the strong drawing of the finest **Sung Dynasty** Sung patterns. It makes an interesting embroidered decoration, **A.D. 960-1279** and at the same time provides excellent practice in framework technique. The lotus flower in profile is filled with long and short shading, tones being worked in a series of stitches beginning with the lightest at the flower's edge and gradating to the darkest at the stem. This is a somewhat wide area to cover with small stitches, and calls for some skill in the management of their direction. The flower is curved, therefore each set of stitches must leave the way open for the next to follow on with ease to flow rhythmically, much as the sap flows in the veins of the flower. This skill in the matter of direction comes only with practice, and it is best to begin with symmetrical and straightforward shapes, such as that of the flower petal in the sampler on Plate 102. Apart from the actual technique of stitching, much depends upon an intelligent choice of direction on the form to be filled, and this idea of the sap in the veins is a helpful one to remember when filling flowers and foliage in this manner. The many-petalled flower, filled with encroaching block shading, is more easily managed, and is no less effective. Care must be taken in choosing a right line of division for the blocks of stitching; that is to say, one which will explain the nature of the form and add to its decorative effect. Here the petals are worked in the lightest tone throughout, and it is the decorative division of the stitches which gives them interest of detail. The centre of the flower is filled by an open couching of yellow held down by blue stitches. All the outline work is in blue in stem stitch, interspersed by lines of yellow worked side by side. These lines suggest leaves beneath the water's surface and the whole pattern gives the feeling of cool flowers floating.

PLATE 103
LOTUS PATTERN FROM PORCELAIN BOWL OF THE SUNG
DYNASTY EXECUTED IN SILK ON LINEN

Laid work is the name given to the method of covering surfaces by laying strands of silk to and fro in parallel lines across them, passing through the background at the outlines only. This is seen in progress at the

Laid Work

centre of the top flower opposite. The threads are laid first of all with spaces, the width of a thread, between them, and these are filled with similar stitches made on a return journey. This avoids the awkwardness of bringing the needle up immediately below the point at which it enters the outline. Worked thus, the lustrous quality of floss silk is seen to perfection, provided the strands lie perfectly flat with no suggestion of a twist in them. They should lie, if anything, a little loosely, and should never be strained tight in the effort to achieve flatness. (See Frontispiece.)

As it is by no means practical to leave long loops of silk lying on the surface in this way, couching is employed to keep them in place at intervals, and may

**Couching
Laid Work**

be done with floss silk, sewn with split floss, or gold or silver thread sewn with Maltese silk. In any case it is a fragile technique, and best used beneath glass, where it will not be subjected to wear and tear—under the glass top of a dressing-table, for instance. Various arrangements of couching are illustrated in the sampler; in the top leaf the veins are couched with floss. The form of the top flower is accentuated by three couched lines in each petal. In the middle flower the effect of absolutely straight radiating lines set more closely is seen. For the lower flower couched lines in scallop form, known as "scale couching," are used.

The effect of this filigree form of couching is seen on the middle leaf. Worked with gold thread it gives great richness. It must be done, of course,

Damascening

directly on the silk, without any guiding line, and the aim is to whirl the thread round for as long as possible without coming to a stop. When it is found that the pattern cannot be continued in this way, the end of the thread must be passed to the back and a fresh start made.

A special kind of shading is made in laid work by laying the threads at different angles. Note the top leaf, where one-half is laid horizontally and the

**Tone, Colour,
and the
Play of Light**

other vertically, and the lower leaf where one-half is laid longitudinally and the other laterally. Flat gradation of tone is possible, using a range of silks, and the change from tone to tone should be made quite frankly. It is possible to manoeuvre so subtle a transition that the effect is like a wash of water colour, but this is not desirable; a more abrupt transition gives the better result. Colour can also be laid in bold contrasting splashes with characteristic effect. Laid work need not necessarily be outlined. The groundwork may allow the edges to be clearly defined by the laid stitches. The effect of a gold thread and of a silk outline is seen opposite.

PLATE 104

A SAMPLER OF LAID AND COUCHED WORK

On Plate 106 some metal threads and methods of padding are seen in in use. At the top left some layers of flannel have been tacked down (as **Metal Threads,** for appliqué, see page 166) to form a padding for *Bullion*, **Couched Gold,** which is a tightly coiled wire cut into the lengths required and **and Further** sewn on like beads. *Plate*, which is a thin flat strip of either gold **Methods of** or silver, is used for the small, straight, raised bar. Both petals **Padding** and bar are outlined by another metal thread known as *Pearl Purl*, which is made specially for edgings and outlines. The small spot which springs from between the petals has a gold *Spangle* sewn at its centre by a loop of Purl (similar to Bullion but a smaller size), and is surrounded by small loops of the same, overlapped in the manner of rose petals. The border beneath is of laid floss silk couched by floss, placed chevron-wise and held by a stitch at each point.

In the second square a disk is worked by couching down *Passing*, a metal thread made of flat pieces of gold, twisted round a cord of silk. Immediately beneath the disk is a small specimen of couched gold, worked by the medieval method known as *couché rentré*. For this a needle threaded with silk of the same thickness as the gold is brought out from the back and passed over the gold thread and back again through exactly the same hole, forcing the metal thread to dip through the ground material, which must be of strong, closely woven linen, or a twofold background, to withstand the strain of this process. None of the silk thread appears on the surface, which is entirely of gold, broken only by the "dips" which form a pattern.

On the left of the *couché rentré* is an embroidered "precious stone" worked with ruby red and white floss silk over a firm padding, and outlined with gold thread. This is a device used by ecclesiastical embroiderers to replace stones, or to eke out an inadequate supply of the genuine article.

Japanese Gold thread (which consists of thin strips of paper on to which gold leaf has been laid and burnished, then wound round a core of red or yellow floss silk) is used for the remaining specimens within the square. In the outer one, gold threads, laid two at a time, are couched in a diamond pattern. The encrusted texture of the inner one is secured by couching a single thread at $\frac{1}{2}$ in. intervals and allowing it to hump up a little between each stitch, placing the stitches which couch succeeding rows between the former ones. A padding of red cloth is used for this stitch, which is helped by its springy texture. The light plays on the closely packed loops, and the couching stitches are lost to view.

A geometric satin stitch border, worked in floss silk by the thread of the linen ground, divides this section from the one beneath, which shows part of a draped cloak worked with gold thread laid horizontally and couched with coloured filoselles. The drawing is expressed by the couching. The outer side of the cloak is sewn with a light and a dark blue. The latter is used for the

PLATE 105
LAID WORK (WITHOUT OUTLINING OR OVER COUCHING) BY THE AUTHOR

shadows of the folds, which are intensified by placing the stitches more closely together. The lining, seen where the cloak is turned back, is sewn with gold filoselle, and a single gold thread is finally couched as an outline to the edge of the cloak. In such a case three needles would be kept going together for the couching, one for each colour. This method of sewing with coloured silks can be used for other types of design, which must first be traced on linen for working.

Another border of couched floss is seen beneath this. In the lower section *Purl* and *Checked Purl* are worked over a padding made by sewing down a hank of linen threads modelled to the required form. The stem and outline are in pearl purl.

Tambour, *gold beads*, bullion, and passing are used for the Tudor rose in the top right section opposite. Tambour, which is much the same as passing but finer, can be sewn *through* the material, and is used here for the inner side of the petals and the calyx leaves. The turned-over tips of the petals have bullion sewn slantwise over a padding of linen threads. The centre is filled by a disk of couched passing, over which stamens are worked, with gold beads at their tips. Green silk is used to outline the inner side of the raised turn-overs, and for couching the pointed leaves. For the raised bands seen beneath, smooth macramé string is sewn down as a padding and covered by satin stitches of floss silk. The same kind of string is used for both specimens, the difference of effect in the lower one being secured by twisting the string at regular intervals when sewing it down.

The next section shows damascening, a form of couching which is described on page 228. The border beneath is worked in satin stitch on the thread of the ground linen.

In the next section blind cord is seen in use as a foundation for the basket-like stitches worked over it, two threads at a time up and down to form the required pattern. *Purse silk*, which is a tightly twisted pure silk thread, is used for the specimen in the centre, and for the filling stitches on Plate 107.

For the border beneath, laid threads of black Mallard Floss are held down by satin stitches worked with gold floss in a geometric pattern. The thistle flower shown beneath is worked with very fine Japanese gold thread couched with purple silk, which is worked solidly at the tips to give more colour; near the calyx, green sewing silk is used and the gold thread allowed to jump over the padding which is first laid for the leaves of the calyx. On the thistle leaf the raised spots are padded by a coil of linen thread sewn down through the centre. Gold tambour is satin-stitched over this padding and the spot finished by an outline of green silk. The body of the leaf is filled with Japanese gold thread couched longitudinally in lines following the curve of the vein. The whole is outlined by double gold thread, single threads of which spring off for the terminals.

PLATE 106
SPECIMENS OF WORK WITH METAL THREADS

The nine open-filling stitches shown in the top panel opposite are carried out in purse silk. Filoselle is used for the finer sewn stitches. A sacred emblem,

Filling Stitches or Purse and Filoselle Silk Agnus Dei

Agnus Dei (Lamb of God bearing a cross and flag) is seen in the centre of the sampler opposite. The technique is interesting in that it combines, within an area of 5 in. × 5 in., appliqué, laid and couched work, raised work (halo and cross), and surface embroidery stitches worked with stout floss, filo floss, Filoselle, and Maltese silk. The outline of the whole design is traced on to a piece of very pale blue satin, of a good thick quality, and cut out by the line of the panel. This piece is applied to the linen ground by means of starch. (See instructions for appliqué work.) The head and body of the lamb, traced on a pale oyster-coloured satin, of an equally good quality, are cut out and attached in turn to the blue. Horizontal lines of floss silk in delicate greens are laid in for the field. The halo is filled with couched Japanese gold thread, laid first on the circumference and then row by row within the circle. The bars of the cross *patee* on the halo are worked over the gold thread with satin stitches of red filo floss, and edged with single couched gold thread, the whole being outlined with black filoselle. The flag is worked in split stitch, with filo floss, a red cross on a white ground. The terminals of the cross *pommée* (at the top of the staff) are raised with padding over which satin stitch in gold filo floss is worked, and an outline of single gold thread is added. The cross itself is a couched double thread of gold, outlined with black filoselle.

Very fine Japanese gold thread is couched in vertical lines over the entire groundwork. The lamb's fleece is then delicately drawn in with split stitches, and a few French knots worked with filoselle and finely split floss in tones of cool fawn. The legs are worked in split stitch, with finely split floss. A dark negro brown is used for the hoofs, some broken outlines, and accents on the head, etc. Finally, a few flowers are sprinkled over the field with stitches of floss, and the border, worked last of all, has first a line of gold silk cord couched on the inner side, followed by two lines of couched gold thread (laid two at a time) and another line of the silk cord, the whole being outlined on either side by stem stitch in black filoselle.

Embroidery in Floss Silk

Three solid fillings carried out in stout floss silk are seen in the lower panel, laid and couched on the left, encroaching block shading in the centre, and long and short shading on the right.

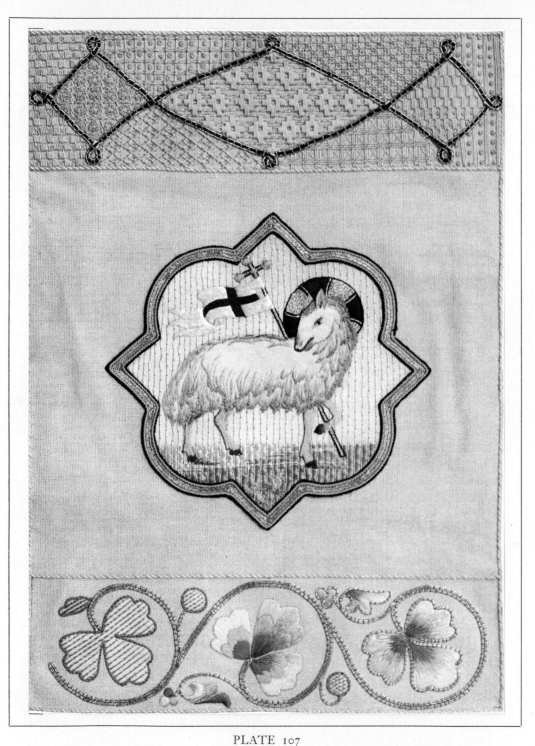

PLATE 107

AN ECCLESIASTICAL EMBLEM IN CENTRE. BORDER AT TOP SHOWS
FILLING STITCHES AND LOWER ONE SHADING METHODS

Japanese gold thread should be laid in such a manner that none of the silk core (around which the gilded strip is twisted) is allowed to show. The thread should be handled as little as possible, and the couching stitches take the same direction as the strip over the silk core. It does not help to twist the thread while sewing it down, for this causes the unseen part to untwist the more on the rebound, when the pressure is released.

Management of Japanese Gold Thread

When couching gold in a series of lines to cover a surface solidly, the couching thread is brought up on the outside and the needle put in slightly under the line of gold already couched. This avoids the possibility of either ground or padding material showing between the lines of gold. A "Melore," which is a small steel instrument similar to a stiletto but with a blunt tip, is used for stroking gold thread into place. Fine, sharp-pointed scissors are needed, and those with blades that close into a rounded shape are the most useful. The thread is not suitable for sewing through the material, but it can be passed to and fro on the surface if not too thick. The turns must be carefully manipulated. The thread can be bent on the needle to sharpen the turn, and the last couching stitch may be secured by a back stitch taken through the ground material; this prevents the end from "jumping." When the gold thread is passed over a padding of cord (as seen on Plate 106) the melore is used to dent the thread before placing the couching stitches which secure it on either side. Here, too, a back stitch taken through the ground material serves to secure the threads more tightly.

Japanese gold is almost invariably sewn down two threads at a time (one exception to this rule is shown in Plate 105), but where a design requires it they may be separated and allowed to flow off singly as shown in the thistle leaf on Plate 106. See also the treatment of the stems and single gold outline of the small shaded leaf on the right in the specimen at the foot of Plate 105.

The end or ends of the thread when being finished off can be passed to the back by putting a large-eyed "chenille" needle into the ground material, and, whilst holding the shaft of the needle beneath the frame, threading the end of the gold which has been cut off short through the eye and pulling it through. In cases where the space to be filled with couched gold is small enough to make it practicable, it is best to take only one thread (instead of a double one) to start with, and having passed the end of it through to the back, secure it firmly and begin couching at the other end of the row each time. The couching stitches pass over two threads as usual, but by this method only one thread has to be turned at the outline, which is a great advantage, for the edge is less clumsy and the gold lies more smoothly, as the stitches cross it constantly from the same side and in the direction in which the gold is twisted. The drapery on Plate 105 and the thistle leaf on Plate 106 are worked in this manner. Sometimes a thread is used for solid couching which is too thick for turning round on the outlines; the threads are then sewn securely at the edges and cut off sharply with scissors. These cut ends are hidden by an outline of a doubled gold thread couched over them, but for durability the method is not recommended.

Maltese silk (or horsetail) is a finely twisted silk, for couching gold thread, made in a variety of tints, and thus allowing various shades to be secured with the same gold. Its burnished surface reflects the colour of these **Colour of** minute stitches, becoming red, copper, orange, bronze, and so **Gold** on, according to the sewing silk chosen, while if no such modi-**Influenced by** fication is desired gold-coloured silk can be used, which leaves **the Couching** its original effect unaltered. Again, it can be made paler by **Silk** ivory silk, cooled by green, blue, violet, etc., a single thread of filoselle being used for these effects.

Chinese gold thread is similar to Japanese, except that it is made with thinner paper cut in finer strips, which makes it softer and more pliable, but necessarily more fragile and easier to damage. Thinner threads **Chinese** can be obtained in it than in any other make. Both Chinese and **Gold Thread** Japanese threads have the great advantage of being untarnishable and comparatively cheap. With much use the gilded paper may wear away, but it will not blacken. The material of "passing" itself wears permanently and, if of pure gold, retains its original appearance. The substitutes for the pure material, such as copper, silver, aluminium, etc., used for reasons of cheapness, will inevitably tarnish. The process will, however, be slow if they are kept protected (when not in use) from the effect of gases, light, etc., by a linen or cotton material that has been dyed by immersion in a strong solution of saffron.

Gold embroidery is pasted at the back before it is taken out of its frame, in the manner already described for canvas work (on page 78). For ecclesiastical and military work, where much metal and closely embroidered **To Paste** areas of silk or gold thread are used, a stronger paste is needed **the Back of** —say, one part of flour paste to one of dextrine. This is rubbed **a Material** over the back of all the stitches with the finger, care being taken that none is allowed to get through to the front surface. Thin muslin may be laid over the paste and all allowed to dry naturally while stretched. This not only secures the ends of threads, but prevents the weight of the embroidery from drawing up the surrounding background when released from the frame, and prevents the stitches from altering through changes of temperature.

PLATE 108
PRUNUS BLOSSOM, EMBROIDERED ON SILK
From the original work by the author.

CHAPTER XI
N O T I O N S

CHAPTER XI

For our own, as for other arts, ideas come in many ways, through imagined and unimagined channels; their coming is bound by no regulations and is **Getting Ideas** free of all rule, for the happiest inspirations reach us unexpectedly at unlikely times and in unlikely places. We learn this and bow to the inevitable. We do not sit waiting to receive ideas, which are too like moths that flit with uncertainty across our light.

Possibly at times original schemes for needlework may actually outstrip their immediate planning and execution; then a careful record of them in our **Keeping Ideas** notebook is of great value when we find we have spare time at our disposal. With these notes should also be recorded useful suggestions found in traditional ornament and methods, for nothing is gained—indeed much is lost—by ignoring the influence of good traditional work, a habit not uncommon in our days and possibly, in a less degree, in past times. Traditional ornament will not always help us when a form of architecture demands a new scheming of furniture, and the furniture a fresh outlook on needlework treatment. In general, however, a regard for the best of the past must unconsciously influence us for our good in selecting from the freshest and most beautiful elements about us, in an unbounded field wherein each finds his, or her, own path.

The previous chapters have dealt with stitches, needlework methods, design, colouring, and detailed technique. This chapter picks out a few designs and divulges the particular notion which led to the making of each. The reader will imagine herself to be idly turning the leaves of a notebook, and if, in so doing, she finds her mind getting ideas of its own for future work, this chapter will have served its purpose.

The design illustrated opposite, taken from a sixteenth-century Turkish plate, is for a small round tray (12 in. in diameter) to hold coffee cups. It was **Ceramics as a Source of Embroidery Design** redrawn, with its embroidery medium borne in mind, but, apart from that, is little altered. The colours suggested by the original were intentionally made more vivid in the needlework rendering. Red, green, and intense lapis-lazuli colouring are worked with filo floss on half-bleach linen. The rose petals are filled by threads laid horizontally. This method is easily distinguished from satin stitch by the fact that only an outline of silk appears on the reverse side as the silk is laid to and fro across the surface and passed to the back at the outlines only; also it is flat in effect compared with satin stitch. The leaves are in long and short, with veins outlined in split stitch; the small leaves and buds are in split, and the stems in stem stitch.

PLATE 109

EMBROIDERY FOR A COFFEE TRAY, DESIGNED FROM A XVIth-CENTURY
TURKISH PLATE

Persian, Moorish, and Saracenic tiles are full of suggestion for embroidery design, from the simplest to the most elaborate. If the correct proportion of colour in the original is carefully kept in the adaptation, it is unlikely that the scheme will fail to please.

Take the tiles illustrated opposite, a fairly simple example, and imagine them as the incentive for the decoration of bedspreads and curtains carried out **Tiled** in silk embroidery on linen. The colour-scheme is cool and well **Designs for** balanced, and therefore a restful one for constant use. It has **Embroidery** two tones of clear yellow (strongly contrasted) for the berries, two of green (Indian jade colour) for the ornament coming at the centre of the four tiles, a clear greyish blue on the larger leaves, and negro brown for the dark outline. A convenient arrangement for working would be to divide the bedspread into panels, a centre-piece and borders in sections to be joined together after the embroidery is finished, by the open seaming stitch shown at *A* on Plate 95. This would be both decorative and strong, and could be executed either with the jade green or a colour matching the ground, which compared with white paper is a pale duck-egg colour.

The ground material could be of silk (Tussore or Liberty's Tyrian) or a fine cotton fabric, as alternatives to linen. In the lighter-weight materials the straight faggot or veining stitch given on Plate 94, worked in twisted embroidery silk, would be strong enough for the joining. The borders of the curtains could be joined in a similar manner, in sections. The tile pattern could occur singly as well as in pairs (as shown opposite) in alternation with plain panels for borders, placed horizontally for casements, and vertically for long curtains. Alternatively, for long curtains that end at the window-sill, a wide horizontal border would look well inserted with the joining stitch. This could be composed of alternate blank and embroidered squares, the latter containing the repeat of four tiles as they appear in the illustration.

The panels containing the embroidery could be arranged in many different ways for the bedspread. A good plan for finding the most suitable one would be to make some rough tracings of the tiles and try them out in alternative positions on the bed.

If a dull surface were required, the same scheme could be carried out in crewel wools on linen with a dull finish, or a lightweight bolton sheeting material. For these materials a decorative closed seam would be more practical for any joining needed. (See Plate 124.)

PLATE 110
OLD TILES FROM SPAIN
Suggesting ornament for embroidery.

This pattern has been embroidered with single threads of filo-floss and filoselle on an off-white (greenish) Tyrian silk ground, and shows a faithful approximation of the colouring of the original painted tile.

Coloured Tile Design Rendered in Silk Embroidery   The dark outline and berry-tops are worked with a single thread of filoselle, the former in chain stitch, the latter in stem stitch worked to and fro, filling the little shape required. The berries are worked with rows of chain stitch, following the direction of their outline, in three tones of clear golden yellow filo-floss, placed in the order of light, half-tone, and dark, giving the berry-like form.

The leaves and circles have a chain-stitched filling of green filo-floss. The voided outline (or space) between the filling and the dark edge (seen in the leaves at the top left corner) gives a freshness and lightness of effect similar to that produced by the glaze on the tile. The wide sweeps of the brush on the blue leaves are expressed by three rows of blanket stitch, dark, medium, and light, worked in that order, the heading of each row being visible. The outline of the square is hemstitched with a thread of filoselle of the same colour as the ground material from which threads were first cut and withdrawn.

PLATE 111

EMBROIDERED RENDERING OF TILE PATTERN SEEN IN
PLATE 110

By taking a good design, originally made for some other process, and carrying it out in needlework, one meets with a delightful exercise in the adaptability of stitches and methods. Instead of making a **Adaptability** working design with one's own technique in mind, one is **of Stitches** faced by a ready-made pattern not intended for needlework. The three plates which follow are a part of such an experiment, which proved to be well-nigh inexhaustible, so many ways and means suggested themselves for our purpose.

These plates show embroidered renderings of a Chinese motif which dates back at least to the sixth century B.C. It was taken from a tomb-tile (of baked pottery) found with others in the Loyang Valley and now in the **Loyang** Royal Ontario Museum of Archeology. This particular tile **Tile** (dating from about 220 B.C.) is described as representing "A stylized bird—perhaps derived from the Jungle Fowl or the Domestic Cockerel—holding a pearl in its beak." It was found with others which appear to be the work of an artist who showed more naturalistic and spirited representation than is seen in other work of the period, which is invariably highly conventional in character.

Before the needlework is attempted it is wise to redraw the design, bearing in mind the new process of working. In this instance a rubbing from the tile showed a thick, uneven outline, and what would have been the **Designer's** finer part of the drawing, that of the legs and feet, became **Original** spread and thickened; this was a natural outcome of drawing **Intention** on wet clay. When transposing a design thus, we aim at reviving the designer's original intention of drawing with finesse. The technique of the needleworked examples was governed to a certain extent by the kind of ground material chosen. No. 1 (Plate 112) is worked on Taffeta silk, blue- and green-shot, reminiscent of those colours as they appear on a drake's plumage. This material, rich and interesting in itself, suggested a light open treatment through which it might be seen. Roumanian stitch, used on the wing and tail feathers, adapted itself perfectly for the purpose; worked rather openly and slanted, it suggests feathers and their quills—at the same time it "drew" (or filled) the varied shapes without any difficulty. The same stitch is used for the little blocks of colour on the body, but here it is worked more closely, not slanted, and the small centre stitches are wider. The spots on the body, between lines of couched gold thread, are spaced out back-stitch. The head, legs and body are outlined by fine Japanese gold laid two threads together, while for the beak and "pearl" a single thread is used. The beak is filled with satin stitch and the comb with blanket stitch. Three tones of yellow gold, and three of brown gold mallard floss complete the colour scheme, and it will be noticed that these are intermingled in places, and so give further tones.

PLATE 112
BIRD FROM LOYANG TILE, EMBROIDERED WITH SILK
THREAD ON A SHOT-SILK GROUND

No. 2 (Plate 113) is worked on a thick Tussore silk of natural colour, and four tones of blue Mallard floss are used for the embroidery. This specimen is the simplest, as regards materials, of the three schemes shown, but the interest is made up by the extra ingenuity spent on the stitchery. The principal stitch is fishbone.

The four tones of blue are used separately throughout; there is no "shading" other than that given by the stitch itself. On the neck and legs the fishbone stitch is worked in alternate blocks of the middle tones, and the body is filled by horizontal bands worked in a like manner. On the wing and tail feathers three tones are used.

The outline is in backstitch of the darkest tone.

All four tones, arranged from light to dark, are seen on the comb. The head is in long and short, and the beak, with its "pearl," in satin stitch.

Unlike No. 1, this specimen is filled with stitches, excepting only the little bands round the neck and eye.

PLATE 113
BIRD FROM LOYANG TILE, EMBROIDERED WITH SILK
THREAD MAINLY IN FISHBONE STITCH ON A TUSSORE
SILK GROUND

No. 3 (Plate 114) is worked on Tyrian silk rich amber in colour. The embroidery is carried out in laid work with stout floss silk. At least ten different mauves, grey, blue, purple and pink are splashed in boldly, and to such good purpose that the strong yellow of the ground material becomes quite tamed and gentle by contrast, the whole effect being strong and rich. A fine thread of Japanese gold thread is laid and couched across the floss silk, in the opposite direction, on the wing and tail feathers, where it serves to hold down the long strands. The whole design is outlined by gold thread laid two threads together.

To each of us a different use would suggest itself for this design. It has many possibilities. It would look well hung on the wall of a small room if worked in a colour scheme incidental to the decoration. The **Suggested** illustrations are destined for table mats, when mounted under **Applications** glass, with cloth or felt on the underside, for use on polished tables. Enlarged, and embroidered with coarse threads, the design would decorate either a fire screen or a cushion. It would serve also, and very effectively, as a *motif* for the ornamentation of an evening coat or a rest gown; and could be used for any of the many "linen embroidery" purposes, not excluding drawn-fabric work.

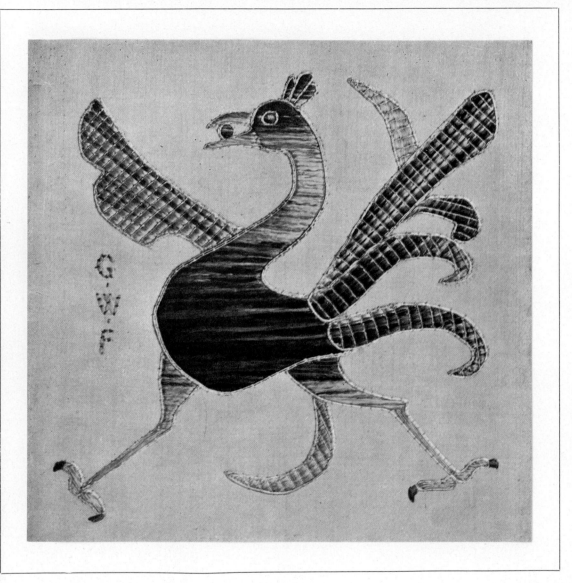

PLATE 114

BIRD FROM LOYANG TILE, EMBROIDERED WITH FLOSS SILK
AND GOLD THREAD ON A TYRIAN SILK GROUND

Over seventy (by the thread) open filling stitches, contained in a panel measuring $12\frac{1}{2}'' \times 9''$. So interestingly arranged that, within its province, this is surely a little masterpiece.

A Black Work Sampler A notion indeed! Also a challenge and inspiration for making, in other idioms, samplers of equal interest and decorative value.

References to Spanish black work from which this example stems, will be found on pages 94 and 128.

Double running and Holbein (or Line) stitches are explained on page 62. A working diagram will be found in the centre of Plate 29, and worked specimens of the stitch (in the form of coloured borders) on Plate 28. See also the final paragraph on page 60.

PLATE 115

POTS!

A contemporary black work sampler by Mrs. St. Osyth M. E. Wood.

A note of wild flowers gathered from a Devon meadow in summer-time (July, to be exact) supplied the idea for the pattern embroidered in coloured

Meadow Flowers

silks in the four corners of the 34-in. cloth illustrated. The square is provided by a straight-line arrangement (see Plate 20), and the working of the line stitch is explained on Plate 22. The short grass in the meadow was so bespangled with flowers that it seemed natural to group them closely when making the drawing, in order that something of their jewel-like effect might be there also. It was this aspect of the note that later suggested its use for the design. Rokfast embroidery silks are used on half-bleach linen. These dyes, not fading with either strong sunlight or washing, suggested themselves as suitable materials for the making of a cloth for tea in a garden. It may be of use to note the stitches employed.

For the petals of the pink campion (centre) Roumanian stitch is used—it so easily suggests their split tips. A ring of knot stitch in two tones suggests the little cups at their centres. The leaves are filled by two sets of buttonhole stitches which follow the direction of the outline. The outer set is worked first, openly, to leave room for the straight stitch of paler green to be set between the stitches. The inner row is not filled; the buttonhole stitches reach to the centre vein, which is a line of overcast back stitch.

The vetch flowers are made by a detached chain stitch, which has a straight stitch of another colour within it and a French knot at the stem. This arrangement gave an opportunity for gradating the tone and blending the colour with the two blues and two mauves used in these flowers. Their stems and leaf stems are in overcast back stitch, and the leaves themselves lines of stem-stitching. The touch of yellow which gives "snap" to the colour-scheme is introduced by the star-shaped flowers in detached chain stitch. The actual cloth is finished by a narrow hemstitched hem ($\frac{1}{4}$ in.), and the predominating colour (mauve) carried round its outer edge by detached loops of buttonhole stitch. These are worked on a foundation of knot stitch placed at $\frac{1}{4}$ in. intervals.

The management of the flowers described above suggests the kind of treatment needed for an embroidered miniature—a fascinating problem in

Embroidered Miniatures

needlework. Having fixed upon the size and shape of the miniature (oval, oblong, round, or square), the scheme of colour should be next decided. It saves time to select this from the silks themselves. (Floss on reels, or filo floss in skeins, is good for the purpose.) Working from these, make a blot effect in water-colours of the proposed arrangement, and from this suggestion draw a simple outline representing a group of flowers for tracing on to the material. This drawing should merely indicate the shapes and their placing, and all detail be left to the needle.

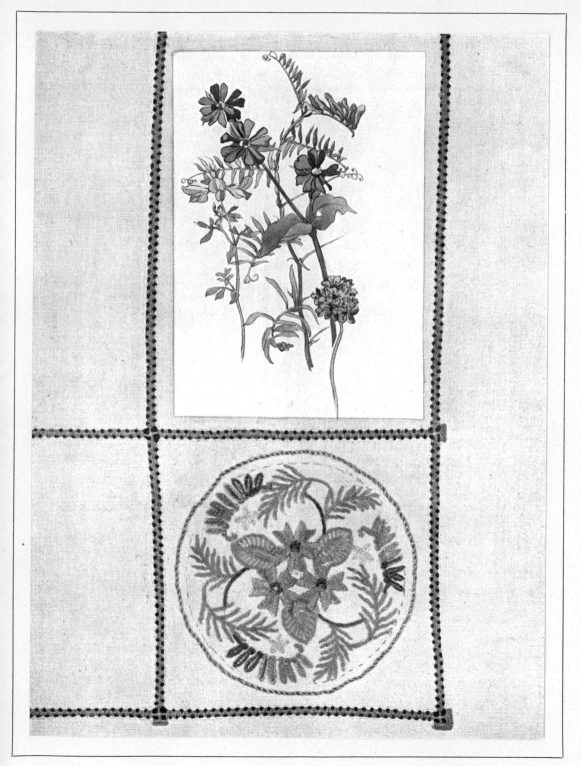

PLATE 116
A DRAWING OF MEADOW FLOWERS AND A DESIGN THEREFROM

The previous designs described were suggested by things seen. That on the opposite page was suggested by the following lines from an old Cornish litany:

**Embroidery
Suggested by
Things Read**

From ghoulies and ghoosties and long-leggetty beasties,
And things that go bump in the night,
Good Lord deliver us.

and is the end panel of a table-scarf for use on an oak table. The cut-work panel occurs at either end, and the two are connected by an embroidered band of lettering along each of the long sides, bearing the above words. One shield is to hold the owner's initials, and the other his motto or a date. This is pure cut work, or in other words, the ornament holds itself together, when cut, without the assistance of worked bars.

For this form of designing the long-leggettiness of the beasties was distinctly useful, but doubtless the ideas suggested by the lines might be given more play were a less restrained technique chosen. Pure linen thread (D.M.C. *lin pour dentelle*) on a linen ground, both écru colour, are the materials used, which means that with ordinary care and freedom from accident the workmanship will last in its original condition as long as the fabric lasts, and that means for some generations. Satin stitch and buttonhole are the only stitches used. In the dragons' bodies satin stitch takes the form of a geometric filling and is worked in diagonal lines in groups of two stitches over four threads of the linen ground. As the latter is rather loose-meshed, the wings, claws, and shield were closely padded by run threads before working the satin stitch, while one line of running only was used beneath the buttonhole stitching.

Here is another quotation for use in a similar manner, which has the advantage of being shorter by four words—

Better is a dinner of herbs where love is, than a stalled ox and hatred therewith.—Proverbs XV, 17.

Poetry as a source of inspiration for sheer decoration in the form of panels (not necessarily to contain lettering) is rich indeed. Take only this instance, from the "Ancient Mariner," a poem full of imagery and colour—

And straight the sun was flecked with bars.

PLATE 117
A PANEL IN CUT-WORK FOR A TABLE-SCARF

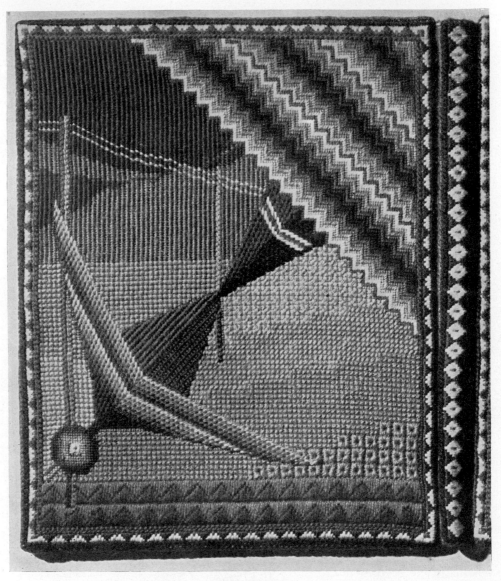

PLATE 118
MAGAZINE COVER
Canvas work by Mrs. Dorothy Britnell (*back*).

PLATE 118A
MAGAZINE COVER
Canvas work by Mrs. Dorothy Britnell (*front*).

Plates 118 and 118A show the two sides of a lively and ingenious piece of canvas work, carried out just for the joy of the thing, and the problems that it set. Birds and backgrounds!

Note the telegraph poles and wires against a stormy sky behind the stylized bird in Plate 118, and the subtle blending of tones and textures (i.e. stitches) leading from horizon to foreground, in the same piece.

Canvas Work Cover   In the other half, shown in colour, the treatment, though more formal, maintains the same liveliness of spirit. The alternating change of pattern from diagonal chevrons to cross stitch of a darker grey, in the squares behind the birds, is a most pleasing feature. The whole design is controlled and steadied by the judicious use of connecting lines and patterned borders.

CHAPTER XII

HINTS ON TEACHING CHILDREN

CHAPTER XII

THE first thing we, as children, do when learning to write is to make a series of similar strokes one after another along a ruled line. The descending (**L**) stroke is tried first, that being the easiest and most natural movement to the hand. When this stroke can be made with ease, we have learned how to hold a writing tool, and are then shown the ascending stroke (**J**). This is followed by a closed letter *o*, to which in due course a tail is added, *a*, and so on by stages until all those movements of fingers and wrist which go to the making of our written alphabet become familiar. The result of this kindly teaching is that few of us in after years can remember any great difficulty in learning to write. We were carried along from weakness to strength until the ability became ours.

First Lessons for Children

With needlework, as children our experience may have been less happy. Some of us can recall the hopelessness with which we contemplated the task of making a long line of minute and even stitches on a white material with a needleful of fine white cotton. We had not been asked to learn our letters by writing them on white paper with white ink! Children no longer suffer these trials to the eye and spirit, but begin by using large needles and gaily coloured threads of a corresponding size, which are not only charming to the eye, but a means of showing clearly the work in progress on both front and back of the material. Stitches, together with their simple applications, are taught by means of decorative stitchery, and so ordered that each process learned helps to clear the way for the next. By learning stitches and constructive processes in this way, the senses of decoration and colour are at the same time given an equal chance of developing, and weariness of spirit is avoided.

All children love colour and the making of gay things, and by being supplied with a square of material, a size 4 crewel needle, and threads of Star Sylko (size 5) of two pleasantly contrasting colours (say a red and a blue), they are filled with a desire to handle them to some purpose. What shall be made? A mat? Then the needle is threaded and running stitch is taught thus—

Beginning about one inch from the edge of the square, we push the needle in and out at half-inch intervals, proceeding from right to left along a straight line, so making the stitches and spaces of equal size. The straight line we keep by following in the track of a thread that has been withdrawn. From the first we make no knot to secure the end of our thread, for it is best to begin as we intend to go on. For this first occasion we leave the end of the thread projecting from the first stitch, and having

Running Stitch

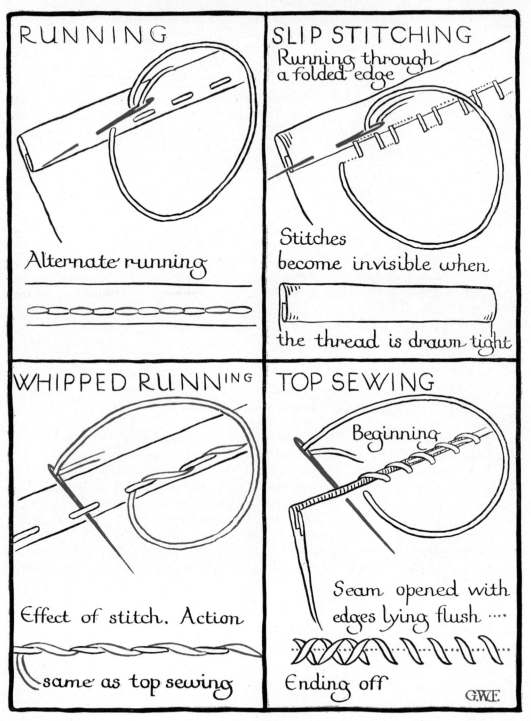

RUNNING

Alternate running

SLIP STITCHING
Running through
a folded edge

Stitches
become invisible when

the thread is drawn tight

WHIPPED RUNNING

Effect of stitch. Action

same as top sewing

TOP SEWING

Beginning

Seam opened with
edges lying flush ....

Ending off

G.W.F.

PLATE 119

finished running round the four sides of the mat, we fasten off each end of the thread in turn by passing it behind our stitches at the back, as shown in the diagram of whipped running. (Plate 119.)

For this effort we have needed to concentrate on two things—first the passing of the needle in and out at regular intervals; secondly, upon pulling the thread through so that it lies flatly on the material without being pulled right through. We practise this until able to make a presentable line of running. Next with a blue thread, supposing the red was used first, we work another line of running in the same track, this time picking up each of the stitches already made, and now being freed from the necessity of measuring the size of the stitch we begin to feel the pleasure arising from the repetition of a definite action, which in turn becomes rhythmical action. On completing the blue running, we find that a line of alternating red and blue stitches is to be seen on the front and back of our square. Further lines of the same stitch can be worked at regular intervals until the space is filled, and to finish the mat we make a fringed edge by fraying out the threads on each of the four sides for a distance of three-quarters of an inch.

Nothing further is attempted until this stitch is mastered. Monotony is avoided by varying the spacing of the lines within the square—spaced-out single lines, borders of many closely worked lines, and lines arranged to form blocks and checks.

From Plates 119 and 120 it will be seen that running is a preparation for slipstitch and herringbone. To slipstitch a hem a running stitch is made, first just below the edge of the fold of the hem and then through the edge of it, in turn. This same action, worked from left to right instead of right to left as previously, results in herringbone stitch. When the time comes for learning these stitches, they will be simplified if this intimate connection is demonstrated.

Rhythmical action is an important element in good needlework. If plenty of practice is provided for each stitch before new and different ones are attempted, **Rhythmical Action** this rhythm comes naturally in time to most children. After running and tacking stitch, they pass on to whipped running and top-sewing, and then to chain and blanket stitch, from which featherstitch is developed. When these actions have become comparatively easy, hemming is introduced, but not before, because it calls for a free movement of the wrist which is not natural to very young children. It develops at

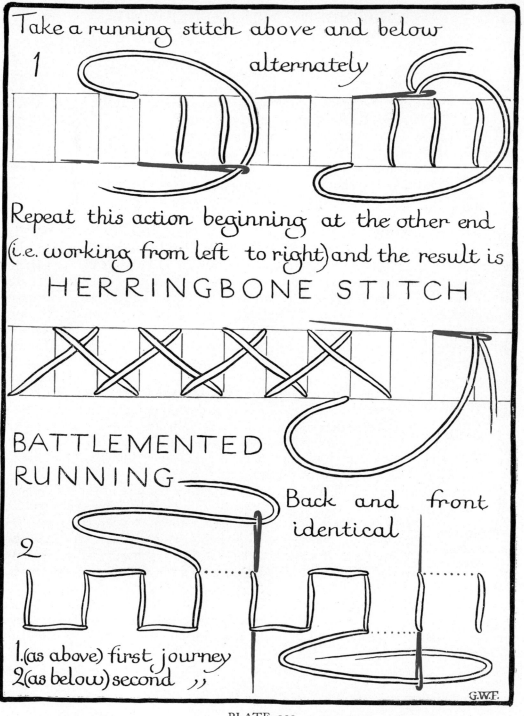

Take a running stitch above and below

1   alternately

Repeat this action beginning at the other end
(i.e. working from left to right) and the result is
HERRINGBONE STITCH

BATTLEMENTED
RUNNING

Back and front
identical

2

1.(as above) first journey
2.(as below) second ,,

G.W.F.

PLATE 120
HERRINGBONE DEVELOPED FROM RUNNING STITCH

some time between the ages of nine and eleven, and it may be later. Chain stitch may be substituted for hemming on a garment.

The second action attempted is introduced by the simplest seaming stitch, known as top-sewing. With the help of this the making of useful little bags,

Top-sewing or Seaming Stitch
pincushions, and cases for handkerchiefs, brush and comb (envelope shape), etc., becomes possible, by joining the folded edges which have been sewn down by running stitch.

The new action needed for this stitch may be shown first by whipped running, with which it is identical. Compare the needles in the diagrams of these stitches (on Plate 119). The method of fastening in and finishing off the end of the thread when seaming is illustrated. Decorative border stitches may be built up with running and top-sewing. *A*, *C*, and *E* on Plate 124 are instances of this combination. The working of these borders as a means of securing hems for the various articles made provides further practice in both stitches before others are embarked upon, and may call forth some inventive skill in suggesting new arrangements. Tacking stitch may be introduced in the making of these borders; it is like running stitch except that the stitches are nearer together.

Prepared Colour-schemes
If the children are given threads which have been previously arranged to make harmonious and contrasting colour-schemes, a practical experience of colour is added to the natural colour-sense which most children possess, and when, later on, colour theories are shown by diagrams, and charts are explained, they will have some foreknowledge to help them with the subject.

Chain and blanket stitch are best taught together because of their similarity in action. The needle is brought out at a point immediately below that at which

Chain and Blanket Stitch
it is put in, and pulled through in a downward direction with the thread lying beneath it from left to right. Thus, working vertically, we have chain stitch, and working horizontally, we have blanket stitch. These stitches give scope for the simple decorative work in which all children delight. If they are shown some examples of flowers and leaves worked in these stitches, and after copying several are encouraged to evolve others of their own, great interest is aroused. The line for the leaves may be made by drawing round a cut (folded) paper leaf, and

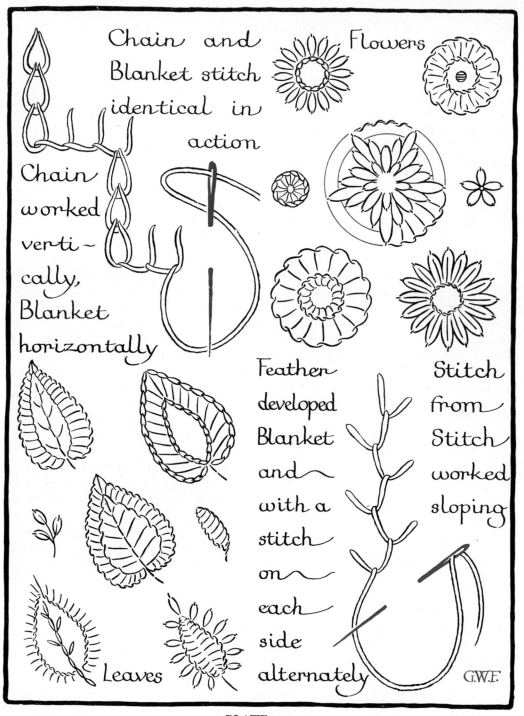

Chain and Blanket stitch identical in action

Flowers

Chain worked verti-cally, Blanket horizontally

Feather developed Blanket and with a stitch on each side alternately

Stitch from Stitch worked sloping

Leaves

G.W.F.

PLATE 121

CHAIN AND BLANKET STITCH TAUGHT TOGETHER

coins serve in the same way for indicating flowers. These exercises lead inevitably to the idea of fitting flowers and leaves together to form a pattern, a suggestion which will probably come from the children themselves. This will be the moment for trying out the free use of colour by allowing the children to select their own scheme from a collection of oddments. This new-found freedom of arranging line and colour proves a great spur to individual effort, and the results are usually surprisingly good.

Feather stitch may be developed from blanket stitch, which it closely resembles. Working vertically, a sloping blanket stitch is made right and left

Feather stitch

alternately. Decorative borders built up from these stitches are useful, attractive, and capable of great variety. By beginning with some simple lines of fancy blanket stitches (see examples on Plate 10), and leading by degrees to chain and blanket stitch, and blanket and feather stitch combinations of a more complicated nature, the procedure shown opposite is well understood. If worked direct with the needle without the help of measured distances, these borders are splendid training in accuracy of eye. It is this which explains the term "needle designing."

By means of these five stitches, running, tacking, top-sewing, chain, and blanket, many useful articles, not excluding an apron or flat pinafore, can be

First Garment

made by children. The seams can be joined by the method shown on Plate 124, the neck and arm openings being turned down in a narrow single fold at the back and made neat by either chain or blanket stitch. One or two pockets (patch) can be attached by chain stitch, and ornament introduced in the form of a floral posy (chain and blanket) either at the front below the neck or on the pockets, or reserved for a built-up decorative border commenced as a means of securing the bottom hem.

The practice given by the work outlined has gradually made fingers and hands more supple and accustomed to the handling of needle and thread. Now

Size of Stitches Reduced

both should be reduced in size, and smaller stitches made, to bridge the gulf existing between the size of the first work and the fine needles and thread required for dressmaking proper. Hemming (Plate 124), back and stem stitch (Plate 4), herringbone (Plate 120), fishbone (Plate 5), and French knots (Plate 15), are now added to the repertoire, and by the introduction of some simple mending an opportunity occurs for the revision of most of the stitches already learned. Running and tacking reappear for the darning of thin places, herringbone for patching

NEEDLE-DESIGNED BORDERS

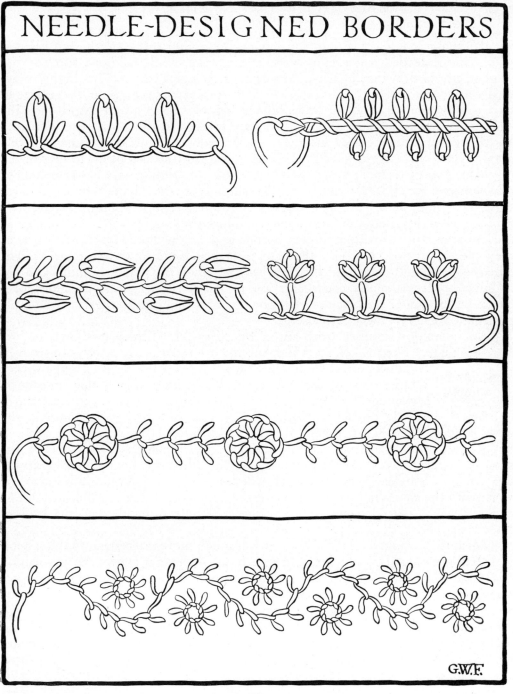

PLATE 122

woollen materials, and tacking, top-sewing, hemming, back stitch, and blanket stitch are all needed in patching various materials, while fishbone stitch is put to good use in drawing together the edges of cuts and tears. This highly practical but somewhat dull section of needlework instruction could be enlivened by a new decorative problem set as homework, of a less limited nature than the chain and blanket arrangements previously attempted, owing to the increased knowledge of stitches. For instance, a 4-in. border could be planned on two parallel lines enclosing a waved or, perhaps, zigzag line as a basis, to be worked in chain, overcast chain, stem, whipped back or running stitch, according to the worker's fancy. The basis of lines should be shown on the blackboard, together with some instances of simple leaf and flower forms in outline, showing the use of herringbone and fishbone as filling stitches by way of a new idea, the children to construct a similar border and fit the floral forms within it as they please, writing, beneath, the names of the stitches they intend to use. The results should be set out for criticism, in which the children join. The use of such borders for the ornamentation of bags, runner-ends, and cushions, could be explained by blackboard drawings showing the border in a suitable position on each of these articles.

An ingenious sampler work-apron by Miss M. Gibson is shown on the opposite plate. The pocket, on which stitches are recorded in a series of straight lines, is attached to the apron by overcast hemstitching, with a happy result. At the corners, the only place that might be weakened by the withdrawal of threads for this stitch, strength is restored by little blocks of blanket stitch and two rows of stitches at the outer angles. The hems, turned on the right side of the apron, are secured by blanket stitch showing various fanciful arrangements. The hems of the shoulder-straps are secured by zigzag chain. The ornamental border at the top contains stitches which were crowded out of the pocket. The apron is worn with the shoulder-straps crossed at the back and clipped to the sides. The clip fastener is placed beneath an embroidered button attached to the ends of the straps.

An Apron Sampler

An apron arranged on these lines proves much more interesting to the school-girl than a mere stitch sampler, and rightly so, because it shows the application of certain constructional processes. The ornament at the top provides an opportunity for an individual decorative design, and when all is completed it can be worn. The linens, holland, crash, and kindred fabrics usually stocked for school use are any of them suitable for the purpose. Balls of Star Sylko provide many varieties of colour-scheme for the needlework—size 5 for the heavier materials, size 8 for the lighter. A No. 4 crewel needle is needed for the former, and a No. 6 for the latter.

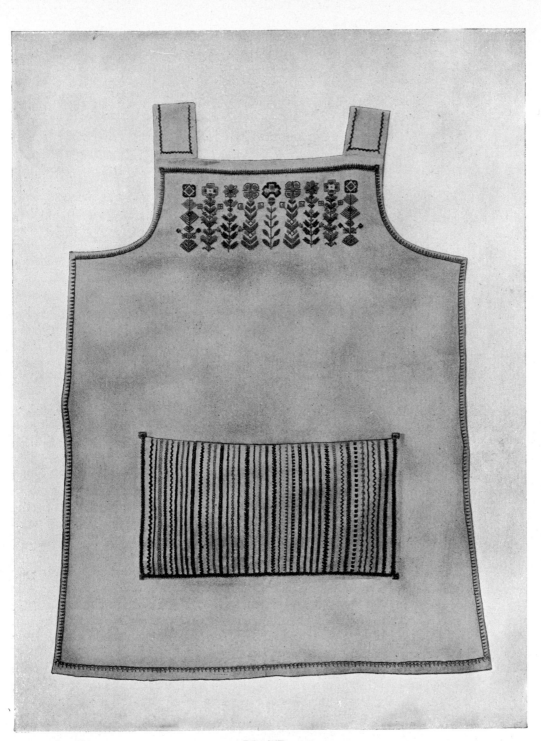

PLATE 123

AN APRON SAMPLER

Hemming   The working of hemming stitch is shown on the opposite plate. It is worked from right to left. Begin by tucking the end of the thread beneath the fold where it will be secured by the first stitches made, and end off by making two stitches, one over the other, and passing the thread beneath the fold and out at the top edge, where it is cut off.

In working the stitch the needle enters the material just below the edge of the fold, and appears again through the triple thickness a little farther to the left, involving a swift dipping movement made from the wrist. This is the "plain" sewing version of hemming. The diagram beneath shows how easily the stitch is turned into a decorative one by reversing the position of the work and making a return journey, this time picking up each stitch already made.

Many stitches other than so-called hemming stitch may be used for the sewing down of hems, notably variations of chain stitch (see Plates 7, 8, and 9),

Decorative Hems   fancy blanket stitches (see hems of the apron on Plate 123), and feather stitches (see Plate 13). Two or more sets of stitches worked in sequence are sometimes used for the same purpose, the first set serving to mark out the position of subsequent stitches. Some very simple borders of this built-up description are illustrated on the opposite plate, at *A*, *B*, *C*, *D*, and *E*. Fly stitch (see Plate 9) is used for completing those at *B* and *D*, and the needles indicate the second action needed for the other three. The border at *E* requires a return journey with the work reversed to form the crosses. Running stitch is used as a foundation for all five stitches, which are shown as instances of a method by which endless variations are possible.

The diagrams at *F*, *G*, *H*, and *I* suggest the highly ornamental effect gained by joining edges which have been first hemmed by simple decorative stitches.

Decorative Closed Seams   The hems at *G* are secured by battlemented running (the working of which is explained by the upper and lower diagrams on Plate 120), at *H* by alternate long and short blanket stitches, and at *F* and *I* by stitches already described above. All four seams are made by top-sewing, which is seen in its normal working position on Plate 112. If the seam is to be opened out flat, the stitches must be left sufficiently loose to admit of this. Here the top-sewing has become decorative by the simple expedient of spacing the stitches in groups of two at *G*, wider apart than usual at *I*, and by making a return journey at *F*, *H*, and *I*.

It will be noticed that the hem is turned with a double fold on the front of the material at *F* and *I*, and with a single fold on the reverse side at *G* and *H*. This is a point to be determined by the texture of the material used, and the

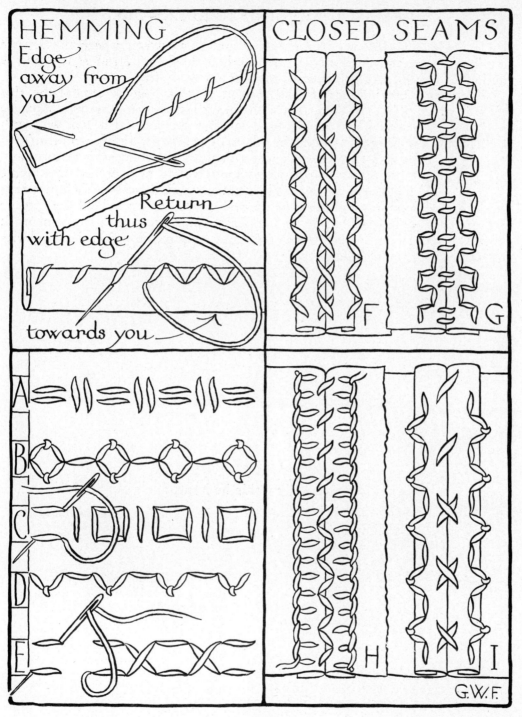

HEMMING

Edge away from you

Return thus

with edge

towards you

CLOSED SEAMS

F

G

A
B
C
D
E

H

I

G.W.F.

PLATE 124

article made. For instance, for cushions and cosy-covers, where the reverse side is not seen, and lined articles, the method shown at *G* and *H* is used. A single fold is sufficient for materials that do not easily fray.

The seams of children's frocks and small coats can be treated by this method, which is in close sympathy with smocking in its appearance. Aprons, overalls, and similar hard-wearing garments also look well with their seams treated in this manner. Bags, cushion-covers (with or without gussets), and furnishings made of heavy textures and those which do not lend themselves to hemstitched treatments may be conveniently joined thus, and in the case of rich materials the decorative join may well serve as the sole adornment, provided the threads used are suitable in quality, size, and colour. The success of this type of work depends equally upon a right choice of thread for the purpose, and the regularity and accuracy of the stitching.

Occasions for Decorative Closed Seams

"And gladly wolde he lerne, and gladly teche."

—(The Clerk) Prologue, *Canterbury Tales*.

INDEX